# The Adventure of Relevance

Martin Savransky

# The Adventure of Relevance

## An Ethics of Social Inquiry

Martin Savransky
Department of Sociology Goldsmiths
University of London
London, United Kingdom

ISBN 978-1-349-84835-5      ISBN 978-1-137-57146-5   (eBook)
DOI 10.1057/978-1-137-57146-5

Library of Congress Control Number: 2016937738

© The Editor(s) (if applicable) and The Author(s) 2016
The author(s) has/have asserted their right(s) to be identified as the author(s) of this work in accordance with the Copyright, Design and Patents Act 1988.
This work is subject to copyright. All rights are solely and exclusively licensed by the Publisher, whether the whole or part of the material is concerned, specifically the rights of translation, reprinting, reuse of illustrations, recitation, broadcasting, reproduction on microfilms or in any other physical way, and transmission or information storage and retrieval, electronic adaptation, computer software, or by similar or dissimilar methodology now known or hereafter developed.
The use of general descriptive names, registered names, trademarks, service marks, etc. in this publication does not imply, even in the absence of a specific statement, that such names are exempt from the relevant protective laws and regulations and therefore free for general use.
The publisher, the authors and the editors are safe to assume that the advice and information in this book are believed to be true and accurate at the date of publication. Neither the publisher nor the authors or the editors give a warranty, express or implied, with respect to the material contained herein or for any errors or omissions that may have been made.

Cover illustration: © Alex Wilkie

Printed on acid-free paper

This Palgrave Macmillan imprint is published by Springer Nature
The registered company is Macmillan Publishers Ltd. London

# Acknowledgements

This book has taken shape over the course of many years, and it has only become possible thanks to the fortune of having been surrounded by others who, not only in paper, but also in person, have been true companions in the sometimes inspiring, sometimes puzzling, but always demanding adventure of trying to think and feel at the edge of what we already know. Their conversations, filled with wisdom, patience, and generosity, have not only helped me develop the thoughts contained in these pages. Perhaps more importantly, they have been a constant reminder that one is not alone in the experience that thinking is hardly ever just a problem of being right or wrong and is always already a matter of feeling—that thinking requires taking creative leaps of trust. It requires the taking of risks that the problems that make us think themselves demand. To these others, friends and colleagues, I thank you. This book is for you.

Among them, I want to start by thanking Monica Greco, who encouraged me to undertake this project at a time when others would have remained sceptical and who has offered me the kind of intellectual and personal friendship that combines, uniquely, the freedom of the possible with the care of the one who takes possibilities seriously. I also want to thank Marsha Rosengarten, for her invaluable friendship and unparalleled generosity, as well as for her unceasing faith in, and enthusiastic engagement with, the adventure of thinking.

For her continuous inspiration and generous, engaged comments, I would like to thank Isabelle Stengers.

My heartfelt thanks also go to Vikki Bell, Mariam Motamedi-Fraser, Felipe Lagos, Celia Lury, Patricio Rojas, and Alberto Toscano for giving me some wonderful comments and thoughts on what has become this book. My deep gratitude is also owed to Alex Wilkie, who not only commented on some chapters but generously helped me to think through, and contributed to, the cover of the book.

None of this would have been possible without the continuous support of members of my family who, in different ways and at different distances, remain always present: Viviana, Luisa, Norberto, Santiago, Carlos, and Paco—my gratitude to you is beyond words.

Special thanks also go to all my colleagues and friends who have supported me throughout these years, engaged with my work by reading and commenting on chapters and papers, and joined me in many conversations that have helped me re-create my habits of thinking and feeling in novel ways. Among them, Svenja Bromberg, Nerea Calvillo, Angela Castrechini, Joe Deville, Andrés Di Masso, Fernando Gabucio, Moritz Gansen, Nicolas Hausdorf, Jose Manuel Hernández, Wiebke Keim, Sean Legassick, Ulli Levri, Santiago Maestrojuan, Micki Manchón, Albano Manganelli, Angelo Martins, Sibille Merz, Felipe Palma, Jose Borges Reis, Sanjay Seth, and Tomeu Vidal—Thank you all!

I am indebted and thankful to the Centre for the Study of Invention and Social Process (CSISP), Department of Sociology, Goldsmiths, as well as the Department of Science and Technology Studies, University College London, for their support and for having given me the opportunity me to be surrounded by such remarkable intellectual communities throughout these years.

My thanks also go to Judith Allan, Philippa Grand, and the entire editorial and design team at Palgrave Macmillan for their support during the preparation of the manuscript.

Last but by no means least, I want to thank Inês Violante, whose unexpected appearance in my life has marked a difference between a before and an after, a veritable transformation of the possible.

# Contents

1 Introduction: The Care of Knowledge — 1

2 The Question of Relevance — 25

3 The Risks of Invention — 57

4 Thinking With Encounters — 89

5 Modes of Connection — 121

6 An Ethics of Adventure — 153

7 For Speculative Experimentation — 181

8 Afterword: Becoming an Apprentice — 209

References — 221

Index — 239

# Foreword, by Isabelle Stengers

Relevance as an adventure! Martin Savransky's proposal sounds both like an appeal and a challenge. Among the many words which, today, have been captured by neo-liberal governance, relevance may be the most entrapping one. Who would claim irrelevance? Who would affirm that the knowledge she is concerned with is unable to make the least difference for our understanding of its object, or can be of interest for nobody, even her colleagues? Obviously, arcane fields in mathematics, physics, or philology may claim 'disinterestedness', but even there examples are promoted that tell how a piece of abstract knowledge that looked like devoid of any imaginable consequences came to matter, acquired an importance nobody would contest.

What to do when a word has been dishonoured—here, when relevance comes to mean that researchers in the social sciences have to answer institutional demands, contribute to the solution of pre-set problems the formulation of which they have to globally accept, and when they have to pre-define the 'impact' of their work? To abandon it would quickly leave us wordless or reduced to the noble exercise of critical denunciation—an inexhaustible resource, certainly, but one that can relate recalcitrant social sciences and humanities to a dangerously inflated idea of the importance of the critical stance as the only buttress against so-called objectifying, non-reflexive, positive scientific practices.

Martin Savransky's proposition spoils this oppositional game. If relevance means the event of a 'coming to matter', it should have significance across the whole diversified field of so-called modern sciences and have them all resisting, each in its own way, to what would thwart their specific adventure. Certainly, in the experimental sciences relevance can be related to the infamous 'Nature has spoken', which transforms into a claim for authority the specific achievement which is the very soul of the experimental adventure: experimental 'facts' able, *in the specific situation of the laboratory*, to verify that their promoters have posed a relevant question to what they dealt with. Right from the beginning, Galileo and his successors have indeed privileged 'the authority of the facts' over the event of relevance, downplaying the very specific and exceptional character of their achievement, encouraging the exportation 'out of the lab' of what has proved to be relevant in the lab.

As we know, the experimenters' usual disregard for the possibility that relevance may be lost in translation, that the 'objective knowledge' they obtain is situation-dependant, has not been challenged by other sciences. Scientific authority has proved such a potent lure for scientists, and also such a potent lever for those who Bruno Latour called 'the allies of Science' (State and the industry), that the proposition that relevance and what it entails must be taken seriously and defended as such can strangely enough be called 'speculative' in a double sense: it activates what may be possible against the power of the state of affairs, and it implies that relevance—something coming to matter—is an 'event of the world', not a subjective appreciation. When critiques deconstruct the experimenters' 'Nature has spoken', they are right to deconstruct the claim that this must matter for everybody, whatever the situation, but they are wrong to deconstruct the event—something coming to matter for something else may well be the (speculative) formula for what William James characterised as the 'universe in the making'.

It may well be that *reclaiming* relevance against the dominant state of academic affairs is today a collective critical concern for all sciences as none has escaped the temptation of downplaying or even willingly ignoring, in the name of progress, the 'messy' answer the social-natural worlds were liable to give to what they proposed as objectively mattering. What Savransky calls the 'ecology of dynamic and fragile patterns of relevance, of modes of mattering for oneself and for others' has often been 'discovered' too late, after a pattern has suffered the so-called unfortunate collateral damages occasioned by a techno-social innovation. The way our worlds have been shaped tells us about the striking absence of this 'care of knowledge' which Savransky associates with relevance, and we should ask to those who would protest that knowledge must be uncaring in order to be 'objective', the question never to be forgotten: 'cui bono?' In the social sciences especially, objectivity can hardly be dissociated from the silencing of those voices who would contest an innovation and demand that attention be paid to some of its, in fact quite foreseeable, destructive consequences. When a sociologist deals about the 'public perception of a problem' it must be said that the study usually turns to be about the statistical analysis of the many ways in which the public opinion is wrong about this problem.

Conversely, Martin Savransky's book cannot be dissociated from our epoch, when it is no longer a question of 'unfortunate collateral damages' brought by the kind of development vectorised by techno-scientific innovations, but of the very future of the inhabitants of the planet, humans, and non-humans. The (capitalist) privilege given to disembedded and disembedding knowledge and strategies has opposed giving relevance to the messy complications of this world. But messiness is returning with a vengeance. Ignoring it, dreaming of its eradication, we discover that we have not only messed up our world but also, unwittingly but quite efficiently, triggered the destruction of the very stability of this world, the only one we have. If there is a chance to escape the worse, it demands a determinate refusal to entrust our endangered future to the very same ones who have created this situation, are still imposing their business-as-usual approach, and now begin to openly dream of geo-engineering and of a 'rational management' of the earth. We urgently need sciences that reclaim relevance, sciences that learn to embrace the entangled 'sociality' of this world, and contribute, through their inquiries, to make it matter, to resist both careless and uncaring techno-social interventions.

In order to take relevance seriously Martin Savransky has called to the companionship of a number of thinkers, among whom I am honoured to figure. The common feature shared by these companions is their pragmatist conception of thinking as a transformative exercise, against what he calls the 'ethics of estrangement' taken as the condition to gain access to the realm of facts and causes beyond that of illusory appearances. The experience of relevance, Savransky writes, 'involves a sense that *there is value beyond ourselves*—that something that is not ourselves, *matters*.' This heralds a second common feature of the companions he is thinking with. One way or another, reclaiming relevance means daring to connect the speculative, the ethical, and the practical, that is, to craft lines of escape from the territory organised by the three *Critiques* of Immanuel Kant.

Against Kant, the master of the ethics of estrangement who prohibited speculation and proposed that we should address nature as judges interrogating suspects, not as students learning from their teacher, he proposes the figure of the apprentice, who has to learn how to know, a learning always situated by the problematic situation which she must succeed in allowing it to become her teacher. A demanding adventure indeed, and a risky one, since it admits no final arbiter, no ground to judge the teaching. But to accept this risk, to renounce knowledge as a right and embrace its achievement as an event, is precisely the specificity of the adventure of the modern sciences when they aim at relevance, what requires the kind of collective—both critical and cooperative—effort which is its very soul.

As for philosophers who recall that Kant made Horace's *Sapere aude!*, dare to know, the motto of the Enlightenment, even if he himself meant 'dare to use your own reason', it may be that they should also recall that 'sapere' was related to 'taste' and that tasting implies the risky and careful encounter with something which can sustain or poison. To dare and taste may well be what is demanded in order to counter the deadly question 'Is relevance "objective" or "subjective"'? We have to dare and taste the poison of this question, which is the mother of the blind alignment of our practices with what Alfred North Whitehead dubbed as the absurdity at the very heart of modern thought: the 'bifurcation of nature'. This may mean accepting the challenge proposed by William James in *Pragmatism and Humanism* about the ideas, theories, and modes of intervention taken as additions to the universe in the making: 'The great question is: does it, with our additions, rise or fall in value? Are the additions worthy or unworthy?'

Isabelle Stengers

Université Libre de Bruxelles,
Brussel, Belgium

# 1

# Introduction: The Care of Knowledge

## Stepping Out into the Open

In 1971 Argentinian writer Julio Cortázar, internationally renowned for his *magnum opus Hopscotch* (1966), as well as for his fantastic short stories, wrote a piece titled *Prosa del observatorio*,[1] a text which according to conventional literary genres would seem to be unclassifiable. While Cortázar is certainly well-known for a form of literature where not only realism and fantasy are intertwined to the point of becoming indistinguishable, but which also transgresses the rules of composition of literary cannons, many of the reviewers of *From the Observatory* (2011) agree in regarding this piece as his most unconventional work. A dream-like visual prose poem-cum-letter-cum-essay that today might be associated with a speculative fabulation on science and life, I read *From the Observatory* as a plea that speaks to the future. Indeed, to a possible future which, while perhaps unlikely, remains a vital source for cultivating a different mode of inhabiting the world.

---

[1] Translated by Anne Mclean as *From the Observatory* (2011).

By moving between a response to an article on the life cycle of eels published in *Le Monde* on 14 April 1971, and the spectral, visual experience of the wonderful structures of the Maharajah Jai Singh's eighteenth-century astronomical observatories in Jaipur and Delhi, the poem articulates a proposition for a different mode of cultivating that very peculiar kind of experience that we normally call 'knowing'. A mode that, throughout this book, I will attempt to make resonate with some of the challenges with which contemporary forms of social inquiry are confronted today.

In encountering the poem, one realises that what sets it into motion is nothing other than an experience of perplexity. And such a perplexity is twofold. First, it concerns the lively, moving, and disconcertingly epic life cycle of eels,

> eels born in the Atlantic depths that begin, because we have to begin to follow them, to grow, translucent larvae floating between two waters, crystalline amphitheater of jellyfish and plankton, mouths that slide in an interminable suction, bodies linked in the now multi-form serpent that some night, no one can know when, will rise up leviathan, emerge as an inoffensive and terrifying kraken, to initiate the migration along the ocean floor [...] [After living] for so many years at the edge of blades of water [the eels] return to submerge themselves in the gloom of the depths for hundred meters down, lay their eggs hidden by half a kilometre of slow silent thickness, and dissolve in death by the millions of millions, molecules of plankton that the first larvae already sip in the palpitation of incorruptible life. (Cortázar 2011: 19–20)

In attending to their adventures, Cortázar wonders about those eels that spend their lives 'at the edge of blades of water' travelling upstream while in the process they 'grow and change color [...] the muddy mimetic yellow [giving] way bit by bit to mercury'; those eels that, according to 'an obscure piece of wisdom from remote bestiaries', at some point in their life 'leave the water and invade the vegetable patches and orchard groves (those are the kinds of words they use in the bestiaries) to hunt for snails and worms, to eat the garden peas as it says in the Espasa Encyclopedia, which knows so much about eels' (2011: 40). He wonders, perplexed, about why, after such a saga, the eels 'commit suicide in their millions in the sluice gates and nets so the rest can pass and arrive' (2011: 29).

Perhaps what is most striking to Cortázar, however, is what becomes of the tragic adventure of the eels as they encounter the knowledge-practices of science, that 'lovely' science whose 'sweet' words 'follow the course of the elvers and tell us their saga' and whose astronomers from the observatory in Jaipur once 'wielded a vocabulary just as lovely and sweet to conjure the unnameable and pour it onto soothing parchments, inheritance for the species, school lesson, barbiturate for essential insomniacs' (2011: 29). What he finds puzzling, as do others—myself included—is the manner in which the quest for a knowledge that could be called 'scientific' transforms the eels' adventures into a set of 'theories of names and phases' that 'embalm eels in a nomenclature, in genetics, in a neuroendocrine process, from yellow to silver, from ponds to estuaries' and attempts to hold the cosmos still by 'gather[ing] into one mental fist the reins of that multitude of twinkling and hostile horses'. For Cortázar, the consequence is inevitable: 'the stars flee Jai Singh's eyes just as the eels do the words of science' (2011: 42).

While the scope of Cortázar's plea exceeds the specific procedures and requirements of neuroendocrinology and astronomy to encompass science as a whole, including the social sciences, it is not a mere rejection of either scientific practice or knowledge. He does not claim that the lively journey of eels or the cosmos should intrinsically escape scientific inquiry, nor does he necessarily anticipate that his own poetic experiment might be better equipped to come to grips with the dynamic, open nature of reality as such:

> dear Madame, what would we do without you, Lady Science, I'm speaking seriously, very seriously, but besides there is the open, the redheaded night, the units of excess, the clowning, tightrope walking, somnambulist quality of the average citizen, the fact that no one will convince him that his precise limits are those of the happiest city or the most pleasant countryside; school does what it does, and the army, the priests, but what I call eel or milky way persists in a species memory, in a genetic program Professor Fointaine has no idea of, and so the revolution in its moment, attacking the objectively abject or enemy, the delirious swipe to bring down a rotten city, so the first stages of the reencounter with the whole man. (2011: 62)

Rather than opposing scientific inquiry, what Cortázar's plea is trying to resist is a specific *kind* of science. He opposes a science that, in exclusively attempting 'to measure, compute, understand, belong, enter, die less poor, to oppose this studded incomprehensibility hand to hand' (2011: 41), would not risk stepping out into the open thereby failing to come to terms with what matters to those it addresses. As he forcefully affirms in addressing his two figurative epitomes of scientific rationality:

> So, Professor Fontaine, it's not diffuse pantheism we're talking about, nor dissolution in mystery: the stars are measurable, the ramps of Jaipur still bear traces of mathematical chisels, cages of abstraction and understanding. What I reject while you gill me up with information on the course of the leptocephali is the sordid paradox of an impoverishment correlated to the multiplication of libraries, microfilms and paperback editions, enlightenment á la Jivaro, Mademoiselle Callamand. Let Lady Science stroll through her garden, sing and embroider, fair is her figure and necessary her remote-controlled distaff and her electronic lute, we are not the Boeotians of our century, the brontosaurus is well and truly dead. But then one goes out to wander in the night, as so many of Lady Science's servants undoubtedly do too, and if one lives for real, if night and our breathing and thought link those meshes that so many definitions separate, it can happen that we might enter parks in Jaipur or Delhi, or in the heart of Saint-Germain-des-Prés we might brush against another possible profile of man; laughable or terrible things can happen to us, we might access cycles that begin in the doorway of a café and end up on a gallows in the main square of Baghdad, or stepping on an eel in the rue du Dragon, or spotting from afar like in a tango that woman who filled our life with broken mirrors and structuralist nostalgia (she never finished doing her hair, and we never finished our doctoral thesis). (2011: 56–57)

In this way, the plea that opens up the space for such an unclassifiable text bears the mark of a challenge—a challenge for scientific inquiries not to demand compliance of what they seek to understand, and instead, to learn to come to terms with it. Again, learning to come to terms with it does not imply ceasing to ask questions and dissolving our inquiries into utter mysticism. Rather, it involves speculating on the possibility of inventing new and different modes of asking questions—'*we must*', he urges us, 'feather and launch the arrow of the question another way, from another departure point, toward something else' (2011: 43, emphasis added).

## Reconstructing Social Inquiry or, What Is Ethics?

In a sense, the plea that *From the Observatory* articulates in its own inimitable style is one that resonates with a series of urgent questions with which the contemporary social sciences are confronted today—a series of questions that constitute the very core of this book. How might the knowledges produced by the social sciences come to terms with this global and complex world, indeed, this world of 'blooming, buzzing confusion', as William James (1957: 488) once described it from the perspective of the early experience of a baby? What new modes of feathering and launching questions might we have to invent, from where and in what directions would we launch them, were we concerned with producing forms of knowledge that will contribute not merely to the multiplication of paperbacks but to the future of those who, in Cortázar's words, 'live for real'?

Insofar as the invention of the modern social sciences in the nineteenth century can be said to be related to the emergence of practical problems of governance of expanding and increasingly complex populations, such questions may be thought to be anything but new. However, the modernist mode of posing those questions, the subsequent history of the social sciences throughout the twentieth- and into the twenty-first century, as well as the global socio-material transformations of the world during this period, testify to the need, or more, the demand, to simultaneously reclaim those questions and *reconstruct* the manner in which they are cultivated and launched.

In a sense, then, the attempt this book will make could be associated to a transformed version of John Dewey's (2004) project of 'reconstruction'. Dewey's aim in his project of reconstructing philosophy after the First and the Second World War was marked by what he saw as the demand upon philosophy and the problems with which it was concerned to become relevant to the continuous changes in human affairs which at times constitute veritable events in the world's history. Concerned with what he perceived as a profound disjunction between the premises of philosophical inquiry and the unstable consequences of the ingression of scientific inventions into the realm of human affairs throughout the first half of the twentieth century, Dewey sought to redress this disconnection by producing a reconstruction of the manner in which philosophical inquiry is conducted.

Philosophy, Dewey argued, cannot continue confining itself to dealing only with that which is 'taken to be fixed, immutable, and therefore out of time [...], that is, eternal.' In contrast, it had to become capable of dealing with the urgent demands of the world with which it was then confronted. Demands that, in science, in technology and in politics, forced one to 'abandon the assumption of fixity and to recognize that what for it is actually "universal" is *process*' (Dewey 2004: vii–viii, emphasis in original). So what is a reconstruction?

As Dewey (2004: xvii) forcefully claimed, 'reconstruction can be nothing less than the work of developing, of forming, of producing (in the literal sense of that word), the intellectual instrumentalities which will progressively direct inquiry.' Dewey's aim was the production of intellectual instrumentalities, of conceptual tools, for the 'construction of a moral human science' which would allow a reorientation of human affairs and provide 'other conditions of a fuller life than man has enjoyed' (2004: xxii). The inquiry that the production of such intellectual instruments would progressively direct was, for him, an inquiry concerned with the 'deeply and inclusively human—that is to say, moral—facts of the present scene and situation' (xviii).

The kinds of criticisms that Cortázar levels against 'Lady Science', namely, the proliferations of technical names, of methods and instruments at the expense of an 'impoverished' experience of the world, one that prevents us from coming to terms with what matters for those who 'live for real', intimately resonate with Dewey's plea for reconstruction. To be sure, they also seemingly resonate with the dangerous backdrop against which C. Wright Mills's *The Sociological Imagination* (2000) attempted to articulate a liberating promise—a promise against the danger of indulging in totalising yet impenetrable and thus, inert, 'grand theories', on the one hand, and of an inhibition prompted by confusing methodology with the substantive issues at stake—what Mills terms 'abstracted empiricism'—on the other. Today, Mills's 'promise of social science' is one which has regained importance in current debates around the so-called crisis of contemporary social science. Such a crisis, I shall argue later in the book, can be read as a series of demands for such sciences to both justify and enhance the 'relevance' of their practices at a time when their institutional and material survival within universities seems to be under threat of dissolution.

Given this historical conjuncture, I am of the view that a project of reconstruction might constitute a productive means of engaging some of the challenges faced by the contemporary social sciences. If they are to intervene productively in the institutional and intellectual challenges that besiege their presents and possible futures, we need now, more than ever, a creative, reconstructive activity of conceptual and practical invention. Nevertheless, because the conditions that the social sciences face today differ in important ways from those that constituted the point of departure of the Deweyian project, we cannot carry out a reconstruction of contemporary forms social inquiry without, at the same time, posing anew the question of what the task of reconstruction might involve today.

Thus, while in the early twentieth century Dewey saw the construction of social and human sciences as a promising mode of reconstructing philosophy, the developments in the mainstream of such sciences throughout the last century suggest that, today, they might themselves be the ones in need of reconstruction. These developments show, moreover, that the 'deep and inclusively human facts' that he regarded as the aim of such enterprise have been taken to be—rather disappointingly—only 'exclusively' human. As I shall argue later on, in an age of global crises of both economy and ecology, a reconstruction that reclaims the concern for the deeply and inclusively human is not about an entrenched defence of the all-too-modern forms of anthropocentric humanism. Rather, what it requires is precisely that we question the exclusive humanisms that the social sciences have instituted in their habits of thinking and feeling and that we take the risk of *reimagining* the relationships between humans and the more-than-human milieus of which they are a part.

A further difference between a classic Deweyian exercise in 'reconstruction' and the one that this book will carry out concerns the kind of work that such intellectual instrumentalities are meant to perform.

In other words, it concerns the kind of tools that such an exercise may produce. Indeed, for Dewey intellectual instrumentalities are conceived, at least partially, as the invention of solutions to a pre-existing problem of relevance that affected the dominant mode of philosophical inquiry at the turn of the twentieth century. A problem of relevance characterised by philosophy's incapacity to come to terms with the transient nature of events that demanded urgent inquiry. In order to overcome this problem, Dewey proposed that philosophy had to abandon its fascination with the eternal and come to terms with process.

Insofar as the present conjuncture that concerns the contemporary social sciences has to a large extent already been framed as a series of demands for relevance by governmental institutions, funding bodies, and some social researchers (see Chap. 2), however, a reconstruction of their modes of inquiry cannot simply become yet another demand for relevance, nor simply an instrument for producing solutions to prior demands. By contrast, we must begin by taking the concept of relevance seriously and entertain the problematic question of what it is that is demanded when such demands are articulated in practice. In fact, as I will show, although a demand for taking the question of relevance seriously may be welcome and timely, the manner in which such demands are usually framed, as well as their implicit conceptions of what the nature of so-called relevance is and what it requires, seems to me to testify to the problem that this reconstruction must develop. As Dewey (2004: iii) would say, then, the concept of relevance must become the new 'locus from which detailed new developments must proceed.'

Most current demands for relevance implicitly or explicitly associate the term, and the problem it is said to pose, with more and better ways of making scientific practices and products, accountable, communicable, and public. Although I believe questions of public engagement do require attention, in this book I argue that reducing the question of relevance to how the knowledge-practices of the social sciences might make their findings more accessible, engaging, or interesting to a public leaves unexplored a difficult but crucial question. Namely, the question of *how* practices of social inquiry may come to terms with the situated ways in which experiences of various kinds and natures *come to matter*. It is this latter concern—a profoundly speculative one—that will be the object of this book.

In order to do this, I suggest, we need to conceive of relevance not as what belongs to a subjective value ascribed either by a social scientist or a public to the theoretical or empirical findings of social inquiry, but as *an event* that belongs, immanently, to the world. To express that 'something matters', that *it* is relevant, is to acknowledge that there is value *beyond ourselves*. The relevance of things, then, cannot be reduced to a judgement that is *passed on* to them, but must be seen as inhering in the situated specificity of the many existences that compose the world (see Chap. 2).

In other words, if it be capable of guiding a reconstruction, 'relevance' cannot be simply conceived as a solution to a pre-existing problem. Rather, it needs to be explored as a constraint on thought and practice that is at once problematic and problematising. In this way, the questions that the notion of relevance poses will force us to interrogate the manners in which the contemporary social sciences come to terms with the many heterogeneous facts and values that compose the worlds such sciences address. Simultaneously, it will prompt us to speculate, to devise propositions, for how such a coming-to-terms might be transformed.

Nevertheless, to say that 'relevance' is not itself a solution to a pre-existing problem must not be taken to mean that it opposes *any* solution. Rather, its problematic and problematising character forces us to take seriously that, as Mariam Fraser (2010: 78) suggests, 'there is no true solution to a problem (although there are true problems). [...] The best—and this is indeed the best, in value terms—that a solution can do is to develop a problem'. In short, then, the aim of this book is to engage with 'relevance' as a problematic question capable of affecting the ways in which some forms of social inquiry are habitually conducted, and to extract from this process real possibilities that may be cultivated with a view towards future, alternative modes of inquiry.

The precise meaning and implications of the above will become clearer, I hope, as this book proceeds. For now, however, it is worth noting that although the instruments that this kind of reconstruction might produce can be called 'intellectual' in that their articulation will be achieved by means of a conceptual exploration of problems and possibilities of certain forms of social inquiry, the change sought is not for that reason to be reduced to the 'merely' intellectual or theoretical dimensions that might underpin, contest, or help justify social scientific inquiries.

By contrast, what such a reconstruction aims at is a cultivation of a different set of *ethical sensibilities* to inform social inquiry—a mutation of the *ethos* that animates their modes of knowing, their *habits* of thinking and feeling.[2] By ethical sensibilities I of course do not mean to say that we are here dealing with codes of good conduct. In fact, the general institutional guidelines that are commonly referred to as 'research ethics' will not here be my concern. More than this, what we mean by 'ethics' in the context of thinking about and of producing knowledge in the contemporary social sciences will, in the course of this exploration, acquire a radically different meaning. By ethical sensibilities I mean the orientations, the intellectual and practical deportments, that both animate and become cultivated through certain practices, and that inextricably entangle certain modes of thinking, certain modes of doing, and certain modes of inhabiting the world.

In other words, I here use the term 'ethics' in a sense that may be associated with the works of philosophers like Pierre Hadot (1995) and Michel Foucault (1984a, 1990, 1997a), and which more recently has been taken up, in different ways, by other scholars in social, cultural, and political theory and the history of science. An understanding that aims not at providing a universal, general answer to the anonymous questions of 'what is the good?' or 'what is evil?', but which rather invites attention to, and care for, an entire 'mode of existing in the world' (Hadot 1995: 265). Ethics here concerns in a broad sense the immanent, practical, and situated question of 'how is one to live?' A question to which no productive response can be given that does not emerge from a transformative *exercise*—Dewey would have called it a 'reconstruction'—aimed at cultivating certain modes of care one takes of oneself and of others when involved in practices of thinking, knowing and feeling. As William Connolly (1995: 127) has suggested in his *The Ethos of Pluralization*:

---

[2] Throughout this book, the notion of habit is not intended to connote a certain conservativeness. Rather, it is employed in the more neutral sense put forth by Dewey (1922: 66), as 'an ability, an art, formed through past experience'. Conservativeness is not intrinsic to habit but depends entirely on the character of the habit in question: 'whether an ability is limited to repetition of past acts adopted to past conditions or is available for new emergencies depends wholly upon what kind of habits exists.' This is why the work to be developed here is not a fight against habits but an attempt to cultivate different ones.

The ethical point is to struggle against the temptation to allow an existing code of authority or justice to dominate the field of ethics entirely; the ethical idea is to maintain critical tension between a congealed code of authority and justice and a more porous fund of critical responsiveness that might be drawn upon to modify it in the light of contemporary injuries it engenders and positive possibilities it ignores.

Emerging out of the scholarly study of Hellenistic and Roman thought, Foucault's understanding of the ethical question of 'how is one to live?' was concerned with the way in which such exercises involve a work of cultivation directed, first and foremost, toward a transformation of the self upon the self. While Foucault's work has been criticised for its possible overemphasis on the culture of the self (see Hadot 1995; Myers 2013), an overemphasis that bears the danger of turning ethics into a therapeutics, my sense is that such a danger may be avoided by rejecting any clear-cut separation between self and world. Selves are nothing if not ingredients in a world that transcends them. In this way, to induce a transformation of one's own way of existing in the world must also involve a transformation, however modest, of the *world's own manner of existence*.

I will come back to this issue at the end of the book, after the speculative exploration of the question of relevance has been undertaken (see Afterword). But I should note here that insofar as self and world are not to be fundamentally split apart, the question of 'how is one to live?' cannot be dissociated—especially not whenever scientific practices are concerned—from the perhaps narrower question of 'how is one to know?'[3] The care of the self, as Foucault would refer to this ethical work upon oneself, involves a care of the world and this, in turn, requires a *care of knowledge*. In fact, it will be this latter interrogation—whose possible responses demand as much practical cultivation as those belonging to the

---

[3] This should be not confused with the Western trope of 'know thyself', which both Hadot and Foucault have so dextrously discussed in terms of a care of the self. I should also point out that by posing the question of 'how is one to know?' I am not suggesting that knowledge or cognition is our primary or in any sense privileged mode of relating to the world. Far from it. I am simply highlighting it because it is, after all, a question that very much concerns the sciences, whatever one takes this latter term to mean or include. More accurate however would be to say that the question 'how is one to live?' must involve the question 'how is one to experience?' and that what we call knowledge is a particular form that experience may take.

interrogation about how to live—that I believe the question of relevance has the potential of setting in motion. My contention in this book is that restoring relevance to the world—instead of confining it to the mind—provides crucial resources for cultivating the possibility of a different care of knowledge in the contemporary social sciences.

## Contemporary Social Sciences and the Ethics of Inquiry

As Dewey's (2004: xxii) own endeavour makes patently present, a reconstruction is an especially arduous, demanding task that requires 'the widest possible scholarship as to the connections of past systems with the cultural conditions that set their problems and a knowledge of present-day science which is other than that of "popular" expositions.' I read this as a demand to think *with* the very sciences that a reconstruction may seek to affect, to understand their habitual modes of inquiry and to extract from their interstices resources that may serve as tools for guiding their transition into a future that be more than a mere extension of their historical present.

To characterise this reconstruction as 'speculative', that is, as oriented towards the cultivation of a different future that without its intervention might have been harder to imagine or achieve, must not be taken as a sign that it operates by an unconstrained practice of conjecture or guesswork (see Chap. 7). To the extent that it involves the taking of a leap, the risking of a thought that may lead us to a novel experience, it also requires that the ground from which one may jump be taken seriously. So how to take seriously a speculative reconstruction whose ground bears the name of 'contemporary social science'? Is not the latter simply too extensive, complex, heterogeneous, even *disparate*, to serve as a possible ground?

To be sure, the term 'social science' tends to include a multiplicity of disciplines, epistemologies, theories, languages, methodologies, objects and aims, and there is no general consensus as to what the criteria for inclusion or exclusion may be. As John Brewer (2013: 20–21) has recently suggested, most public bodies—such as the UK's Academy of the Social Sciences, the US Social Science Research Council, or the

International Social Science Council (ISSC)—tend to omit definitions of the term even in high-profile reports on the present statuses and futures of such sciences.

The 2013 World Social Science Report (ISSC 2013: 44), for instance, states in a footnote that 'throughout this Report, and in line with the ISSC's scientific membership base, reference to the "social sciences" should be understood as including the social, behavioural and economic sciences', but it does not define what any of the these constitute. The website of the UK's Economic and Social Research Council (2014) does offer an extensive list of potential disciplines and post-disciplinary undertakings, ranging from Sociology, Psychology, and Social Anthropology to Linguistics, Law, Management, Economics, and Social History, among others. However, the fact that in their website they also include a video with 'viewpoints' on the question of 'What is social science?' seems to testify to the fact that no single grouping, however inclusive, will do.

Moreover, if we put the question not only at the level of disciplines but at the level of the epistemologies, theories, languages, and methods that both compose and cut across those disciplines, the chances of a non-arbitrary definition become even slighter. And although at first sight it might appear that despite the aforementioned disparities the objects of inquiry may indeed be shared, including "society" and "humans" as preferred choices, some social scientists have not only contested that these shall constitute appropriate objects for social science, but have also disputed the very fact that something called 'society' or 'humanity' may be conceived as having any distinct and stable existence (e.g., Haraway 2008; Latour 2005).

In an effort to find a solution to this problem, many of the historiographical and theoretical works that take 'the social sciences' as their ground for thought begin precisely by delimiting their frontiers as much as possible. In those instances, the criteria employed for drawing the borders of the social sciences are commonly those of geography and periodicity. Thus, the rise of 'social theory' in France between 1750 and 1850 (Heilbron 1995), the co-development of the social sciences and the capitalist world-system from the nineteenth century onwards (Wallerstein 2001), and the emergence and role of the social sciences within an epochal understanding of 'modernity' (Wagner 2001) are some of the most famous and, to my mind, most sophisticated studies that take such criteria for delimiting their grounds.

These criteria do have methodological and heuristic value in providing a fairly succinct border for delimiting a ground from which to exercise, in thought, a jump into a possible future. Unless presented very carefully, however, they may also have the pernicious effect of naturalising traditions whose frontiers and lines of continuity are otherwise singularised retrospectively by the very practices of history-writing that mobilise them.

In other words, they may be seen as presupposing that geography and periodicity—rather than, say, intellectual traditions not bound by geography, or other non-chronological forms of cultural memory (see Schlanger 1994)—constitute, by definition, what matters in any historiographical and/or theoretical inquiry into the social sciences. As the famous *Report of the Gulbenkian Commission On the Restructuring of the Social Sciences* (Wallerstein et al. 1996) convincingly argued, however, if one considers the processes of circulation of knowledge across national boundaries, the proliferation of disciplinary overlaps brought about by pressure for increased specialisation, as well as the creation of so-called area studies following the Second World War—which for their part turned certain geographical locations into multi-disciplinary, multi-theoretical, multi-method fields of social research—geography and periodicity become premises that can no longer be taken for granted.

In sum, what such a plethora of possible demarcations seems to suggest is that there is no single, correct, natural, exhaustive way of delimiting a ground. Rather, such gestures of bordering might be more productively taken as abstract propositions. Abstract, because they necessarily omit part of the truth; propositions, because they combine actuality and potentiality—they are 'tales that perhaps might be told about particular actualities' (Whitehead 1978: 256). Tales which make certain problems, exercises in thought, and certain possible transformations available for development.

My own definition has no ambition of being anything more than this, a tale that might be told about some pasts, presents, and futures of social inquiry. As we shall see, however, it matters how tales are told. To the extent that the current study is concerned with producing instruments that may induce not only a shift in thought but employ thinking as a means to cultivate a different ethos, or a different care of knowledge, I here propose to understand the 'contemporary social sciences' not primarily along disciplinary, epistemological, objectual, geographical, or chronological lines, but in ethical terms. That is, as a historically situated *attitude*, an intellectual deportment that informs certain modes of coming to terms with how experiences come to matter.

I am thus using the term 'contemporary social science' deliberately, and not simply as a synonym for, say, 'the present of social science'. By contrast, I take the seemingly unproblematic notion of the 'contemporary' to be traversed by a productive tension that emerges from the two senses it conjoins. A tension that I have no intentions of dispelling, but which I will attempt to inhabit. As Paul Rabinow (2008) has suggested, one acceptation of the contemporary designates that which is distinctively *modern*, where 'modern' connotes not an epoch but a historically cultivated ethos, not a chronological period but the form of an intellectual and ethical attitude to oneself and to the world. The conception of the world such an attitude may be associated with could perhaps be characterised by what philosopher Alfred North Whitehead (2004) famously termed the 'bifurcation of nature'. Although we will have many opportunities to discuss this notion and its implications for the contemporary social sciences in more detail in the next chapter and throughout the book, briefly put, the bifurcation of nature consists in dividing reality in two—a causal realm of fact, on the one hand, and an experiential realm of appearances, on the other.

In this way, the bifurcation of nature involves a conception whereby experience discloses only that which is apparent, whereas the 'relevant' factors in the process of knowing the world must always lie, and be sought, somewhere else. I believe such a conception admits a translation into ethical terms, involving a particularly modern care of knowledge which I call the *ethics of estrangement*—a mode of inquiry consisting in *becoming estranged* from the realm of appearances made available by direct experience in order *to gain access* to a realm of facts and causes.[4] As I

---

[4] I will explore the specificities of such exercises in more detail in the coming chapters. Only by way of illustration, however, we may think about the positivist fascination with 'scientific method' as

show in this book, such an ethos arguably characterises much—although of course not all—of what we usually associate with social science.

I want to suggest, however, that resisting the bifurcation of nature by restoring relevance to the world may enable us to cultivate a different care of knowledge. One that, instead of presupposing that what matters in a given situation lies hidden behind a realm of appearance that a knowledge-practice would seek to uncover, rejects the very ontological bifurcation between the two realms. It proposes, in turn, that all the relevant facts and the only relevant facts that a practice of inquiry has to come to terms with *are the facts of experience*. Thus, while this alternative mode of knowing is one which adopts a resolutely empiricist outlook, it does so by reclaiming a deep version of empiricism that can be associated with the work of William James and Alfred North Whitehead. That is, a radical empiricism which expands 'experience' to include not just isolated facts or things but also the experienced relations between them; not only human or subjective experiences, but also other-than-human experiences; not only perceptive experience, but also the experience of thought, concepts and ideas; not just the experience of things as they are, but also of what they could be. It entertains experiences *all the way down*. As Whitehead (1967a: 256) put it in his *Adventures of Ideas*:

> Nothing can be omitted, experience drunk and experience sober, experience sleeping and experience waking, experience drowsy and experience wide-awake, experience self-conscious and experience self-forgetful, experience intellectual and experience physical, experience religious and experience sceptical, experience anxious and experience care-free, experience anticipatory and experience grieving, experience dominated by emotion and experience under-self-restraint, experience in the light and experience in the dark, experience normal and experience abnormal.

---

providing value-free access to the real, objective, social facts; the interpretativist and symbolic traditions that sought to account for social phenomena by accessing a non-apparent realm of 'meaning' informing them; the Marxist tradition that sought to explain social and cultural phenomena by recourse to an underlying set of economic forces; the structuralisms that searched for unconscious, universal, and transhistorical patterns organising human culture and society; the social constructivist stances that placed 'social construction' as the real 'cause' of what might otherwise appear as natural phenomena; the post-structuralisms which, although rejecting the possibility of accessing a realm of factual reality beyond value, still seek to strip away experience from its self-evidence.

But there is more. To the extent that, in its second acceptation, the 'contemporary' also designates a space characterised by the co-presence of heterogeneous elements, regions, and practices of thought and feeling that populate it with relative mutual independence, speaking of 'contemporary social science' has the advantage of preventing us from equating the modern ethos with a self-enclosed, totalising system. As Whitehead (1967a: 195) has noted, it is out of this constitutive heterogeneity of the contemporary that the possibility of freedom and thus, of a different future, arises. It is also out of such heterogeneity that a speculative experiment in reconstruction is practicable—for speculation begins by thinking with unique situations, which make possibilities present by having already succeeded in actualising them somewhere else, in other forms, under different names.

Moreover, the co-presence of *contemporaries* also has the advantage of enabling the tools produced by a reconstruction to become more refined. In this sense, and precisely as a response to what I have called the modern ethics of estrangement, novel forms of empiricism have already begun to proliferate in the social scientific literature of recent years (Adkins and Lury 2009). The exercise of cultivating a different care of knowledge in the contemporary social sciences will thus require that we draw, whenever pertinent, specific contrasts between this and other forms of empiricism already available. For the moment, however, a general contrast may help orient the more specific ones that will follow. This is that, unlike some other forms of empiricism in the social sciences, the kind of empiricism underpinning this project is not of the type that takes the task of knowing to simply be that of disclosing, discovering, or describing the world as if all experiences were immediately present and available for representation.

Although it does postulate the priority of experience, and it proposes that everything that exists *is* relevant, that it *matters in some degree and manner*, the possibility of knowing is associated with the challenge of *inquiring* into how—again, in what degree and what manner—multiple and heterogeneous experiences come to matter in specific situations. In other words, the question 'how is one to know?' is not *epistemological* in nature but rather *practical*, pertaining to the speculative construction of a mode of inquiry. And inquiries begin in problematic situations, whose relevant definitions become unknowns in the direction of which the inquiry shall be oriented (Dewey 2008a).

As I hope to show, the ethics of inquiry to be developed here does not seek—unlike much critical work in social theory and unlike other recent empiricist projects—to force the contemporary social sciences to abandon their ideals. By contrast, it invites them to experience their possible mutation in a world that in many ways no longer resembles the one in which they were born. In this way, among the propositions that will emerge from such an exploration are an attentive constructivism that is constrained by an inventive sense of objectivity, fact, and experience; an account of the efficacy of knowledge that does not forget the active roles of the many milieus with which the former connects; and a concern for a more-than-human world of events that does not disavow our attachments to human experience nor the possibility of emergent and always precarious forms of order. The task to be developed in what follows, thus, is to interrogate those conceptual, methodological, and practical requirements that have to be problematised, and to produce those that have to be cultivated, for such an ethics of inquiry to become possible.

Such a task cannot be produced in a vacuum. By contrast, it requires a practice of thinking *with* heterogeneous companions. As I have already suggested, some of those forms of companionship will be provided by empirical studies that *show*, rather than explain, forms of cultivating a different care of knowledge. Other companions constitute a diverse range of thinkers, including A. N. Whitehead, Gilles Deleuze, Isabelle Stengers, as well as the American pragmatists John Dewey and William James, among others, that will contribute insights and help name sensibilities that this study shall, in turn, affirmatively and selectively draw upon while both expanding and reworking.

Taking the cultivation of the possibility of a different care of knowledge as its aim, however, it must be noted that, while conceptual and theoretical, this project is not exegetical. As Gilles Deleuze (in Foucault 1980: 208) once affirmed, a theory 'must be useful. It must function. And not for itself. If no one uses it, beginning with the theoretician himself (who then ceases to be a theoretician), then the theory is worthless or the moment is inappropriate. We do not revise theories, but construct new ones; we have no choice but to make others.' To construct theories as tools is not to imply, however, that the toolbox is entirely flexible to whatever tool one might need, or that the tool itself is useful so long as it allows one to say or do what one had planned in advance, so long as it allows one to 'apply' it to some particular case.

My sense, by contrast, is that to the extent that theories may provide tools for thought and practice, they still always pose the challenge of how to learn to operate with them in relation to the problems at stake. The philosopher of technique Gilbert Simondon (2005: 53. my translation) already warned us about the use of tools when he suggested that to know how to use a tool is not simply about acquiring the practice to perform the required gestures. Rather, 'it is about knowing how to recognise, by way of the signs that arrive to man through the tool, the implicit form of the matter under elaboration, at the precise spot where the tool operates.'

To my mind this is true both when 'the matter' refers to the demands that an empirical situation might make, and when it signals a matter of thought and concerns the obligations that thought places upon thinking when struggling to coming to terms with, and to develop, a problem. Moreover, in actual fact, and certainly in what follows, 'the matter' refers to both at once. In the context of this work, then, reading is not simply what makes a certain mode of thinking possible but it is itself an exercise in taking care of how we think.

## Coming Steps

The task to be undertaken in this book cannot be produced in one blow. It will require piecemeal, progressive transitions making apparent those obstacles that need to be overcome, and those steps that demand to be taken, such that certain possibilities may become perceptible. Thus, the reconstruction to follow is composed of a series of chapters, each marking a step or transition in the process of inquiry. Therefore, each chapter builds on the preceding ones while adopting a distinct focus and set of questions that, by examining current debates in the contemporary social sciences, may allow us to progressively interrogate specific problems and to identify the ethical sensibilities required to cultivate a different care of knowledge.

The first problem to be developed is, to be sure, the problem of how to address the concept of relevance such that it may open up a reconstruction of the care of knowledge in the contemporary social sciences. In order to do this, in Chap. 2, I address some aspects of the so-called crisis of the contemporary social sciences by attending to the implicit ways in which 'relevance' seems to be conceived. By focusing specifically on some of the recent calls for forms of 'public' social science, I argue that although a demand for taking the question of relevance seriously might be welcome and timely, the way in which the question is often understood reproduces an ethics of estrangement and thus prevents the concept of relevance from becoming a potential lure for cultivating a different care of knowledge. By contrast, I argue that taking the question of relevance seriously forces us to come to terms with the possibility that the former inheres in the situated natures of facts. Relevance, in this sense, belongs to the order of an event and it is expressed in the experience that *facts matter*.

This shift in our understanding of 'relevance' will open up the possibility of cultivating a different ethics of inquiry, an *inventive* mode of knowing that takes the risk of negotiating the question of how, in what degrees and manners, things come to matter in specific situations. It is such a mode of inquiry that I associate with a different ethics, one that, for reasons that shall become apparent below, I call an 'adventure'. The aim of this reconstruction, therefore, is to arrive at a characterisation, however partial and provisional, of an ethics of adventure.

In Chap. 3 I seek to clarify the specific understanding of invention required by an adventure of relevance. Insofar as the question of relevance prompts us to affirm that there is value beyond ourselves, it involves the affirmation of a relative *outside*, an exteriority in relation to which knowledge-practices must put their questions at risk. An account of 'invention' attuned to the question of relevance must thus foreground the fact that inquiries are inventive of their own process but they do not create the objects or situations to which their questions are posed. As I show, this seemingly simple realisation challenges crucial assumptions about the nature of knowledge-making in many traditions of contemporary social science, from interpretivism to social constructivism and Actor-Network Theory. As a result, to think about the *risks of invention* requires that we reclaim a concept we have learned to treat with suspicion, namely, objectivity. The challenge is to develop a concept of objectivity that does not preclude but entails invention, and simultaneously, a concept of invention—that is, a form of constructivism—that would not make 'objectivity' absurd but crucial.

For their part, Chaps. 4 and 5 follow adventures of relevance in more practical terms. As I have suggested above, the task of a speculative reconstruction is to be performed not simply *on* but *with* practices. Thus Chap. 4 explores the real possibilities of practical invention, by thinking with actual, empirical research *encounters* in the contemporary social sciences that exhibit signs of already having embarked on adventures of relevance. It will risk thinking with encounters in disciplines such as Social Psychology, Cultural Anthropology, and Sociology; with methods such as experimentation, ethnography, and archival and text-based research; with objects of inquiry including humans, soybeans, words and their entanglements. As I show, such explorations not only help us illuminate some of the more general arguments previously made but, more importantly, they make perceptible the kinds of relationalities involved in negotiating the question of relevance.

In Chap. 5 I come back to the relationship between social inquiries and their relative outsides. This time, however, the exploration focuses on how to think about the ecological relationships between an accomplished invention and the worlds to which it might come to *connect*. To the extent that demands for relevance tend to reduce the latter to a suspicion about whether or not the contemporary social sciences are capable of making a difference beyond the academy, addressing the question of the efficacy of inventions is crucial. While those traditions that have embraced a logic of 'performativity'—whereby social science creates what it purports to represent—may seem better equipped to give an account of the effects that knowledge makes, I argue that many of their proponents exaggerate the claims to efficacy by oversimplifying the ecological relationships between inventions and the *milieus* with which they connect. In contrast, in this chapter I argue for the need to pay attention to the intricate, dynamic, and circulating forms of causality that obtain in such processes of connection and examine this by interrogating the complexities of one historical connection—the forced introduction of the concept of 'belief' in Colonial India.

Building on the lessons and intellectual instruments emerging from the preceding chapters, Chap. 6 takes up the challenge of risking a general characterisation of adventures as a care of knowledge. In order to do so, we need to elucidate the ontological nature of 'relevance' as an *event*, as well as the demanding and complex temporal and ethical requirements that events may pose on forms of social inquiry. As I show, events constitute the very pulse of reality and, as such, the relationship between inquiry and event cannot be one of attempting to *explain* the coming about of the latter by reducing it to pre-existent conditions of possibility, for events involve both ordinary and exceptional transformations of the possible. By contrast, I propose that a mode of social inquiry that is oriented by and towards events needs to come to terms with the latter's double temporality, and by the same token, with its double ethical demand—the demand to invent ways of inheriting the past while becoming exposed to possibilities concerning the future. It is this conjunction between what I shall call an 'ethics of inheritance' and an 'ethics of exposure' that articulates, both ethically and temporally, the care of knowledge that I have associated with adventures.

In Chap. 7 I explore the possible place and role that conceptual exercises such as the one performed throughout this book, may have within the radical empiricist framework that adventures adopt. In other words, I will raise a series of questions and propositions concerning the notion of 'theory': why do 'theory'? How does theory matter? And also, how *might* theory matter? I argue that such questions are particularly pressing today, as the activity of theory in the contemporary social sciences undergoes its own period of crisis—or worse, as theory is often taken to be already dead—and as some of the new empiricisms that have emerged within the contemporary social sciences have taken a resolutely anti-theoretical, or anti-intellectualist, stance. I articulate an empiricist and future-oriented mode of theorising that, after Alfred North Whitehead, Isabelle Stengers, John Dewey, and others, I will associate with the practice of 'speculation'. Thus, this chapter seeks to specify what speculation is, what its relations to experience are, what its requirements might be, and what it might be capable of offering. In so doing, it proposes a practice of *speculative experimentation* as a means of imagining novel and future modes of social inquiry.

In exploring these questions throughout the coming chapters, my hope is that the plea for possible futures that I have associated with Cortázar's poem might not only resonate but help us cultivate a different care of knowledge, a different care of the world, and a different care of the self. Thus, in the Afterword I return to the entanglements between these three dimensions to ask the dramatic question of what kind of social scientific self, what kind of conceptual persona, an adventure of relevance may give rise to. To embark on an adventure, I suggest, is to conjoin the problem of knowing with the problem of *learning* how to know. It is, in order words, to become an apprentice.

# 2

# The Question of Relevance

## Introduction: The Demands for Relevance

At a time when a series of entangled economic, political, ecological, and social transformations threaten the institutional and intellectual futures of the social sciences, there has been growing concern among social researchers around the question of how to foster, articulate, and promote the relevance of their practices and modes of knowledge-production. In such debates, the demand for relevance often emerges as a desired response to a problematic situation that is perceived as a state of crisis related to 'societal challenges' posed by the transversal effects of a globalising world (Vilnius Declaration 2013).

To be sure, the diagnosis of 'crisis' ascribed to the contemporary social sciences is not in itself unproblematic, and indeed it has accompanied the social sciences throughout their history.[1] Be that as it may, the pres-

---

[1] If, following conceptual historian Reinhardt Koselleck (1988), crisis is endemic to modernity, it is not ludicrous to argue that crises are constitutive features of the history of the social sciences as well. In this sense, despite the generalised interest that Thomas Kuhn's (2012) *The Structure of Scientific Revolutions* attracted amongst critical social scientists, not many social scientists seem to have taken into account the fact that Kuhn's argument about the dynamics of crisis and change in scientific communities were, in his view, restricted to what he described as 'paradigmatic sciences' (e.g., physics):

© The Editor(s) (if applicable) and The Author(s) 2016
M. Savransky, *The Adventure of Relevance*,
DOI 10.1057/978-1-137-57146-5_2

ent historical conjuncture confronts the social sciences with a challenge that has brought their researchers into a discussion around the life of knowledge in an age where modern universities, once progressive and expanding loci for cultures of public, research, and critical thought (Wagner et al. 1991; Wallerstein 1999), have become, under neo-liberal models of governance and audit, contracted spaces whose activities must find justification in their services to the boosting of national income and employment capacities, the development of techno-scientific innovation, the informing of public policy, and the engagement with wider non-academic publics (Brewer 2013; Readings 1996).

In this context, the contemporary social sciences are often required to justify and enhance the 'relevance' of the knowledge they produce. Taken together, such demands for relevance are rather ambiguous, if not contradictory, both in their assessments and in their proposals. On the one hand, demands for relevance emerge in the context of a proposed reformation of the institutional and intellectual organisation of scientific activity that might foster more interdisciplinarity and greater accountability for scientific and technological innovation—and, certainly, cut down funding—by 'embedding' social research in other scientific and innovation programmes, thereby 'better' contributing to informing policy and innovation (Felt 2014; Gibbons et al. 1994; Nowotny et al. 2001; Rappert 1999). Thus, in the 2013 Vilnius Declaration on the 2020 Horizons of the Social Sciences and Humanities in Europe it was stated that

> Making use of the wide range of knowledge, capabilities, skills and experiences readily available in SSH [Social Sciences and Humanities] will enable innovation to become embedded in society and is necessary to realise the policy aims predefined in the 'Societal Challenges'. (Vilnius Declaration 2013)

On the other hand, calls for a more relevant social science emerge from a number of heterogeneous positions that see the latter as *already*

---

scientific communities that organise temporally and collectively around a guiding paradigm which eventually encounter a series of anomalies that bring about a crisis and a revolution. Insofar as the history of the social sciences is characterised by the problematic coexistence of a variety of competing 'paradigms' with no strict order of succession, it could be argued that a sense of 'crisis' is constitutive of their history, producing no final resolutions but a continuous problematisation and revisiting of their guiding principles.

*complicit* in forms of neo-liberal governance and hence detached from wider moral and political public concerns. In any case, questions as to the extent to which the contemporary social sciences may be said to be 'relevant' pervade virtually every discipline in the contemporary social sciences, including anthropology, sociology, social psychology, historiography, economics, and political science.[2]

Despite the aforementioned demands, however, it is somewhat puzzling that almost none of them ensues from any in-depth exploration of what 'relevance' entails, what place it occupies in the worlds that the social sciences encounter, which modes of inquiry it might require, and what kinds of habits of thought and feeling its understanding might help cultivate. 'Relevance' has become so ubiquitous and multifarious a demand, it has become such a 'tyranny'—as political scientist Matthew Flinders (2013) has recently put it—that it has failed to raise any substantial, conceptual investigation on what it itself might involve. Enforced by some and dismissed by others, the notion of 'relevance' has become something of an empty placeholder that heralds an ideal solution to general, anonymous, and pre-existent problems. A solution, moreover, whose conditions of success are said to be definable in advance, thus turning 'relevance' into an abstract criterion of demarcation.

Prompted by such a sense of puzzlement and wonder, I here will attempt to take the question of 'relevance' seriously. I shall take the risk of exploring and experimenting with it not as if it were itself a solution to a problem we already understand how to define, but as a problematic and problematising question that rather than contribute to instrumentalising contemporary forms of social inquiry, might provoke a more difficult, but potentially more fruitful, exercise in reconstruction. As I will show, to take the notion of relevance seriously—beyond its tyrannic demands—will require that we cease proposing 'relevance' as a new imposed criterion of judgement, in order to follow the requirements that ensue from its conception as a speculative and practical problem. In this chapter, I will begin such an exploration by paying close attention to

---

[2] In anthropology see Rabinow (2003); in sociology see Burawoy (2005a), Savage and Burrows (2007); in social psychology see Teo (2012); in postcolonial studies and historiography see Chakrabarty (2008); in economics see Colander et al. (2009); in political science see Trent (2011).

one of the recent demands for relevance which has prompted discussions and attracted attention within and beyond the limits of its disciplinary origins. It constitutes a call for relevance that situates the latter beyond a mere instrumentalisation of social scientific practices while connecting it, instead, to the revitalisation of a 'moral' and political promise. The demand in question is, thus, the one articulated in the recent debates around the public life of sociology.

Michael Burawoy's (2005) widely debated presidential address at the American Sociological Association, titled 'For Public Sociology', was primarily an attempt to reclaim Wright Mills's (2000) 'promise of social science'—the promise of bridging biography and history, and transforming private issues into public concerns. Burawoy urged sociologists to regenerate 'sociology's moral fiber' (2005: 5) by proposing an organic mode of doing sociology that would become 'relevant' to wider yet 'visible, thick, active, local and often counter-public' concerns. The task was that of 'bring[ing] sociology into a conversation with publics, understood as people who are themselves involved in conversation' (2005: 7). As Burawoy (2005: 8) stresses it, echoing Mills's promise:

> [b]etween the organic public sociologist and a public is a dialogue, a process of mutual education. The recognition of public sociology must extend to the organic kind which often remains invisible, private, and is often considered to be apart from our professional lives. The project of public sociologies is to make visible the invisible, to make the private public, to validate these organic connections as part of our sociological life.

There is surely much that is laudable about Burawoy's call. First, it was successful in opening up a space of problematisation and discussion around the need to take seriously the relations that the social sciences establish with the publics they attempt to address. And second, it prompted the emergence of diverse articulations of how those relations might be cared for and addressed.

Nevertheless, as many commentators have noted, Burawoy's proposal presents a number of limitations that prevent 'relevance' from becoming the locus from which a reconstruction might be developed. In what follows, I will explore some aspects within the debate around so-called Public Sociology to understand the way in which the demand for relevance is articulated, and to attempt to extract from its own limitations a different sense of what a reconstruction centred around the question of relevance might require. Specifically, I will show that by approaching relevance as a subjective act of interpretation, as a value that is added to facts, Burawoy's call for public sociology reduces the question of relevance to a problem of how social scientific findings are communicated to publics. In so doing, it leaves untouched a different question—namely, the question of *how* the knowledge-practices of the contemporary social sciences may come to terms with the situated ways in which experiences of various kinds and natures *come to matter*.

## Matters of Fact, Facts that Matter: Contemporary Social Science and the Adventure of Relevance

As said, Burawoy's (2005: 5, emphasis added) call for relevance in relation to sociology and social sciences stems directly from his description of what he refers to as 'public sociology'. For him, public sociology is a 'complement, and not the negation of *professional* sociology'. 'Professional Sociology', he argues, 'consists first and foremost of multiple intersecting research programs, each with their assumptions, exemplars, defining questions, conceptual apparatuses, and evolving theories.' It is this 'puzzle-solving' mode of sociology that 'supplies [public sociology with] true and tested methods, accumulated bodies of knowledge, orienting questions, and conceptual frameworks' (2005: 10).

While he regards 'professional' sociology as indispensable for the realisation of the public role of sociology, and at some point even concedes that in the practice of many sociologists both kinds of activity may be interlinked, Burawoy rejects the possibility of turning all sociology into public sociology. In accepting the fate of the over-specialisation and internal division of social science disciplines, he argues that the two kinds of sociology actually enact different modes of knowing and thus, that 'we have to move forward and work from where we really are, from the division of sociological labor' (2005: 9).

As would be expected after such categorical distinctions, many commentators have taken issue with the division of sociological labour that Burawoy puts forth. What is striking, however, is that most criticisms have been concerned solely with what we might call the 'institutional' or 'organisational' consequences of the proposal[3]—the reproduction of existing hierarchies among sub-disciplines (Hays 2007), the rather immodest changes required in appointment strategies in academic departments (Stacey 2007), the 'politicisation' of the professional branch of the discipline (e.g., Massey 2007; Smith-Lovin 2007; Stinchcombe 2007), and so on.

Nevertheless, the implications of Burawoy's division of labour are arguably much more far-reaching. In separating 'public' from 'professional' sociology, that is, a mode of social science that is involved in a conversation with publics yet remains fundamentally, indeed, epistemically distinct from the rigorous, methodic and truth-driven mode of social science, Burawoy's proposal effectively reduces the question of the relevance of contemporary social scientific practices to a matter of communication and public engagement. The argument might read like this: *first*, something called 'professional sociology' produces true, objective, scientific knowledge *and then* 'public sociology' must find ways of engaging publics to make such knowledge relevant, by being communicated or brought into dialogue, and 'we do have a lot to learn about engaging them [publics]' (Burawoy 2005: 8).

In dissociating attention to facts from attention to publics, Burawoy's call for a 'public sociology'—whose business would be that of developing strategies for communicating the otherwise true and objective findings of professional sociology to multiple publics—turns the question of relevance into a subjective or intersubjective phenomenon whose mode of success depends only on an act of recognition or interpretation by a public. In this way, while Burawoy's division of labour seems to be a means of preserving the production of forms of 'true' and 'objective' knowledge, to presuppose that producing knowledge and making it relevant to those with which such knowledge may be concerned constitute two distinct activities is to leave unanswered

---

[3] For an exception in this regard see Wallerstein (2007).

the question of what relevance is, where it comes from, and what its implications might be for the ways in which practices of knowledge-making in the contemporary social sciences are imagined, organised, and carried out.

In other words, it presupposes that the question of relevance concerns only the ways in which knowledge is communicated, but not the manner in which it is *produced*. By the same token, it seems to assume that either the perplexing worlds of facts that the social sciences must come to terms with do not *by themselves* matter or, more likely, that by means of their true and tested methods, accumulated bodies of knowledge, orienting questions, and conceptual frameworks, social scientists can anticipate and single-handedly justify which facts matter and how they might come to matter in any given situation.

This subjective understanding of relevance may find precedence in the phenomenological theory that Alfred Schutz (1970) began to develop in the sixties and never quite finished. Indeed, Schutz saw relevance as a subjective process whereby an individual consciousness encounters an unfamiliar object within an otherwise familiar surrounding and deploys mental efforts to interpret it thereby 'assigning' relevance to certain objects. This interpretation, in turn, transforms the subject's phenomenal field and his or her future behaviour.[4] While such a theory might have some psychological value as an exploration of how cognitive and volitional human subjects interpret and relate to their milieu, it forgets, however, that for any such response to take place, there must be a situation posing a question. As Whitehead (2004: 28) put it, '[n]o perplexity concerning the object of knowledge can be solved by saying that there is a mind knowing it.' If that is indeed the case then we might ask, both to Schutz and to Burawoy, what is it about the *objects of inquiry* themselves that makes them relevant?

This question forces the problem to drastically change. If we resist reducing relevance to a subjective response and include in it the questions posed by the world, as I will attempt to do in what follows, the problem can no longer be reduced to that of effectively communicating findings to

---

[4] Another famous theory of 'relevance' as a basic feature of human cognition and as a pragmatic dimension of communication is that developed by Dan Sperber and Deirdre Wilson (1995).

publics.⁵ It needs to be approached, rather, as a question of how to come to terms with the events by which, in given situations, things of diverse nature become relevant in specific ways. As a question, that is, of how they come to matter.

It is this latter question that, because it forces us to problematise the division of scientific labour that Burawoy takes for granted, I believe might be capable of opening up a speculative experiment in reconstruction. In this way, if the achievement of relevance is usually complicated, as sociologist John Scott (2005: 407) has complained, by the fact that publics 'have their own answers' and seem unwilling to listen to what social scientists may have to say, have the latter not been posing the wrong kinds of questions? If people engaged in conversation already possess their own senses of how things matter, should we not ask why the social sciences have been unable to come to terms with what may matter to others? Rather than ascribing to the social sciences 'an obligation to ensure that publics listen' (Scott 2005: 407), and the implicit right to determine what is relevant and what needs to be communicated and listened to, might the former not be obligated instead to learn to attend to the senses of relevance of those they address? Indeed, might it not be that their own knowledge-practices, their modes of inquiry, and not just their communication strategies, fail to bring concerned publics into being?⁶

In order to explore this issue, I suggest that what is required is an exploration of 'relevance' as an event that belongs not just to an act of recognition that could reside in an individual or collective mind, but to the world itself. Namely, I want to entertain the proposition that relevance is not a value or judgement that the social sciences, or their publics, 'add' to the knowledges the former produce, but that it already inheres, as an event and as a problem to be developed, in the situations into which they conduct inquiries. In this way, the perplexing questions that the world poses cannot be explained away by recourse to a psychological theory of responses, for the very experience of relevance involves a sense that *there*

---

⁵ This is of course not to claim the opposite, namely, that questions of public engagement are irrelevant. It is simply to suggest that perhaps it is not in the process of communication of findings that the question of 'relevance' is to be explored. For an interesting approach to thinking through publics see Marres (2012).

⁶ On the coming into being of publics see Dewey (1989), and more recently, Marres (2005).

*is value beyond ourselves*—that something that is not ourselves, *matters*. To develop such a proposition we may begin from the seemingly obvious but potentially powerful realisation that the facts of the world which practices of social inquiry must come to terms with, *matter*.[7] That facts and relevance are always reciprocally entangled such that there is value to facticity and facticity to value.

To suggest that facts matter seems almost self-evident, yet it constitutes a proposition that, I fear, our modern habits of distrusting direct experience make particularly difficult to grasp. We should therefore tread carefully. What does it mean to say that 'facts matter'? In this sense, the double acceptation of the English verb 'to matter' might prove illuminating. On one pole, facts matter as they *materialise*, come into, and remain temporarily in existence. On the other, they become relevant to some degree and in some manner. The key is to read this double sense of mattering simultaneously. To matter is to come into existence, and to come into existence is to become relevant.

In other words, it is by virtue of the event of coming into existence in some determinate way, that the facts that compose a situation matter. Indeed, to the extent that a fact comes into existence, the event of its coming to matter is always specific and situated and it is that situated specificity which makes the fact both what it *is*—even if only momentarily—and what opens a question as to the varying degrees and manners in which it matters to a situation. Minimally, then, everything that has acquired a determinate existence (this human, this table, this paper, this idea, this feeling) has some relevance by virtue of having come (in)to matter, and this event is never unrelated to the situation in which it partakes. Indeed, only a generic, indeterminate 'anything' does not matter. 'Anything' is 'no-matter-what', namely, it does not matter what it is (Garcia 2014).

Thus, facts exist to the extent that they come to matter in specific situations, and they matter insofar as they come into existence. In this way, relevance might be said to belong to what Whitehead (1968) described as the primary experience—it should be noted, not necessarily

---

[7] The notion of 'fact' here is used in a realist and radically empiricist sense, namely, everything that is included in experience (see James 2011).

a 'psychological', 'subjective' or even 'human' experience—of the actual world. Namely, a *value* experience whose expression is none other than 'Have a care, here is something that matters' (1968: 116). As he argues (1968: 111):

> Existence, in its own nature, is the upholding of value intensity. Also no unit can separate itself from the others, and from the whole. And yet each unit exists in its own right. It upholds a value intensity for itself, and this involves sharing value intensity with the universe. Everything that exists has two sides, namely, its individual self and its signification in the universe.

A fact comes to matter for itself, for other facts with which it composes a situation, and for the world of facts to which it becomes added. It is with this event of a coming to matter, and with the problem it poses to those with whom it is concerned, that I want to associate the question of relevance.

Approached in such a manner, the concept of relevance involves a series of important implications. The first implication is that, as suggested, relevance is not something that is *added* to facts by reason of true and tested methods, or by a process of interpretation or recognition performed by a subject. By contrast, relevance is an event of the world—it inheres in and among its many existents. Second, if everything that exists matters in some degree and in some manner, then, conversely, everything that matters must have some manner and degree of existence, even if this mode is not entirely 'material' or, to put it more bluntly, physical. Matter matters, but depending on the situation, so do feelings, relations, ideas, ghosts, beliefs, words, numbers, and so on. Thus, we should not reduce the proposition 'facts matter' to a materialist eliminativism that would deny the relevance of everything that is not endowed with physical properties.

Third, because facts are always situated and specific, their relevance must also be associated to a situation in which they partake and that, in turn, partakes in their own nature. In other words, 'there is no such thing as bare value. There is always a specific value, which is the created unit of feeling arising out of the specific mode of concretion of the diverse elements' (Whitehead 1926: 90)—there are no pure, general, universal values or criteria for relevance. The relevance of facts is only specific, immanent to the situations in which and for which facts come to matter in different degrees and manners. Thus conceived, the concept of relevance cannot become a general criterion that could demarcate what matters from what does not, and it cannot be reduced to how findings are communicated. When approached in this way, the question of relevance becomes a constraint that invites not just better communication but an entirely different *mode of inquiry*. An inquiry into *how, in what degree and in what manner, things come to matter within specific situations*. It is from this question, with its requirements, problems and possibilities, that I seek to produce tools to cultivate a sensibility capable of opening up a different care of knowledge for the contemporary social sciences.

To suggest that facts *matter* is to resist the long-standing bifurcation between fact and value, an aspect of a many-headed monster that Whitehead (2004) famously named 'the bifurcation of nature' and which I associated to the ethics of estrangement that could be said to characterise much of the contemporary social sciences. As I intimated in the introduction to the book, the bifurcation of nature consists in separating the world into two realms. One side of this bifurcation, Whitehead (2004: 30) suggests, would be 'the nature apprehended in awareness'. The other, 'the nature which is the cause of awareness':

> The nature which is the fact apprehended in awareness holds within it the greenness of the trees, the song of the birds, the warmth of the sun, the hardness of the chairs, and the feel of the velvet. The nature which is the cause of awareness is the conjectured system of molecules and electrons which so affects the mind as to produce the awareness of apparent nature.

It is this bifurcation that makes Burawoy's division of scientific labour possible and that allows relevance to be dissociated from the very facts with which the social sciences must learn to come to terms with, and added only later as a 'value' that ultimately awaits public recognition and judgement. So-called professional sociology, thus, deals with bare facts, with the nature that is the cause of awareness. The task of public sociology, in his account, seems to be one of communicating those bare facts to publics so that they may acquire relevance in the process of being apprehended in awareness.

Cultivating an ethics of estrangement, much of the contemporary social sciences understand their task to be that of estranging themselves from the nature apprehended in awareness, which is to say, from the apparent character of experience, in order to access the nature which is the cause of awareness. Although, as we shall see later on, not all versions of this ethos agree on what aspects belong to which side of reality, that Burawoy and Scott place the truth and objectivity of professional sociology as belonging to the causal side of reality should not come as a surprise. Since the inauguration of modern science, the bifurcation of nature has been key to define the 'value-neutrality', 'objectivity', and 'truth' of scientific knowledge (Proctor 1991).

To suggest that facts *matter*, then, is a way of resisting this bifurcation, and an attempt to cultivate a different care of knowledge. It is however certainly neither the first nor the only form of resistance to it, probably not the last one either. Biologist and complexity theorist Stuart Kauffman (2008), for instance, has argued against a reductionist physicalism that would reduce everything to the 'particles in motion' of physics by suggesting that the biosphere is pregnant with agency, meaning, and value. For him, however, those particles in motion are indeed mere 'happenings', bare facts, while it is the creative emergence of 'life' in the universe that introduces agency, value, meaning, and thus, relevance, into the world: 'the agency that arises with life brings value, meaning and action into the universe' (2008: 72). If facts *matter*, however, the very facts that physics comes to terms with must matter too—they must themselves be pregnant with relevance, even if they cannot be said to be 'alive' in a biological sense.

Another prominent attempt at resisting the distinction between fact and value has been, for example, Bruno Latour's (2004) call to move from the anonymous and supposedly pure 'matters of fact' of modern epistemology, to always controversial and hybrid 'matters of concern' or 'things', as he calls them after Heidegger. Latour's call was an attempt to simultaneously draw social scientists' attention to the liveliness of objects and to draw scientists' attention to their sociality, thereby multiplying and distributing the many heterogeneous agencies that labour towards the making of things. In other words, what he was articulating was 'a multifarious inquiry launched with the tools of anthropology, philosophy, metaphysics, history, sociology to detect *how many participants* are gathered in a thing to make it exist and to maintain its existence' (2004: 246, emphasis in original).

Latour's call was also in part an overt attempt to 'finally' be able to present his work in a way that would not be read as a critique of science—a critique that would follow the same ethics of estrangement that he claimed to be resisting—but rather as a means of conveying respect for it. I am not here concerned with the question of whether this attempt may be deemed successful or not. While I am appreciative of Latour's project and of his notion of 'matters of concern' as a way of anchoring a different kind of social study of science, his project differs considerably from mine and, consequently, so does his way of resisting the modern distinction between facts and values.

Indeed, by speculatively inquiring into the question of relevance in contemporary social science I am not calling anthropologists, philosophers, metaphysicians, historians, sociologists, political scientists, or psychologists to abandon their projects and delve in to the making of 'things'. In my account, the event of facts that *matter* does not invite an inquiry into the many participants that may or may not converge in their making, but becomes a constraint that practices of social inquiry have to learn to inherit. Thus, what concerns me is the exploration of what might be required, intellectually, ethically, politically, and practically, for social research practices to take up 'relevance' as an inquiry into of the heterogeneous patterns that relate human, other-than-human, material, ideal, concrete, and abstract modes of relevance in ways that matter for those with which a problematic situation might be concerned. What I am interested in is not so much a different job description for contemporary practices of social inquiry, but the possibility of a different *mode* of social inquiry that would seek to negotiate the question 'how is it, here, that things matter?', without imposing on 'things' either a specific nature or a number in advance, and without single-handedly delimiting the horizon that defines where 'here' ends.

As I show in the chapters that follow, the key to this question is that any possible answer be negotiated in practice. Whenever a social scientist encounters a problematic situation as an object of inquiry, it is not simply her practice that makes that situation 'matter'. Rather, the situation is already constituted by an ecology of dynamic and fragile patterns of relevance, of modes of mattering for oneself and for others, to which her questions, her assumptions, theories and methods, in sum, her mode of knowledge-production, become added. Such an addition, to be sure, is never innocent, that is, it has effects—it affects the ecology of such patterns in different ways. I will get back to this later in the book. For now, the point is that to speak of a 'negotiation' is neither to suggest that it is her questions or methods themselves that *produce* that ecology of relevance out of thin air, nor that their goal is that of discovering the relevant way of defining the problem that characterises a situation, as if such a way could be said to fully pre-exist her questions. As I will argue, inquiry is always a matter of 'invention'—a notion which, in my reading, takes the risk of conjoining discovery and creativity (see Chap. 3).

For this reason, to affirm that the negotiation of relevance requires the invention of a manner of encountering a situation with the aim of disclosing how things matter suggests that relevance poses, first and foremost, a relational problem. As Isabelle Stengers (1997: 6) argues in the case of experimental sciences, 'one speaks of a relevant question when it stops thought from turning in circles and concentrates the attention on the singularity of an object or situation.' Thus, as I will show in the next chapter, the risk of negotiating relevance is that of navigating a middle space of invention whereby questions can be reduced neither to an 'objective truth', single-handedly dictated by reality, nor to mere 'arbitrary decision', 'imposed by the all-powerful categories of which the investigative instrument is bearer.' By contrast, relevance requires us not to undo the subject-object relation, but rather to imagine 'a subject that is neither absent nor all-powerful' (Stengers 1997: 6).

I shall return to these questions later on. For now, it is crucial to notice that the relational nature of 'relevance', which entangles it inextricably with the ways in which objects of inquiry come to matter in specific situations, suggests that the possibility of producing a form of knowledge that could be said to be 'relevant' is never guaranteed. No discipline, theory, or established body of knowledge can attempt to single-handedly anticipate or justify what may matter to those to whom the question is posed. Relevance is an achievement, and as such it belongs to the order of an event, of an effect that may obtain but which can neither be promised nor be reduced to a cause (see Chap. 6).

Relevance, therefore, should be understood as a problem that affects the very situated processes of negotiation that make every answer dependent upon the question that calls for it, and every solution to a problem dependent on, or *deserving of*, the manner in which the problem is defined (Deleuze 1994). This is because every definition of a problem guiding inquiry, and every question that may point to an unknown which an inquiry may seek to address, also produces a pattern of contrasts that productively constrains the range of possible answers that might matter to it. Nothing guarantees, however, that the pattern of contrasts that the initial question generates, the range of possible responses that it makes available as relevant to it, will address the one to whom the question is posed in a manner that resonates with how things in that situation matter.

In other words, the manner and degree in which things matter to a question may not necessarily resonate with the ways in which they matter to the situation to which the question is posed. If relevance is to become capable of affecting the manner of directing practical inquiries in the contemporary social sciences, of *feathering and launching the arrow of the question another way, from another departure point, toward something else*, then the term cannot designate, *ex post*, or worse, *ex ante*, the value that a certain finding has in relation to the public to which it may be communicated. Concerning the very ways in which knowledge is cared for and cultivated, relevance needs to be thought as an active constraint upon practice—a constraint that forces inquiry to put the pattern of contrast that a question generates, that is, the assumptions that underpin it, at risk.

Conceived in this way, the possibility of a 'relevant' social science cannot be understood as the production of a series of bare truths that would then support, and help legitimise, the voice of social scientists in the public sphere. Neither can it become, to be sure, a method for making publics willing to listen. For the invention of a proposition by a practice of inquiry constitutes an achievement that legitimises no one, and guarantees nothing. The question of relevance and the question of the effects that certain inventions may have upon the world—or what I shall call the question of 'connections'—while interconnected, are irreducible.

I will address the question of connections in Chap. 5. For the moment, however, it is worth noting that a first requirement posed by the concept of relevance is that any response to the situated question of 'how is it, here, that things matter' is an *unknown* towards which an inquiry may be oriented. In other words, part of the challenge of attending to the demands posed by the situated specificity of an object or a situation involves not being able to fully know in advance who or what is going to respond to the call, in what way the pattern of contrasts that the initial question generates might be contested, and in relation to which other objects, patterns, and situations the direction of inquiry might have to turn. It is this relational process, which might obtain only when the questions are put at risk by an object or situation so that its assumptions might be challenged and a sense of wonder about its specificity might emerge, that rearranges the relationships between subjects and objects, knowers and knowns, and connects them all to a milieu to which such questions and responses relate and might be said to matter.

I believe this set of requirements helps us envisage the image of a different care of knowledge, one that I shall aim to develop throughout the coming chapters. For unlike the ethics of estrangement, which designates a researcher that addresses an object or a situation that—traditionally—'he' already knows how to relate to, taking relevance seriously entails an openness to embark on an *adventure*. Despite its more recent romantic connotations, an adventure, in the etymological sense, comes from the Latin *adventurus*, which signals an exposure to that which is about to happen, that is, an investment in the possibility of an event, where the latter becomes associated with a sense of a difference that matters. An adventure places whoever embarks on it in a middle space, between a problematic situation that demands to be inherited, and the possibility of working towards its transformation. As such, the researcher becomes situated in a place which is neither the position of the mere ignorant who does not know but has not yet wondered, nor that of the arrogant who claims to know yet is only ignorant of 'his' own ignorance.

By contrast, the middle space opened up by the adventure of relevance is thus a hesitant experience of wonder in relation to the problems posed by an object or situation—the experience of wondering how to inherit a problem, 'wondering how practically to relate to it, how to pose relevant questions about it' (Stengers 2011a: 374; Bynum 2001). Simultaneously, the experience of wonder is animated by a willingness to be exposed to the possibility that something might be learned, that this puzzling encounter with a problematic situation may yield something new. As we will see below, it is moreover an adventure in the sense conveyed by Cortázar's (2011: 57) plea. For if we embark on it, 'it can happen that we might enter parks in Jaipur or Delhi, or in the heart of Saint-Germain-des-Prés we might brush against another possible profile of man; laughable or terrible things can happen to us.'

Remaining open to the adventure of relevance, as Cortázar's plea invites us to do, makes perceptible another limitation of the debate around the public life of social science as it is currently framed. Namely, for all the claims around the novelty of the crisis with which the social sciences are said to be confronted, a crisis variously characterised as being brought about by 'globalisation', 'global economic crises', and the pervading, digital technologies of surveillance of 'knowing capitalism' (Savage and Burrows 2007; Thrift 2005), much of the debate relies upon a conception inherited from the modern birth of the social sciences in nineteenth century, whereby both the objects and publics of social science—understood variously as 'civil society', 'the market', 'the State', and so on—dwell in a cultural world inhabited and made solely by humans, a worldless world where nature is but a passive and indifferent container of the events of human history. As I suggested above, however, the question 'how is it, here, that things matter?', needs to remain as open as possible regarding the nature and number of the 'things' that compose the situation as well as the extension of the 'here' that might define its limits.

Moreover, I will argue in the next section that if that worldless world ever existed or could be reasonably sustained in theory, it is certainly not the one we inhabit today. In other words, both the nature of the components and the specific location of a situation have become increasingly difficult to define and, as such, they can no longer be presupposed. By revisiting recent debates around the proposition of the 'Anthropocene', or what might be better termed 'Capitalocene' (Moore 2014), I will argue that, today, the challenge of cultivating an adventure of relevance does not just concern a matter of articulating multiple social or cultural 'values', but is simultaneously a challenge of becoming *worldly*, that is, of inhabiting a world the very fabric of which is profoundly shaped by the connections between human and more-than-human patterns of relevance that compose it.

## Ecologies of Relevance in a Buzzing World

At the end of the first part of his *Adventures of* Ideas, a section that involves a long 'survey' of the guiding ideas in the history of Western civilisation and which, not accidentally, is titled 'Sociological', Whitehead (1967a: 92), draws a 'momentous' conclusion:

> Our sociological theories, our political philosophy, our practical maxims of business, our political economy, and our doctrines of education, are derived from an unbroken tradition of great thinkers and of practical examples, from the age of Plato in the fifth century before Christ to the end of the last century. The whole of this tradition is warped by the vicious assumption that each generation will substantially live amid the conditions governing the lives of its fathers and will transmit those conditions to mould with equal force the lives of its children. We are living in the first period of human history for which this assumption is false.

Indeed, it could be argued that in the 80 or more years since Whitehead drew this conclusion,[8] the world has not ceased witnessing the effects of such an assumption guiding practice. And while, today, the modern tradition we have inherited may have started to show signs of breakage, the current demands for relevance placed upon the contemporary social sciences suggest that many links to that tradition still persist. Among them, one pervades social scientific practices and debates with particular force. It is another head of the monster of the 'bifurcation of nature'. Namely, the modern cosmology which imagines the world as composed by two discrete and separate realms, that of a passive Nature constituted exclusively by non-human entities which are animated by mechanical forces, and that of Culture, which consists of the realm of human affairs, of differences, interests, and passions.

---

[8] *Adventures of Ideas* was originally published in 1933.

Situated within such a cosmology, thus, the horizon of the patterns of relevance that compose a problematic is confined to a realm of human affairs, practices, and interests entirely divested of nature. As Michel Serres (1995: 3) dramatised it in his *The Natural Contract*:

> In these spectacles, which we hope are now a thing of the past, the adversaries most often fight to the death in an abstract space, where they struggle alone, without a marsh or river. Take away the world around the battles, keep only conflicts or debates, thick with humanity and purified of things, and you obtain stage theatre, most of our narratives and philosophies, history, and all of social science: the interesting spectacle they call cultural. Does anyone ever say *where* the master and slave fight it out? Our culture abhors the world.

By adopting a modern cosmology which bifurcates the world in two distinct realms, recent calls for contemporary social science to become relevant not only tend to distinguish practices of knowledge-production from activities of public engagement but, by and large, they implicitly presuppose that social scientific problems are fundamentally human and cultural, and thus *worldless*. The political issues that seem to concern the public life of social scientific practices both in Burawoy's famous call, as well as in most of his respondents, consist exclusively in questions of what, following Dipesh Chakrabarty (2012), we could call the problem of coexistence of the many human 'anthropological differences': questions of class, race, gender, history, culture, and so on. But how are we to understand the possible locations and limits of the ecologies of relevance addressed by the contemporary social sciences in an age where the modern cosmology does not seem to hold any longer, an age where Nature has violently intruded in human affairs and where humans, with all their cultures and differences, have themselves become natural forces that transform the material fabric of the world?

This question resonates with the proposition that, first elaborated by ecologist Eugene F. Stroemer and later popularised by the Nobel Laureate in chemistry Paul Crutzen (see Crutzen and Stoermer 2000), has become the focus of heated debates in the earth sciences—particularly in geology—and that has also attracted the attention of a number of scholars within the humanities and the social sciences: the Anthropocene. Such a proposition suggests that, as a consequence of the many technological and global societal shifts that have followed the Industrial Revolution, the world may be said to have progressively entered a new geological epoch, one primarily characterised by the anthropogenic, material transformation of its geological foundations brought about by the unprecedented increase in human population, massive expansion in the use of fossil fuels, the exponential rise in $CO_2$, and so on (Zalasiewicz et al. 2008). These transformations, which have endowed human practices—but not just human practices—with a 'tectonic' force, have brought about 'a new phase in the history of both humankind and of the Earth, when natural forces and human forces became intertwined, so that the fate of one determines the fate of the other' (Zalasiewicz et al. 2010).

There are, to be sure, many interpretations and possible implications that follow from the Anthropocene proposition and the debate it has elicited.[9] To name but a few, geologists still debate amongst themselves whether this age is deserving of a new name or not, and if so, what its date of birth should be. For their part, Jason Moore (2014) and Donna Haraway (2014) have argued that the name Anthropocene is a misleading one, both historically and metaphorically speaking. It is historically misleading, Moore suggests, because the Industrial Revolution is part and parcel of the rise of Capitalism over the long sixteenth century.

But it is also metaphorically misleading, Haraway argues, because the figure of the Anthropos invoked is not simply that of 'people', of humans embroiled in earthly muddles, but of the one who looks up, of 'fossil-making man, burning fossils as fast as possible'. The name for such processes might then rather be the 'Capitalocene'. Isabelle Stengers (2009a), moreover, insists that we must encounter it as 'Gaia', as James Lovelock and Lynn Margulis baptised it, in order to come to terms with what may well be a being that exists in its own terms, that has its own sense of mattering, and that cannot be reduced to the terms used to represent it, no matter how 'reliable' they may seem. These debates are important not least because what they make perceptible is that no solution is independent of how a problem is determined. Nevertheless, my aim here is

---

[9] For volumes collecting diverse positions see Turpin (2013) and Hamilton et al. (2015), among others.

not so much to add another version to these debates but, more narrowly, to explore some of the possible implications of the processes that the Capitalocene seems to make perceptible in relation to the ways in which the problematic situations inquired by the contemporary social sciences might be engaged.

At first sight, the immediate implications of the Capitalocene for the contemporary social sciences would seem to concern, at most, the kinds of sciences and specialisms that we have come to qualify by the term 'environmental'. In this sense, a critic may argue, the contemporary social sciences cannot be said to have ignored the question of the material world of nature, as each of them, from psychologists to anthropologists, have created their own specialised fields around the question of 'the environment'. Nor have the recent demands for relevance ignored 'the environment'. Indeed, at least four of the seven societal challenges postulated by the European Commission, and to which the contemporary social sciences are asked to become relevant to, include questions belonging to it.[10]

But my sense is that even though those specialisms may surely make important contributions to understanding questions related to global warming and climate change, the processes captured by the image of the Capitalocene by far exceed the creation of such specialised disciplines. Indeed, the creation of an environmental psychology, sociology, or anthropology, seems to presuppose that the challenge put forth by such an image can become yet another 'field' of social scientific knowledge, alongside those of a more long-standing history. However, if the Capitalocene can teach us anything, if it is capable of affecting an ethics of social inquiry, it is certainly not by extending social inquiry upon it. Rather, it is by forcing us to take seriously what up until now belonged both to our immediate experience, to literary imagination, and to the arguments of certain metaphysically-minded scholars—namely, that the modern cosmology that founds the social sciences is in need of serious reconsideration.

---

[10] Namely, 'Food security, sustainable agriculture and forestry, marine and maritime and inland water research, and the Bioeconomy', 'Secure, clean and efficient energy', 'Smart, green and integrated transport' and 'Climate action, environment, resource efficiency and raw materials' (European Commission 2014).

If the human practices that the social sciences conceived of as their sole object of study are not exempt from participation in the transformation of the material fabric of the world, then neither do such practices take place in a worldless space of human representations, nor can the natural world be the mute, inert, stable, and ahistorical realm of reality that they deemed the exclusive concern of—natural—'scientists'. On the contrary, '[hum]ankind is that factor *in* Nature which exhibits in its most intense form the plasticity of nature' (Whitehead 1967a: 78).

In this way, rather than *attend* to the entanglements between humans and more-than-human worlds, natures and cultures, the institution of specialisms termed 'environmental' seems to presuppose their separation. That is, it presupposes that there can be other fields of inquiry with which such entanglements are not concerned. If humans are not apart from, but *a part of*, more-than-human worlds that sustain and intervene in their affairs as humans do intervene in worlds, the consequence is not so much that everything turns 'environmental' but that, as Serres (1995: 33) argues, the very notion of 'environment' becomes inadequate:

> So forget the word *environment*, commonly used in this context. It assumes that we humans are at the center of a system of nature. This idea recalls a bygone era, when the Earth [...], placed in the center of the world, reflected our narcissism, the humanism that makes of us the exact midpoint or excellent culmination of all things. No. [...] we must indeed place things in the center and us in the periphery, or better still, things all around and us with them like parasites.

Things all around and us *with* them, like parasites. A buzzing, turbulent world constituted by ecologies of relevance and concatenations between humans and other-than-humans, each of which affects and is affected by the doings of the other. A connectionist, processual world which, as William James (2011: 75) once proposed, 'is one just so far as its parts hang together by any definite connexion. It is many just so far as any definite connexion fails to obtain. And finally it is growing more and more unified by those systems of connexion at least which human [and more-than-human] energy keeps framing as time goes on.'

Might this be what it means to enter the Capitalocene? Perhaps. To speak of a connectionist, processual world, however, is to resist the temptation to reduce it to yet another, static, 'worldview', or to the fixity of a new 'epoch' which may one day pass. Indeed, what is at stake is the realisation that together with other practices, social inquiries partake not so much in a different cosmology, but in an ongoing, buzzing, cosmogony—a partial, open, and dynamic worldly ecology assembling a multiplicity of patterns of relevance, entities, and relations, both stubborn and mutable, that progressively transform the world's mode of composition while they themselves become transformed by it.

## Patterns, Relationality, and Radical Empiricism

No practice can escape the consequences of its doings and consequences are always more-than-human. The theories, questions, methods, and findings, in sum, the modes of inquiry of the contemporary social sciences both engage ecologies and transform them by producing 'new relations that are added to a situation already produced by a multiplicity of relations' (Stengers 2010: 33). Knowledge in this sense ceases being a matter of epistemology, of more or less accurate or true representations of an independent world of facts, and becomes an ecological achievement whereby different parts of the world become connected in such a way that some of its terms become the knower, and others become the known (James 2003: 3). In this way, then, questions of inquiry must be approached not in cognitive or epistemological terms, but in terms of practical encounters that, in connecting heterogeneous forces and beings that are *already* multiply connected, bring something—or someone—new into existence, a novelty which may in turn affect the milieus to which it connects.

I will explore this understanding of knowledge-practices at greater length in the next chapter and indeed throughout the book, but we first need to address a number of overarching implications of thinking the possibility of social inquiries in the Capitalocene. Indeed, how might the contemporary social sciences come to address this buzzing world whereby all the modern demarcations that found their practices and conventional objects of study have been meshed up in relations with entities and practices that they thought belong to an entirely different realm? How are they to take up the adventure of relevance, of entertaining the question of 'how is it, here, that things matter?', when their modern ethics of inquiry hardly prepare them for the heterogeneous, naturalcultural encounters that the question is likely to generate? How might they invent a manner of encountering worlds that matters?

There are at least two transversal implications of this issue that affect the politics of knowledge-production in the contemporary social sciences and thus, also, their possible modes of dealing with the question of relevance. The first, suggested above, is that the matters of fact that compose the situations the social sciences may address cannot be reduced, as many classic empiricist philosophies and positivist social sciences have assumed, to pre-existent, fully formed, isolated entities. To come to matter, which is also to say, to come into and endure in existence, is simultaneously to partake in various forms of togetherness with other existences—human and other-than-human—that compose a situation. Those modes of togetherness, that is, those relational patterns of relevance that simultaneously bring facts together and contribute to their own composition are very much *real*. Indeed, they are as real as, as well as constitutive of, the heterogeneity of entities, human and other-than-human, that make up the very fabric of the world. As I suggested in the introduction to the book, then, the form of empiricism pertinent to an adventure of relevance belongs to what James (2003: 22, emphasis in original) has termed 'radical empiricism':

> Empiricism […] lays the explanatory stress upon the part, the element, the individual, and treats the whole as a collection and the universal as an abstraction. […] For [radical empiricism], *the relations that connect experiences must themselves be experienced relations, and any kind of relation experienced must be accounted as 'real' as anything else in the system.*

What this implies, then, is that the mode of mattering of an entity, human or not, is dependent upon a set of relations, practices, and other entities to which it relates. This is why existence, and hence, relevance, is always specific and situated. In this sense, many scholars in the humanities and the social sciences have already begun to foreground the relationalities, flows, and processes through which socio-material realities are cultivated and transformed, and have thus also attempted to understand how knowledge-practices are themselves made possible by specific kinds of relationships among humans and other-than-humans.

As James's quote above makes explicit, however, conceiving of the world and their entities as relational and conceiving of relations as real, does not *imply*—as some of these attempts in the humanities and the social sciences seem to suggest—throwing the baby out with the bathwater and affirming that relations are *the only existents* and that everything that appears to be an entity is *actually* an assemblage of relations yet to be disclosed.[11] Relationality cannot be a means of ignoring the specificities of the many modes of mattering that compose the actual world, for such reading turns radical empiricism into another means of cultivating an ethics of estrangement (Savransky forthcoming).

If things matter by virtue of their coming into existence and not just because they constitute knots of relations—which is not to say that they do not constitute such knots—then relationality is to be approached technically, that is, with a careful attention to the local, situated, and specific manners in which concepts, as technical tools, may indeed be productive, while refraining from extending them into an all encompassing universals. In other words, '[t]he relationship is not a universal. It is a concrete fact with the same concreteness as the relata' (Whitehead 1967a: 157). Just as relations shape and alter the nature of entities, so do the latter shape the nature of relations.

Thus, whereas the existence of both humans and atoms is affected and sustained by the relationships they maintain, and they both matter, they surely do not, in all situations, matter in the *same manner*, even though one entity may be certainly present in the other (Whitehead 1978: 50).

---

[11] While Karen Barad is perhaps the most sophisticated contemporary proponent of such forms of relationalism, arguing that 'relata do not precede the relations; rather, relata-within-phenomena emerge through specific intra-actions' (2007: 140. See my critique of this proposition in Savransky forthcoming), a very succinct illustration of the paradox posed by such an understanding can be found in Timothy Morton's *The Ecological Thought* (2010: 94. emphasis added): '[t]he ecological thought realizes that all beings are interconnected … the ecological thought realizes that the boundaries between, and the identities of, beings are affected by this interconnection … The ecological thought finds itself *next to other beings*, neither me nor not-me. *These beings exist, but they don't really exist.*' It does beg the question of what is it then, that his 'ecological thought' finds itself thinking next to.

Different beings in different situations come to matter in different ways and to different degrees. It is this question of 'how is it, here, that things matter?' that opens up the possibility of an ethics of social inquiry that operates not by opening up black-boxes but by seeking to come to terms with the varying degrees and modes of relevance that compose the world.

Relatedly, to the extent that things matter in different ways, they can be thought as endowed with diverse *modes of existence* (see Chap. 3). The situated specificity of their mode of existence may in turn affect the kinds of relations in which they enter and how other things matter to them. As Stengers (2010: 23) argues: 'the distinctions [among modes of existence] begin with physics itself and their number increases whenever we try to understand the impassioned interest in new artefacts capable of being referred to as "living" or even "thinking".'

Thus, we cannot solve the problem of relevance by arguing that the social sciences need only focus upon the way things are assembled, which is to say, upon the relations among things (Latour 2005). Rather, as both James and Whitehead remind us, the challenge of taking both relations and things seriously amounts to inhabiting a world composed both by heterogeneous relations and beings, relations capable of affecting the nature of beings and bringing new ones into existence, and beings capable of affecting the modes of relating, of immanently generating obligations and stubbornly affirming the manners in which a situation matters to them.

For this reason, cultivating a care of knowledge cannot be reduced to devising a general *theory* of knowledge, a new epistemology for the contemporary social sciences that would attempt to provide a universal model for the posing of relevant questions. If, as I argued above, relevance becomes a constraint that forces whoever takes it seriously to wonder about how things matter in a given situation while one's wonderings are themselves added to that situation, then an ecological exploration of knowledge-making requires an ethical and practical interrogation based on encounters and connections: 'the connection between what has come into existence [by the encounter] and the many differences it can make to the many other existences with which it is connected' (Stengers 2008: 48).

Insofar as the knowledge-practices of the contemporary social sciences are themselves relations that are added to an ecology of beings and relations, the challenge of negotiating ecologies of relevance involves inventing ways of wondering about how those encounters matter—it requires that attention be paid to how a practice may affect a situation, and how the latter may affect a practice. Addressing the question of relevance in practice requires an attention to the *obligations*, to the constraints, that the ones an inquiry encounters may pose to the way in which the encounter situates them, and what patterns of contrasts matter to them in the invention of propositions that may address the problematic situation with which they are concerned.

The term 'obligation' here is not to be understood in the moral, transcendental sense with which the term has commonly become associated after Kant. For the task of cultivating a different care of knowledge cannot be carried out by appealing to universal moral imperatives. By contrast, an obligation arises immanently from the claim '*it matters!*' What it foregrounds, what it makes resonate, is the heterogeneity of modes of existence that compose actuality and, therefore, the specific, stubborn claims and demands that each of the disparate beings and relations that compose a situation make. An obligation is therefore nothing other than that which an inquiry into the question of 'how is it, here, that things matter?' must learn to come to terms with. In James's words (1956: 194),

> we see not only that without a claim actually made by some concrete person [or thing] there can be no obligation, but that there is some obligation wherever there is a claim. Claim and obligation are, in fact, coextensive terms; they cover each other exactly. Our ordinary attitude of regarding ourselves as subject to an overarching system of moral relations, true 'in themselves', is therefore either an out-and-out superstition, or else it must be treated as a merely provisional abstraction from that real Thinker in whose actual demand upon us to think as he does our obligation must be ultimately based.

Thus, an adventure of relevance does not endow an inquiry with the right to demand compliance of those to whom its questions are posed. If it is to learn something, an inquiry must *first* learn to deal with how, in a situation that it inherits and in which it partakes, things matter, and to take those senses of relevance as constraints upon its own inventive activity.

This relates to the second implication of cultivating the possibility of a social science in the Capitalocene. An implication which concerns the kind of politics in which a social science might engage today. If the modern social sciences, founded upon a bifurcated cosmology, might have regarded the question of what we have called human or anthropological 'difference' and coexistence to be the privileged political arena in relation to which their knowledge-practices could contribute, the buzzing cosmogonies we inhabit force us to recognise that any conception of politics that categorically excludes the more-than-human world from its concerns is itself already founded upon a modernist, humanistic exclusion. Accordingly, a social science that limits its potential publics to diverse human groups and their institutions is not only in danger of becoming *worldless*, and thus, banal. More disturbingly, it is in danger of becoming poisonous to the heterogeneous relational ecology that brings such human groups with their interests, passions, hopes, and dreams into coexistence with a more-than-human world.

Cortázar's plea for a science that would allow us to step into the open, where the dramatic life-cycle of the eels meets the cosmic complexity of the 'redheaded night', takes here particular urgency. For what it suggests is that the question of coexistence has to be expanded in order to address the becoming together of a variety of interconnected beings endowed with different modes of mattering. This is, in other words, what Isabelle Stengers (2011b: 356) has named 'cosmopolitics'. As she argues:

> The prefix 'cosmos-' indicates the impossibility of appropriating or representing 'what is human in man' and should not be confused with what we call the universal. The universal is a question within the tradition that has invented it as a requirement and also as a way of disqualifying those who do not refer to it. The cosmos has nothing to do with this universal or with the universe as an object of science. But neither should the 'cosmos' of cosmopolitical be confused with a speculative definition of the cosmos, capable of establishing a 'cosmopolitics.' The prefix makes present, helps resonate, the unknown affecting our questions that our political tradition is at significant risk of disqualifying [...]. It creates the question of possible nonhierarchical modes of coexistence among the ensemble of inventions of nonequivalence, among the diverging values and obligations through which the entangled existences that compose it are affirmed.

To attempt to situate social inquiries in a cosmopolitics is not to propose a turn to a holistic, re-enchanted approach that would produce a social science in love with nature. Neither is it a call to relinquish, in the name of complexity or distributed agency, the interests in the passions, imaginations, hopes, fears, and dreams that are said to constitute the specificity of human and other higher-level organisations of experience. Notwithstanding the importance of not categorically excluding the more-than-human to interrogate human experiences, I agree with William Connolly (2013: 49–50) when he argues that 'to act as if there is no species identification flowing into our pores through the vicissitudes of life is to falsify much of experience'. To our *species* identification we should also add those other attachments that Chakrabarty (2012) names 'anthropological differences'—differences of class, race, gender, history, culture, and so forth.

Indeed, all those differences matter to us in many situations, and when present they too can create obligations in any attempt to learn how things come to matter. My point is that to wonder about how things matter forces us neither to exclude all those differences nor to take for granted their capacities to lure knowing, thinking and feeling situations in productive ways. That they often matter is not to say that they *must always* matter to same degree, or in the same way. The degrees and manners in which all those differences may matter is not what *explains* a situation, and should not be thought as 'underlying' it. They are, by contrast, part of the many differential patterns of relevance that require the situated negotiation that I call invention.

In my view, what the cosmopolitical question creates as a challenge but also as a possibility for the contemporary social sciences is not the suggestion that now politics should only be posthuman, but an ethico-political reconceptualisation of the interconnectedness of humans, human-others, and other-than-humans, by inventing new modes of feathering and launching the arrow of questions, of constructing problems and producing knowledges that take the adventure of relevance seriously. Thus, it lures inquiries to attend to the heterogeneous and specific modes of mattering of those who might compose the situation in the direction of which the arrow is launched.

Cosmopolitics, I think, is about the *difficulty of*, and not the recipe for, crafting a form of 'problematic togetherness of the many concrete, heterogeneous, and enduring shapes of value that compose actuality, thus including beings as disparate as "neutrinos" (a part of the physicist's reality) and ancestors (a part of the reality of those whose traditions have taught them to communicate with the dead)' (Stengers 2002: 248). It does not offer a solution to the problem of human politics, but makes both the human and the political less available to capture by the promise of an all-too-easy solution. In my view, the notion of cosmopolitics proposes what is neither an individualistic nor a holistic enterprise, but one that, following James, we might call 'connectionist'—composed of piecemeal transitions, partial efficacies, and reciprocal responses (see Chap. 5).

## Conclusion: Casting Off

By interrogating some of the many demands for relevance that ensue from recent debates around the public life of social scientific knowledge, in this chapter I have sought to trouble the assumption that what makes something relevant is to be understood as an added value to the otherwise 'true' and 'objective' findings of social inquiry. I have argued that any definition of relevance that conceptualises it in terms of a subjective value that is added to an object ignores that the very value experience with which the notion of relevance is associated involves the affirmation that there is value beyond ourselves—that the facts that compose actuality matter.

By contrast, I have sought to extract from the seemingly obvious realisation that 'facts matter' a series of implications, constraints, and questions that may emerge from it. Indeed, the first task of affirming that facts matter involves conceiving of relevance as something that belongs not only to a subject but to the world. It inheres not in someone's head, as it were, but in the situated and specific achievements that constitute the determinate existence of things. This proposition, in turn, prompts a mode of thinking that resists any strict bifurcation between fact and value, and invites us to attend, simultaneously, to the specific facticities of value and to the specific values of facts. Mattering is, then, as much a process of materialisation as it is one of valuation.

To the extent that actuality and value are intimately intertwined in the situated specificity of things, then a practical question becomes available for social inquiry to experiment with and be oriented by. Namely, the question of 'how—in what degree and in what manner—do things in a given situation matter?' The transformation that such a question might be capable of inducing in relation to the contemporary habits of thinking, practising, and feeling of the contemporary social sciences is potentially very far-reaching. In this chapter I have only begun to sketch some of the implications of such a proposition with the purpose of situating the inquiry into the speculative space that the question of relevance has opened up. Taking the latter seriously, I have argued, turns every inquiry, even this one, into an adventure.

But this adventure is just casting off, and what it beckons requires that we address difficult questions with care. Indeed, throughout the coming chapters I will follow this adventure by developing the implications of the initial propositions raised here with the hope of exploring the requirements and possibilities that the question of relevance might open up for a different care of knowledge in the contemporary social sciences. The next step will be to speculate about the risks that inventions may involve. In order to do this, I will suggest that we need to rethink the role of a notion that we have come to forget how to take seriously, and which the question of relevance prompts us to reconsider. Namely, the notion of 'objectivity' and what we have come to know as the 'subject-object relation' in the making of knowledge: how might objectivity come to matter?

# 3

# The Risks of Invention

## Introduction: In Order to Know, We Must Invent for Ourselves

In the opening lines of a book titled *Images in Spite of All*, art historian Georges Didi-Huberman (2012: 3, emphasis in original) writes:

> [i]n order to know, we must imagine for ourselves. We must attempt to imagine the hell that Auschwitz was in the summer of 1944. Let us not invoke the unimaginable. Let us not shelter ourselves by saying that we cannot, that we could not by any means, imagine it to the very end. We *are obliged* to that oppressive imaginable. It is a response that we must offer, as a debt to the words and images that certain prisoners snatched, for us, from the harrowing Real of their experience.

This proposition might at first seem paradoxical, or indeed, contradictory. If those words and images are the objects that demand inquiry, that require to be addressed and made known, what and why is it that we need to imagine for ourselves? Should we not just *look*? Is the act of imagination itself not the very temptation we would need to avoid if we are to remain truthful to those horrifying images—if we are to know them 'objectively'? Conversely, is it not that, because we *cannot* possibly free our attempts at knowing from our own imaginative presuppositions, we are bound to fail at meeting our obligations? And if the latter is the case, are we really obligated? How? And by what?

These sets of questions conjure up two traditional understandings of what it means to engage in practices of inquiry and knowledge-production in relation to the situations those images and words bear witness to and of which they are a part. For the reader who might be puzzled, perhaps even annoyed, by Didi-Huberman's invitation to *imagine*, the proposition might seem like an extravagant and outrageous disregard for the harrowing Real of the experiences to which the images and words testify. For the other, who might regard 'imagination', assumptions, and presuppositions as an inescapable, mediating feature of any knowledge-practice, the language of *obligation* might perhaps come across as an unwarranted, moralising injunction. In a self-congratulatory act of intellectual and epistemic consistency and rigour, both readers might feel tempted to close the book, thereby rejecting the perplexity induced by Didi-Huberman's opening.

I fear the proposition put forth in Chap. 2 of this book might bear the same danger. Indeed, the apparent paradox in the paragraph above resonates intimately with what I have attempted to convey through the speculative lure to a mode of social inquiry that be traversed by what I have called 'the adventure of relevance'. On the one hand, I have argued that relevance is *not* something that we subjectively add to things but that it inheres in the very situated specificity of things. Consequently, the challenge of wondering about how, in what degree and manner, things matter in a situation constitutes, I have suggested, an immanent obligation that social inquiries must learn to become responsive to.

On the other hand, I have suggested that to the extent that such a practice of wondering becomes with the situation, to the extent that it partakes in it, the question of relevance does not fully predate the very encounter that makes an inquiry possible. Becoming responsive to an obligation to the patterns of relevance that compose a situation involves a risky process whereby questions and problems are negotiated, the patterns of contrast that underpin them are put at risk, and propositions concerning those problems are brought about through *invention*.

## 3  The Risks of Invention

Paraphrasing Didi-Huberman, my proposition might read—'in order to know, we must invent for ourselves.' I fear, then, that what I have suggested will seem to some like a contradiction in terms too, one which can only be the product of a weakness of thought.

But to suggest that Didi-Huberman's proposition and mine might prompt the same kind of response from such sceptical readers would be slightly disingenuous on my part. For the historical situations out of which the senses of each other's propositions are extracted might potentially incite different consequences. What distinguishes them concerns both their milieus of inquiry and the differential authority often ascribed to the practices that we respectively address.

Even though Didi-Huberman presents himself as a historian and is dealing with an intensely morally and affectively charged event of Europe's recent past, the reader who might feel annoyed by his call to imagine and may thus be tempted to charge him with 'revisionism', might nevertheless also pardon him, as it were, for most of his work concerns the realm of the 'arts', a set of practices that, 'everyone knows', ensue from just those capacities of human imagination, creativity, and passion. In other words, the positivist realist who upholds a certain version of 'objectivity' that opposes imagination might nevertheless concede that some amount of imagination in the arts might not, after all, be that reproachable. Conversely, the post-Kantian reader who distrusts the very possibility of knowing those images objectively and suspects that a certain amount of 'moralism' underpins the reference to an *obligation* to those images and words, is still likely to restrain herself from voicing scepticism, given the nature of the event in question.

By contrast, my proposition emerges from, and seeks to affect, a milieu—the modes of inquiry of the contemporary social sciences—for which not only the stakes are less high, but insofar as it concerns some form of 'science', it may struggle to find much support in a call for invention. For unlike art practices, scientific practices have been historically presented as the only ones who have succeeded in becoming emancipated from the contaminating burden of human invention, imagination, intentionality, and freely engaged passion. Their exceptional achievement, it is often proclaimed in defence of their superiority regarding other knowledge-practices, has been to devise the means to affirm that there is only one relevant interpretation, the 'objective one' (Stengers 2002: 251; see also Harding 2008). Thus, I might be not easily pardoned[1] by the reader who distrusts the proposition regarding the potential inventiveness of knowledge-practices and who would most surely be ready to charge me with 'social constructivism', 'relativism', 'postmodernism', 'subjectivism', and so on. Neither would the Kantian reader pardon what might surely strike her as a kind of 'naive realism' when I propose that 'facts matter'.

In any case, the apparent incongruity of these suggestions could, at first sight, be motivation enough for readers to abandon the texts. To those who have already done so, there is unfortunately nothing else that I can say. To those who are still reading, I ask for a bit of patience. How is it that the immanent obligation posed to practices of social inquiry by the specificity of an object[2] and the complexity of a situation, an obligation that asks of them that they pay due attention to the objects' own mode of mattering, also forces practices to invent, to construct the manner in which they will engage and come to inherit them? In other words, what might be required by what I call *a process of invention*?

It is precisely the tension inhabiting this question that I will explore in this chapter. As I suggest, such a tension confronts us with the difficult problem of trying to make possible a concept of objectivity that would not preclude but require invention, and simultaneously, a notion of invention—that is, a form of constructivism—that would not make 'objectivity' absurd but crucial.

In order to attempt this, and given that, as I will show, the concept of objectivity is more than one, we first need to explore how certain versions of this concept have contributed to making its coupling with invention absurd. Thus, in what follows I will briefly explore a number of critiques of objectivity which have arisen in the recent history of the contemporary social sciences. In so doing, I will address three different versions of

---

[1] Although perhaps the fact that I am studying 'social' sciences instead of 'proper', 'hard' Science (e.g., physics, chemistry, biology, etc.) might also grant me a pardon from the reader. I will come back to the relationship between the two below.

[2] It is worth keeping in mind at this point that by 'object' I do not necessarily mean an other-than-human being. Rather, 'object' stands here for 'object of inquiry', the precise nature and number of which may, in principle, include any and all modes of existence. In practice, the question 'which object?' is already part of the situated process of wondering about how things matter.

'objectivity' and their respective criticisms in order to understand why the coupling of objectivity and invention has become absurd. In turn, I shall problematise them in light of the question of relevance and its particular mode of resisting the distinction between facts and values.

Needless to say, it is not the purpose of this exploration to write an exhaustive history of objectivity in the social sciences, or of its many criticisms. Obviously, the exhaustive history of anything could hardly be written. But more than this, rather than a description, comparison, and judgement of a series of theoretical and methodological proposals for their own sake, what interests me here is the exploration of 'objectivity' as a problem that the concept of relevance demands us to come to terms with.

For this reason too, it is not my aim to challenge, as a matter of principle, the presuppositions underpinning the various versions of objectivity available, or their respective criticisms; to denounce them as false, inadequate, or outdated. As Dewey (2004: xxii) warned us, a 'reconstruction is not something to be accomplished by finding fault or being querulous'. In other words, I am not interested in playing any sort of 'epistemological chicken' (Collins and Yearley 1992). I have learned and still learn a great deal from all such studies and it is thanks to them, *with* and not *against* them, that the current study can be articulated. If I am required to oppose anything in this endeavour, then it is the very undertaking of what Michel Foucault (1984b) has termed 'polemics'. As he stresses it, 'the person he [the polemicist] confronts is not a partner in the search for truth, but an adversary, an enemy who is wrong, who is harmful, and whose very existence constitutes a threat' (Foucault 1984b: 382).

In contrast to this image, what I intend to do in what follows is closer to what Gilles Deleuze (1994) has associated with the pragmatics of an art of consequences—the construction of a problem that seeks not the negation of an other that it might present itself as opposing, but the crafting of an affirmation by means of the drawing of creative contrasts, one that may allow for the production of a difference that adds new elements to the becoming of an ongoing conversation.

Thus, in attending to three contemporary versions of 'objectivity', I will argue that while their criticisms launched against them are various, the strategies that animate them bear—save some exceptions—the form of a contestation. Indeed, in such critiques objectivity is not only rightly identified as a pillar of modern epistemology. Perhaps for the same reason, it tends to become a term of abuse, something to get rid of, something to move beyond. Although I cannot do justice to it in the context of this chapter, my sense is that such attempts at 'putting objectivity down' have made rather counterproductive contributions to another well-known polemic which I would very much like to avoid, namely the so-called Science Wars (see for instance Latour 1999; Stengers 2000; Sokal and Bricmont 1998; Brenkman et al. 2000).

By contrast, I am more interested in the possibility of transforming what we might take objectivity to mean rather than doing away with it altogether. Such an interest emerges from the sense that the adventure of relevance, as I have attempted to singularise it in Chap. 2, *requires* a concept of objectivity as an intellectual and practical instrument that might allow the adventure to become actualised in practice. This is because the proposition that 'facts matter', and that their relevance inheres in *them*, rather than in *us*, involves the affirmation of a *relative outside* in relation to which practices might put their questions at risk. It involves the sense that that which an inquiry might strive to come to terms with cannot be conceived as a mere by-product of the inquiry itself, but it is there, with its own mode of mattering, potentially obligating the research process to change course, to reinvent itself. An outside, that, while never absolute, matters practically because it is capable of putting an inquiry at risk. It is this question of how to think about the relationship between scientific practices and their relative and always specific outsides that I want to associate with the question of 'objectivity'.

# Of God-Tricks and Other Tyrants: The Contemporary Politics of Objectivity

Objectivity is a tricky concept, not least because debates around objects and objectivity tend to conflate a great number of different versions of what it is and, accordingly, what its implications—ontological, epistemological, methodological, ethical, political—may be (for a nuanced exploration see the edited volume by Megill 1994). While 'objectivity' has become, ever since the eighteenth century, the ultimate epistemic virtue embraced by scientists in their pursuit of knowledge, debates around its value and meaning reveal, paradoxically, its heterogeneous nature. As Lorraine Daston and Peter Galison (2010: 51) phrased it in their monumental study on the history of objectivity in the making of scientific atlases:

> [w]hether understood as the view from nowhere or as algorithmic rule-following, whether praised as the soul of scientific integrity or blamed as soulless detachment from all that is human, objectivity is assumed to be abstract, timeless, and monolithic. But if it is a pure concept, it is [...] less like a bronze sculpture cast from a single mold than like some improvised contraption soldered together out of mismatched parts of bicycles, alarm clocks, and steam pipes.

In order to extract a productive notion of objectivity, then, the key is to become sensitive to the differences characterising some of its versions so that a possibility for another form conceiving it might be opened up. In this sense, my aim here is not to produce an exhaustive map of the different versions of objectivity but rather to engage the politics of knowledge by suggesting that while some of its versions are indeed to be resisted, there are also residual elements that remain *themselves* vital tools for resistance.

For those who have been brought up in what are usually associated with the 'critical' strands of the social sciences, the concept of objectivity seems to inevitably carry with it a number of ghosts belonging to a positivist conception of social science and its obsession with method and related epistemic virtues. Objectivity, as one of the central features of positivism in the social sciences, has become an epistemic *vice* that critics claim to have learned, as a matter of course, to move 'beyond'.[3]

Informed by a number of key works in the history and philosophy of science (see for instance Feyerabend 2010; Foucault 1994; Kuhn 2012)[4]

---

[3] This is of course not to say that they have effectively moved beyond positivism and its understanding of objectivity. For an interesting overview of the 'life' of positivism in contemporary social science see the edited volume by Steinmetz (2005).

[4] Although the rejection of positivism in the social sciences has, to be sure, more ancient roots, including late nineteenth-century thinkers like Wilhelm Dilthey and Max Weber.

that the social sciences have appropriated as epistemological manifestos for driving the dagger through positivism's heart, the responses by many of the late twentieth-century social sciences to positivist epistemic commitments have thus entailed a conflation of the notion of objectivity *tout-court* with what could be read as three of its versions. First, a version of 'objectivity' as a fantasy of transcendental, infinite vision, that is, as a practice of self-abnegation that would guarantee the universal validity of the scientist's claims—or what Donna Haraway (1991) has famously termed the *'god trick'*. Second, 'objectivity' as the affirmation of an 'objective reality' stripped of values, a *Really Real* that can *only* be grasped through 'objective methods'—or what Elizabeth Lloyd (2008: 177) has termed the *ontological tyranny* of objectivity. Third, 'objectivity' as a mode of characterising the epistemological relationship between knower and known, whereby the object of inquiry is presumed to be a passive entity awaiting capture by an active subject. That is, the depiction of the subject–object relation as the right of a 'free' subject to know an object she already knows how to relate to, a passive object that is reduced to the mere 'cause' about which 'subjects discuss and pass judgment on' (Stengers 2000: 134)—or what I call 'still objectivity'. Let us explore these versions and their criticisms in turn.[5]

The 'god-trick' version of objectivity has been a central matter of critique and contestation within the contemporary social sciences, especially in the context of feminist and postcolonial studies. The 'god-trick' is, as mentioned, the version of objectivity that presents it as the Archimedean point of an infinite, universal gaze which, simultaneously[6] ensues from no-body: 'the gaze that mythically inscribes all the marked bodies, that makes the unmarked category claim power to see and not be seen, to represent while escaping representation' (Haraway 1991: 188).

Feminist and postcolonial critiques have thus contested 'objectivity' as a scientific virtue by denouncing the work of erasure that this

---

[5] I am only separating these versions for the purpose of attaining greater clarity in the exploration. However, as will become evident below, all three versions are intimately entangled so that critics of one are also often critics (or inadvertent proponents) of the other.

[6] Because, as Daston and Galison (2010) aptly affirm, every version of objectivity presupposes a complementary version of scientific subjectivity (see also Daston and Sibum 2003. See also the Afterword).

version produces in relation to the subjectivity of the scientist and to the unacknowledged parochial values associated with *his* claims: a white, male, Western, and bourgeois subject that is presented—or absented—as entirely unmarked, indeed, as the very self-abnegation of subjectivity. According to such critiques, insofar as scientific knowledge is produced through the practices of always culturally, historically inscribed knowing bodies, their claims cannot be dissociated from their conditions of production but need to be examined as *products* of those conditions.[7] The universalist, unmarked, disinterested objectivity of Western, white, male Science that equates its own particular form of reasoning with Reason, as such (Seth 2004), needs to be provincialised and critically interrogated through the intellectual attitude that decolonial theorist Walter Mignolo (2009: 160) has called 'epistemic disobedience':

> who, when, why is constructing knowledges [...]? Why did eurocentred [and we should ask, white, masculinist] epistemology conceal its own geo-historical and bio-historical locations and succeed in the idea of universal knowledge as if the knowing subjects were also universal?

To be sure, what Mignolo calls 'epistemic disobedience' constitutes a particular operation of what I have characterised as the ethics of estrangement, whereby the critical social scientist or theorist is prompted to estrange herself from the apparently universalist claims to objectivity made by scientists in order to gain access to the parochial values truly informing those claims.

Now, while many of the various criticisms launched toward the god-trick have taken the form of denunciations and rejections of both objectivity and scientific knowledge, arguing for a social science unencumbered by its fantasy of impartiality, not all the critiques of the god-trick have taken the form of denunciation. Perhaps one of the most full-fledged alternatives to this version of objectivity is the one proposed by Sandra Harding's (1991) notion of 'strong objectivity'.

---

[7] The literature is vast and diverse, but see as examples Collins (2000), Haraway (1991), Harding (1991, 2008), Mignolo (2009), Seth (2004).

Harding's (1991: 144) argument emerges from her critique of the god-trick as requiring 'the elimination of *all* social values and interests from the research process and the results of research.' According to her argument, insofar as scientific institutions 'are constituted in and through contemporary political and social projects, and always have been' (1991: 145), their practices are already permeated and shaped by the social and political values that brought them into being. In this sense, then, the god-trick cannot possibly be upheld as a scientific virtue but should be regarded as a deeply problematic form of 'weak objectivity'. Weak because it 'offers hope that scientists and science institutions, themselves admittedly historically located, can produce claims that will be regarded as objectively valid without their having to examine critically their own historical commitments, from which—intentionally or not—they actively construct their scientific research' (Harding 1991: 147).

In contrast, what she calls 'strong objectivity' entails a form of scientific research that includes a critical examination of the values and interests that historically constitute a certain scientific community or field; in other words, it is about the levelling of subjects and objects through 'the extension of the notion of scientific research to include systematic examination of such powerful background beliefs' (1991: 149).

To be sure, there is much to be praised of Harding's effort to reclaim a notion of objectivity that, without enacting the god-trick, might perhaps still provide a distinction 'between how I want the world to be and how, in empirical fact, it is' (1991: 160). However, whether it does so convincingly is not self-evident. Indeed, by associating strong objectivity with the critical examination of one's own background presuppositions, objectivity becomes less the need to come to terms with the mode of relevance of an object than an operation by the subject upon its own subjectivity.

Put differently, although Harding criticises the concept of objectivity by resisting a simple bifurcation between facts and values, for her values are still *subjective*, they relate not to how things matter, but to how things matter *to the scientist*. It is the scientist that *unwittingly* brings his own values to bear upon the objects of inquiry. In order to produce a strong objective claim, the scientist must estrange herself from those claims by accessing the realm of subjective values that inform them. Thus, although a reflexive practice of 'strong objectivity' might be crucial to avoid imposing the scientist's own sense of what matters upon a situation, insofar as it prolongs the ethics of estrangement it does not provide the necessary tools to inquire into how the facts themselves matter but merely accepts that they can only matter to some knower, from some particular standpoint.

In a related sense, 'objectivity' has also been mobilised as a guarantee of accessing reality beyond the confounding values of the knowing subject. It is this version that Elizabeth Lloyd (2008) has termed 'the ontological tyranny of objectivity'. As she argues, the version according to which it is only through 'objective methods' that we can legitimately access the *Really Real* so that it will unequivocally dictate the terms of capture and announce the success (or failure) of knowledge presupposes a certain ontological commitment to thinking about objects of inquiry as 'that-which-is-independent-from us'(Lloyd 2008: 178).

In other words, it presupposes a particularly modern version of realism. Here we re-encounter one head of the bifurcation of nature illustrated above. Namely, the modern separation between reality and experience. On the hand there would be *bare facts*, said to pertain to the matter-of-factness of Nature—the nature that is the cause of awareness—and thus to be entirely independent from the knowing subject. On the other, subjective experience—those components of the world which were believed to arrive not from Nature, but from our *senses*—the nature apprehended in awareness—being thus nothing but mere epiphenomena of the real objects of Nature. In this sense, 'objectivity' is *itself* an operation of estrangement, conceived as the means of accessing the very matter-of-factness of reality beyond an experience that is conceived as subjective and epistemologically unreliable.

The critiques of the ontological tyranny of objectivity that emerged within the social sciences have usually involved not a resistance to bifurcate the world but an inverted bifurcation. Insofar as the objects of the modern social sciences were conceived of as hardly belonging to Nature as such (see Chap. 2), such a way of bifurcating nature located them in a position of inferiority as compared to the 'hard', natural sciences that not only preceded them historically but were by this definition better equipped to access the real objects of Nature.[8]

As a part of their anti-positivist spirit, researchers and thinkers in the contemporary social sciences also rejected the realism underpinning the ontological tyranny of objectivity. Positivists are wrong, the critics argued, not only because of their emphasis on the search for universal laws, or because of their ascetic obsession with method and passivity in relation to the objects encountered, but also because the brute objects they thought constituted the Real that the social sciences aimed at discovering were always beyond our grasp, or had never been there to begin with. I cannot think of a better example of such a post-Kantian rejection of the tyranny of objectivity than the famous passage by anthropologist Clifford Geertz (1973: 5), so often invoked as embodying the very ethos of social scientific inquiry:

> Believing, with Max Weber, that man (sic) is an animal suspended in webs of significance he himself has spun, I take culture to be those webs, and the analysis of it to be therefore not an experimental science in search of law but an interpretive one in search for meaning.

Even though positivism in anthropology never managed to get as strong a hold of the discipline as it did in other social sciences such as economics, psychology, and political science, Geertz's celebration of an 'interpretive' social science is by no means an isolated gesture. Indeed, by different names, the last 40 years of contemporary social science have witnessed the emergence and proliferation of a manifold of interpretive, herme-

---

[8] The strategies to 'emulate' the natural sciences and thus become able to access the 'Nature' of 'mankind' or 'Society' were various, some more successful than others (Steinmetz 2005). Interestingly, the most sophisticated versions are still very much alive today. One relates, of course, to the many biological reductionisms of Sociobiology, Eliminative Materialism, and certain prominent strands of Cognitive Neuroscience. The second, which surely inherits a 'structural' rather than a 'naturalist' conception of objectivity (i.e., objectivity as an access to nature's invariants, see Daston and Galison 2010) can be associated with defenders of the 'truly objective' methods of statistical analysis for supposedly revealing the underlying invariants of the social (see Porter 1996). Thirdly, while experimentation in the social sciences does no longer enjoy the acceptance and high regard that it had 50 years ago (especially in disciplines like social psychology where it became distinctly famous for its conspicuous experiments. See Chap. 4), it is still alive in a number of disciplines such as political science and economics (e.g., Morton and Williams 2010).

neutic, semiotic, discursive, and/or social constructivist epistemologies. What perhaps underlies these various efforts is a denunciation of what they take to be an implicit, and above all, 'naïve' realism governing the practices of their predecessors.

Moreover, while such arguments might have been first advanced under the purported modesty of a certain 'humanist rationality', that is, as an argument concerning the specificity of the human as an object of inquiry—one that would make 'objectivity' the sole concern of the natural sciences—social constructivist arguments soon gained more ambitious, general epistemological import. Arguing that insofar as knowledge-practices are but a human endeavour, they challenged the separation between science and society—the facts and claims to truth and objectivity the former aim at producing owe nothing to 'reality' as such, as if it could ever be accessed, and everything to the social and cultural processes, practices and technologies involved in the making of scientific claims.[9] As Lorraine Daston (2009: 802) succinctly summarises the social constructivist argument: 'no satisfactory account of why some scientific claims triumphed over others could appeal to the truth or superior epistemological solidity of the winning claims'.

In contrast, the triumph—and failure—of scientific claims to knowledge, the 'discoveries' they affirm as being part of the reality of the objects under investigation could, like any other social undertaking, be explained *socially*. That is, both in terms of the 'macro' factors of historically and culturally sedimented commitments, belief systems and orientations, and in terms of 'micro' social actions, interests, human negotiations, and strategies of selection, inscription, translation, representation, argumentation, and rhetoric that feed into scientific labour (a case in point might relate to the works associated with the 'strong programme' of Sociology of Scientific Knowledge, for example, Bloor 1977; Barnes et al. 1996). It is by means of such factors and strategies that, it is said, scientists *create* what they purport to *discover*. The early work of Karin Knorr-Cetina (1981: 3; but see also Gilbert and Mulkay 1984, Latour and Woolgar

---

[9] Needless to say, this is a significantly simplified version of the argument that does not do justice to the cornucopia of sometimes important differences among their proponents in various disciplines. For an in-depth, critical philosophical study of the underpinning logic behind this argument and some of its many variants see the wonderful book by Hacking (1999).

1986; Potter 1996, among others) might be read as a good illustration of the position:

> Rather than view empirical observation as questions put to nature in a language she understands, we will take all references to the 'constitutive' role of science seriously, and regard scientific enquiry as a process of production. Rather than considering scientific products as somehow capturing what is, we will consider them as selectively carved out, transformed and constructed from whatever is. And rather than examine the external relations between science and the 'nature' we are told it describes, we will look at those internal affairs of scientific enterprise which we take to be constructive.

Several implications follow from this. First, the rejection of an account of scientific practice that would 'put questions to nature' that might 'capture what is' radically contests the modern realism underpinning scientific claims. *Reality acquires inverted commas*: the real, bare facts that scientists claim to interrogate become but the product of their own—necessarily, social—practices of selection, transformation, and construction. Second, because there is no reality but only scare-quoted 'reality', scientific practice becomes indistinct from any other social practice and is thus susceptible of being investigated by social research: the social sciences thus become super-sciences capable of extending their scope of inquiry to other sciences, indeed, capable of providing explanations for, or rather, of *explaining away*, the explanations that others produce. Third, insofar as objects are 'constructions' that ensue from the activities of scientists, the 'ontological tyranny of objectivity' loses its hold, and not just because there is no *Really Real* to which 'objective methods' might guarantee access. It loses its hold because insofar as 'objectivity' is a constitutive element of scientific culture, it no longer regulates its practice as if it related to an outside but is itself *produced from within* and mobilised as a rhetorical device for the production of certain truth-effects (Osborne and Rose 1999; Potter 1996).

Thus, while contesting the 'tyranny of objectivity' is certainly a welcome move—for, as I have argued, there is no such thing as bare facts—what makes Knorr-Cetina's paragraph particularly characteristic of the problems that inhabit social constructivist accounts of scientific practice and objectivity and which denotes its corrosive character is the adverb—'rather'—that qualifies every one of her propositions. What the adverb introduces is an opposition between the constructive, practical, and negotiated character of scientific undertakings *and* their realist, constrained, and 'objective' nature.

This is precisely the kind of opposition that makes the question that gives birth to this chapter an apparently contradictory one. According to the adverbial politics of social constructivism, if there is an object which obligates me then 'construction' is out of the question, but if what is at stake in the practice of knowing is 'construction', then there can be no obligation, and indeed, no object. Reality is reduced to a 'whatever is' that does not matter and thus poses no constraints upon what is carved out, constructed, and transformed.

The question of relevance is thus here dissociated from the *encounter* with the specificity of objects and the question of how facts come (in)to matter and is reduced to the effects of scientific practices themselves: the political, ethical, and ontological question of the differences brought into being by social science itself. While this is an important issue that I will attend to in Chap. 5, to reduce the adventure of relevance to a question of the effects of knowledge-practices alone, as if they could be produced out of thin air, as if there was no relative outside to which a scientific practice would be obligated, amounts to a knowledge politics that is freed from constraints, and a mode of thought for which the very question of relevance becomes irrelevant. Moreover, by conceiving the relation between the reality of scientific practices and their constructive character as an opposition, that is, by arguing that 'rather than attending to an object, science produces it' and by implying that such production can be explained *socially*, social constructivism is unable to undo the bifurcation of nature it sought out to contest. What it does instead is to *invert* it—'*rather than* having the *Really Real* Natural objects explaining social experience we have associated with—social and cultural—subjective construction', their argument goes, 'from now on social constructions are going to explain the "objects" of "nature"'.

The result of the introduction of the little adverb qualifying their propositions is thus a '*sui generis society*' that would 'produce everything arbitrarily including the cosmic order, biology, chemistry, and the laws of physics!' (Latour 1993a: 55, emphasis in original). In so doing, hermeneutic and social constructivist accounts of knowledge-production end up implicitly enforcing—indeed, extending *ad absurdum*—the third version of 'objectivity' that needs to be resisted, namely, a version that presupposes an account of the subject–object relation whereby the subject has on her side all the power, initiative, and creativity, while the object remains still, passive, and in this case, 'rather' inexistent. It is this third version that I call 'still objectivity'.

Thus, if the adventure of relevance requires that we take seriously both the obligations posed by the specificity of the objects *and* the constructive, ecological character of scientific practices, if both objects and invention *matter*, our aim now becomes clearer: the task is to transform that opposition into a conjunction—from 'rather' to 'and'.

## Beyond Still Objectivity? Actor-Network Theory, Subjects and Objects

Despite the fact that his earlier work with Steve Woolgar (Latour and Woolgar 1986) could be said to imply the same kind of adverbial politics that I have associated with social constructivism, Bruno Latour and others pertaining to what has acquired the name of 'Actor-Network Theory'(ANT) have ever since been acutely aware of the impracticability that the dualist 'rather than' of social constructivism entails. In contrast, they have proposed a symmetrical approach that refuses the Modern—and postmodern—settlement and is said to put everything on an equal footing—neither is humanity the epiphenomenon of a *Really Real* nature nor is the latter and its non-humans mere receptacles of social categories and activities. Instead, both society and nature are constantly performed, are continuously being made and remade, through the heterogeneous, socio-material associations that both human and non-human *actants* weave among themselves in the process of relating and mutually shaping each other (Latour 2005).

The notion of 'actant' is crucial in such an exploration because it has been assigned the purpose of distributing, de-centring and de-humanising notions of 'agency' and responsibility thus contesting the still objectivity of modern and, by implication, social constructivist, epistemologies (Law

1999). In contrast, for Latour (1993b: 167), '[w]e must not believe in advance that we know whether we are talking about subjects or objects, men or gods, animals, atoms, or texts[...]: who speaks, and for what?' In order to account for the making of such practical assemblages of humans and non-humans, all a priori *categories* must be set aside in favour of the actual, empirical composition of multiple, heterogeneous networks. As Latour (1993b: 156) puts it in his 'Irreductions': 'nothing is more complex, multiple, real, palpable, or interesting than anything else'.

According to ANT, the same is of course true for the study of scientific practices, a field where this approach first gained prominence (e.g., Callon 1986; Latour 1988, 1993b). In his *Pandora's Hope* (1999: 98–108), Latour describes the approach as a manner of attending to the *threading* (1999: 80) together of heterogeneous processes of circulation and transformation by an indeterminate number of actants. In this sense, the success of the coming into being and endurance of a scientific proposition depends (1) on the 'mobilisation of the world', namely, the deployment of instruments, equipment, expeditions, surveys, and methods for placing 'the field' under scrutiny through the production of data; (2) on the professional 'autonomisation' of the scientist as well as the institutionalisation of the science to which she belongs, namely, it depends on the series of professional activities that the scientist might be involved in order to *interest* other colleagues; (3) on the construction of 'alliances' with other groups and institutions that might deem worth investing and becoming involved in scientific labour while simultaneously placing the latter in a sufficiently large and secure context; (4) on the 'public representation' of those novelties that the scientist brings into being and has to introduce into 'another outside world of civilians: reporters, pundits, and the man and woman in the street'(1999: 105).[10]

Up until this point, ANT does not differ much from the social constructivist versions discussed above. What distinguishes it, though, is the introduction of a fifth condition for the coming into existence of a scientific proposition. A condition which we need to pay close attention to because it is what renders the other four *necessary* yet *not sufficient* for accounting for scientific inquiries—the 'pumping heart' of such circula-

---

[10] Although for Latour (1999) and indeed for other proponents of ANT (see Law 2004), there is no such thing as the 'outside world.'

tory system is the coming into contact of the entities of the world with the scientific community, or what I will call an *encounter* (see Chap. 4). Let us briefly explore such a condition by attending to Latour's studies on the work of Pasteur and his microbes.

In such studies it becomes clear that the task for Latour is not the account of Louis Pasteur's discovery of microbes by means of a social account capable of explaining 'hygiene in terms of class struggle, the infrastructure, and power'. According to him, '[w]e cannot reduce the action of the microbe to a sociological explanation, since the action of the microbe redefined not only society but also nature and the whole caboodle' (1993b: 38). In contrast, the task for ANT is to follow the *actions* of both Pasteur and the non-human actants, the microbes, through the different trials of strength that the former designs to prove the existence of the latter. ANT is, in this sense, a contemporary empiricist response to the ethics of estrangement (see Chap. 7). As Latour argues in a later text (1999: 124, emphasis in original):

> [i]n the course of the experiment Pasteur and the ferment *mutually exchange and enhance their properties*, Pasteur helping the ferment show its mettle, the ferment 'helping' Pasteur win one of his many medals. If the final trial is lost, then [the experiment] was just a text, there was nothing behind it to support it, and neither actor nor stage manager has won any *additional* competences. Their properties cancel each other out, and colleagues can conclude that Pasteur has simply prompted the ferment to say what he wished to say. If Pasteur wins we will find two (partially) new actors on the bottom line: a new yeast and a new Pasteur!

In addition to the first four tasks mentioned earlier, the actor-network theorist also needs to account for the exchanges that constitute the mutual 'help' among actors and actants and that bring into existence a new scientific proposition. Indeed, by using the language of mutual exchange, enrolment, mobilisation, articulation, circulation, and so on, to describe the interactions between the many actants involved in a scientific encounter, ANT certainly contests the version that I have here termed 'still objectivity', according to which a 'free' subject is endowed with the right to know a passive object she already knows how to relate to. Instead, they depict the process of scientific knowledge-production through a series of steps that accord a different character to the folding of humans and non-humans:

> first, there would be translation, the means by which we articulate different sorts of matter; next, [...], crossover, which consists of the exchange of properties among humans and nonhumans; third, [...] enrollment, by which a nonhuman is seduced, manipulated, or induced into the collective; fourth, [...], the mobilisation of nonhumans inside the collective, which adds fresh unexpected resources, resulting in strange new hybrids; and finally, displacement, the direction the collective takes once its shape, extent, and composition have been altered by the enrollment and mobilization of new actants. If we had such a diagram, we would do away with social constructivism for good. (Latour 1999: 194)

This does do away with social constructivism. In the process, however, it also takes with it the entire subject–object relation.[11] ANT's contestation of the latter is praiseworthy insofar as it displaces its epistemological centrality. Arguably, however, it also does away with its pragmatic value. By reframing the subject–object relation as the mutual production of practical assemblages of humans and non-humans and by describing the scientific encounter through the notion of 'enrolment'—that is, as a seduction, manipulation, or induction of non-humans into the world of scientists (and society)—Latour's account could be read as either presenting Pasteur as a *Don Juan* that manages to seduce the ferment into his own sense of what matters, or, more symmetrically, as presenting both Pasteur and the ferment as collaborators with a shared sense of how things matter, working towards the same goal.

But why shall we assume that it matters to the ferment what will become of the yeast, or indeed, what will become of Pasteur? How do they define what each other's—or indeed their own—goals are before negotiating how things come to matter, and how they matter to each other? In other words, ANT seems to smooth out the process of negotiation between different senses of how things matter, that is, those of the scientist and her inquiry, and those of the relative outside to which the objects of inquiry might be said to belong. This smoothing out allows for

---
[11] A consequence they themselves celebrate (see Latour 1999: 294).

a characterisation of scientific inquiries as highly laborious indeed, but without any reference to the risk of inventing a proposition that matters.

This is evident not only in their own claim that there is no separation between science and politics,[12] but also in the fact that, since its conception, ANT has rapidly extended its scope of investigation to a myriad of other fields including the making of technology (e.g., Bijker and Law 1992; Law 2002), medicine (Mol 2002), law (Latour 2009), religion (Latour 2010), and so on.[13] In this sense, the construction of a technological apparatus may not require a distinction between subject and object. For even though it may involve negotiations that lead to a new way of distributing humans and non-humans, what is ultimately at stake is the production of an artefact whose responses must satisfy the producer's sense of what matters.

However, in the case of scientific practices, and particularly in the case of the experimental sciences that ANT has studied extensively, the construction of a scientific proposition cannot be achieved without a negotiation, which involves both the scientist and the many objects that compose a situation, *of* how things matter. The precise outcome cannot be anticipated in advance, and whenever it is successful, neither can it be reduced to the production of an artefact that will fulfil the scientist's demands, but involves the invention of a proposition that might matter to those with which the problem is concerned. As Hans-Jörg Rheinberger (1997: 32) expresses it:

> [r]esearch produces futures, and it rests on differences of outcome. In contrast, technical construction aims at assuring presence, and it rests on identity of performance. How could it fulfill its purposes otherwise? A technical product, as everybody expects, has to fulfill the purpose implemented in its construction. It is first and foremost an answering machine. In contrast, an epistemic object is first and foremost a question-generating machine.

Thus, in the case of engineering, the unknown concerns the precise technical procedure that will lead to the production of a difference that is

---

[12] A claim that Latour (2014) has recently been at pains to revisit.

[13] Its unlimited extension induces another potential danger. Whilst it advocates an ethics and politics of heterogeneity and difference, ANT nevertheless 'behaves' as a theory of everything, capable of effacing Otherness and including everything into 'the progressive composition of a common world' (for criticisms in this direction see Lee and Brown 1994; Savransky 2012; Watson 2011).

known and expected in advance, and the process of innovation requires a negotiation with objects such that the engineer's problem may find a solution. For the scientist and, as we will see, the social scientist associated with the adventure of relevance, in contrast, the relevant definition of a problem *is the unknown around which her practice is articulated*. For this reason, a scientific *invention* does not involve a process of seducing the objects of inquiry to agree to the scientist's proposed definition of how things matter, but of putting the latter to the test of what matters to those with whom the problem to be invented is concerned.

The risk of scientific invention is, in this sense, not simply the production of compliant artefacts that might make a difference but 'the invention of the power to confer on things the power of conferring on the experimenter the power to speak in their name' (Stengers 2000: 89). It is this particular kind of power, which requires that the object of inquiry *not* be internalised as a mere instrument for the production of a difference that matters *to the scientist*, that demands that we retain both a certain notion of 'objectivity', and that we do not do away with a *relative*, pragmatic separation between subjects and objects.

In other words, while we can and indeed should distribute agency throughout the scientific encounter, the process of invention that is elicited through and by the encounter needs to be related to the many divergent senses of how things matter that the specificity of the encounter has to fulfil. Thus, the question of the relevance associated with the invention of scientific propositions does not force us to maintain either the god-trick version of objectivity, the tyrannical realism that would seem to underpin it, or the concept of still objectivity. But insofar as it does force us to raise questions of obligations and unknowns, the relational question opened up by 'relevance' does prompt us to designate a subject that is neither absent nor all-powerful, and an object that is neither still, inexistent, nor tyrannical.

## The Risks of Invention

The notion of 'invention' I have been using should definitely not be thought as yet another synonym for 'social construction', even though what is at stake may crucially be identified with a form of constructivism.

As it often happens, tracing the history of a term sheds some light on the possibility of inheriting it differently than heretofore. According to the Oxford English Dictionary, the term 'invention', which comes from the Latin verb *invenire*—to come into—conveyed, throughout the sixteenth and seventeenth centuries, the 'action of coming upon or finding; the action of finding out; discovery (whether accidental or the result of search and effort)' as well as the sense of 'fabrication', 'construction', and so on. It is only in the course of the eighteenth century that the disjunction between 'invention' and 'discovery' came into being as we now know it. As I have tried to show, however, the kind of constructivism that the question of 'relevance' makes possible reveals the problematic character of such a disjunction for thinking about scientific inquiries. Thus, I want to reclaim 'invention' in its pre-modern, conjunctive sense, as involving both discovery and creative fabrication. For it allows us to imagine scientific practices neither as submitting to the tyranny of 'bare facts' nor as constructing propositions out of a 'whatever is' that does not in fact matter. In contrast, with 'invention' it becomes possible to think of them as requiring both a singular attentiveness to the many versions of how things come to matter in a specific situation, and a constrained creativity that might allow the latter to find a *manner* of encountering the situation such that a problem that matters can be defined.

Because it is a question of practical invention, then, our exploration of practices of inquiry cannot be formalised in the terms of a general epistemology that could, from the outset, lay the necessary and sufficient conditions that a problem must meet in order to address the question of relevance. Invention belongs not to the order of a well-implemented procedure for the posing of questions, but to an immanent and practical event (see Chap. 6). In other words, it is because we cannot anticipate in advance what the relevant pattern of contrasts of the questions might be, because initial questions might fail to resonate with how things come to matter, forcing practices to wonder and hesitate, that 'invention' can be said to constitute a risky process.

The specific form this risk takes is entirely dependent on both the specificity of the situation, the mode of inquiry, and the mode of existence of the object. As Stengers and others have argued, 'the invention of the power to confer on things the power of conferring on the experimenter the power to speak in their name' (Stengers 2000: 89) cannot be dissociated from the constraints with which experimental sciences are identified. That is, neither from the particular mode of invention that characterises laboratory practices nor from the mode of existence of the objects these sciences encounter. While experimental practices are certainly required to invent a problem that might allow for such objects to respond, the latter's stubborn sense of what matters allows them 'to turn around the (im)precisions of our foresight and understanding' (Rheinberger 1997: 23) in a way that, whenever the experiment succeeds, the event of invention is such 'that [it] affirms their [the object's] independence with respect to the time frame of human knowledge' (Stengers 2010: 21). In this sense, it is precisely the highly recalcitrant mode of existence of experimental objects that allows for the experimental encounter to be characterised in terms of what Andrew Pickering (1995: 22) has named the *dance of agency*:

> [t]he dance of agency, seen asymmetrically from the human end, thus takes the form of a dialectic of resistance and accommodation, where resistance denotes the failure to achieve an intended capture of agency [of an object] in practice, and accommodation an active human strategy of response to resistance, which can include revisions to goals and intentions as well as to the material form of the machine in question and to the human frame of gestures and social relations that surround it.

Following Pickering, then, in the experimental sciences the event of invention could be characterised by the risky process of devising a creative, choreographic practice that might invent a manner of attending to the obligations generated by the recalcitrance of the object of inquiry. It is in the encounter between the experimental practice and the object—an encounter which requires both the posing of questions and the carrying out of specific adjustments related to the object's own sense of what matters—that a problem might be invented in such a way that it may testify to the object's existence without reducing it to a deliberate technical construction.

As Pickering's 'dance of agency' suggests, knowledge-practices are inventive processes for encountering an object that is nevertheless experienced by virtue of its antecedence to the encounter. Unlike the social constructivist versions I have discussed in previous sections, the inventive process of knowledge-making 'creates itself, but it does not create the objects which it receives as factors in its own nature' (Whitehead 1967a: 179). For this reason, the subject–object relation is pragmatically maintained, but the risk of invention in the experimental sciences is neither predetermined by the tyranny of a bare fact nor does it depend upon an all-powerful human knower who, by right, already knows how to encounter and relate to a still object. In contrast, the manner of the relation between subject and object is transformed. In other words, the subject–object relation 'is recognized not as a right, but as a vector of risk, an operator of "decentering." It does not attribute to the subject the right to know the object, but to the object the power (to be constructed) to put the subject to the test' (Stengers 2000: 134).

What this means is that even if scientific propositions are indeed the result of a creative process of encountering objects and thus cannot be entirely dissociated from the careful posing of questions, they nevertheless are, when successful, propositions of a very particular kind—ones that, *because* they have invented the manner of attending to the obligations generated by the objects they encounter, of engaging in the choreography of 'resistance and accommodation', they can be said to be *relevant*. In other words, whenever relevance is at stake, the challenge is always that of putting the questions we create *at risk*, of making their assumptions and the contrasts they make available vulnerable to resistance by an object, so that a rapport to it can be invented in such a way that it becomes irreducible to a unilateral process of construction.

If the risk associated with a scientific inquiry can never be dissociated from the mode of existence of the objects it encounter, how may we characterise the risks associated with the possibilities of invention in the social sciences? Let me first clarify that the notion of 'mode of existence', as I am using it here (for a different use of the term see Latour 2014), should not be read as a way of responding to the question of 'what makes us human', but rather to a concern for the specific ways in which diverse objects come to matter. In this sense, being sensitive to the specific modes of existence of the objects into which the social sciences usually inquire does allow us to draw relevant contrasts between the singularity of the risks involved in their practices and those that concern the experimental sciences, without relying on a sharp ontological classification of 'kinds' (cf. Hacking 1986). Indeed, to rely on such distinctions would amount to returning to a form of 'shallow empiricism' that presupposes the very bifurcated conception of reality we have sought out to resist—a worldless empiricism that would regard the values, aims, subjectivities, dreams, hopes, and fears of human and other complex animal forms of life as being excluded from nature.

In other words, the notion of 'mode of existence' proposes another conjunctive proposition—the possibility of affirming qualitative differences among entities while maintaining that such differences do not rely on discrete ontological categories but on continuous, emergent forms of organisation that build upon and 'shade off into each other':

> [t]here is the animal life with its central direction of a society of cells, there is the vegetable life with its organized republic of cells, there is the cell life with its organized republic of molecules, there is the large-scale inorganic society of molecules with its passive acceptance of necessity derived from spatial relations, there is the infra-molecular activity which has lost all trace of the passivity of inorganic nature on a larger scale. (Whitehead 1968: 157)

While a full discussion of Whitehead's (1968) six modes of existence and their coordinated complexities exceeds the scope of our current discussion (for more in-depth discussions of this issue see Henning 2005; Savransky forthcoming; Stenner 2008), it is important to keep in mind that, unlike the concept of 'kinds', the borders that separate different modes of existence are fuzzy, and that while we may certainly assume that, generally, the social sciences deal with the more complex levels of organisation of experience, such a mode is not confined to the limits of the human.

To sum up the previous discussion, the particular kind of invention that takes place in the laboratory is only possible thanks to the recalcitrant nature of the objects that the experimenter encounters. It is their radical *indifference* to an irrelevant pattern of contrasts inhabiting the questions that the researcher poses to them, that characterises the achievement of an experimental invention as an event—that of allowing the researcher to affirm the existence of what has come into being by the encounter without reducing their becoming to the power of the scientist to bring it into existence. The same cannot be said, however, of the objects encountered by social scientists.

By contrast to experimental objects, social scientific objects are usually not indifferent to the questions that are posed to them, but are capable of *becoming affected* by them. Indeed, the difficulty here lies in the fact that, for some of the objects that the contemporary social sciences encounter, it matters that a question is posed to them. For others, moreover, science, as such, matters. In other words, whereas for the neutrino the questions posed by the scientist do not matter unless they become capable of inventing a problem in a way that does, for more complex organisms, those who inhabit a situation that inherits in one way or another the authority associated with modern science, scientific questions might themselves *become* relevant even if their becoming does not stem from the invention of a problem that matters to the organism.

As I argued in the previous chapter, no answer is independent from the question that calls for it because the question generates an immanent pattern of contrasts which constrains the range of possible answers that might be considered relevant to it. In the case of the social sciences, the danger is that of transforming the productive constraint of a pattern made available by a question into an imperative mould—'please respond to the question!'—that prevents the object from contesting the question and its pattern.

This practical difficulty that stems from the fact of dealing with beings to whom questions matter should be crucially taken into account in order to understand the specific risks that characterise practices of social inquiry. This taking into account needs, nevertheless, to be done carefully, because one might be in danger of associating this difficulty to an intrinsic feature of the human *as such*. Thus, to my mind, the difficulty *does not* arise from the suggestion that '[h]umans, as soon as they are in a scientific lab, agree [...] to answer questions or produce performances that reproduce the lab dissymmetry' (Stengers 2011c: 83). Because just as not all rats are susceptible to being conditioned by experiments (Brown 2011), not for all humans scientific labs or scientific questions more generally, *matter*.[14] Otherwise, the difficulty might seem rather insurmountable, or one might be tempted to solve it, perhaps too easily, by discouraging experiments with humans. But the point is not to run away from risk. As I will suggest later in the book, part of what makes the proposition of invention in the contemporary social sciences speculative, rather than merely descriptive of what is, is that a lot of contemporary social inquiry is already carried out through methods and techniques that require no risk whatsoever. As we will see in Chap. 4, experimentation with humans might be especially conducive to experiencing this difficulty but it need not be caught up in it as a matter of principle.

By contrast, this difficulty contributes to defining the risks of invention in social inquiry not because it is always actual but because it inheres as a possibility that cannot be dispelled in advance. The possibility, that is, that those situated objects of inquiry a practice encounters, and in relation to which it might seek to interrogate how things matter, might too readily submit to the social scientist's *own* sense of what matters, because it *matters* to the object that questions be posed 'in the name of science'. It is the possibility of the research question overriding the modes of mattering of the situation into which one seeks to inquire that renders the event of invention extremely fragile and unstable.

What is at stake, ultimately, is the risk of forcing the object to waive the claims and demands that might obligate an inquiry, while prompting it to submit to the pattern of contrasts that inhabits the question, regardless of whether such contrasts matter to it or not. Vinciane Despret (2008: 131) expresses such a danger with great clarity when she argues:

> [certain research habits] rest on a procedure that demands submission from those who are questioned: submit to questions, submit to the inevitable play of interpretations that will judge one's testimony, […], submit to the theories that guide research, submit to the problem that is imposed on them and to the manner in which the researcher constructs and defines it. The [object] is summoned by a problem that he or she often has nothing

---

[14] For all that has been written about Stanley Milgram's experiment on 'obedience' in this regard, for example, hardly anyone—certainly not Milgram himself—has found any interest in the fact that, while recruiting random subjects for the experiment, only 12 % responded to the thousands of directly addressed letters that Milgram's team sent out (Milgram 2004).

to do with, or in any case has nothing to do with the manner in which the problem is defined, just as the researcher isn't usually preoccupied by the manner in which his problem may or may not be a problem for whoever it summons. And most of the times the [object] mobilised in this way will agree to respond to questions without calling into question their interest, their appropriateness or even their politeness, as evidently, the scientist 'knows better'.

As Despret suggests, the challenge lies not in an intrinsic feature of the human as being somehow incapable of developing her own sense of what matters, but might be better approached as associated with the particular habits and sensibilities that certain contemporary modes of social inquiry take. This is especially true for those modes of inquiry I have associated with the ethics of estrangement. For to the extent that the exercise involves replacing one order of reality for another, it is inherent in their propositions that they be at odds with the objects' own modes of mattering.

Thus, if the 'dance of agency' may appropriately characterise the risks of invention in the sciences of the laboratory, in the social sciences the manner of the encounter cannot be dissociated from the difference it makes to the object to whom the questions may be posed. Indeed, if we were to unproblematically extend the choreographic metaphor, the dance might resemble less a dialectic of resistance and accommodation and more one of rights and duties, as in the many dance traditions where one leads—usually, the 'man'—and the other 'follows'. My view is that whenever such an extended metaphor can be said to be a good descriptor of an actual habit of practice in social research, the results might be rather disastrous. For its effect is not that of making the object internal to the technical process of construction, as in the case of engineering, but rather that of replacing the object's own mode of relevance with the social scientist's account of a situation.

In an attempt at making perceptible the questions I have been exploring throughout this chapter, in the above quotation I have replaced Despret's original term 'subject' by the term 'object'. And I have done so for a very specific reason, namely, that the problem posed by our conventional research habits that Despret describes so well makes felt the residual potential of this notion we have learned too rapidly to disqualify as naïve and positivistic. A notion which, throughout this chapter, I have tried to reclaim while dissociating it from its truly *disqualifying* versions: 'objectivity', other than a god-trick, a tyrant, or the name for the stillness of objects, might be mobilised as the achievement of a manner of encountering objects which, instead of *subjecting* them to the power of social scientific questions, may enable them to *object*—to put scientific questions at risk by making their own obligations present.

But we cannot conclude this discussion without adding another dimension of complexity to the process of invention in the social sciences. For as crucial as the attention to the encounter as an individual occasion is, we must resist the temptation to implicitly model our thinking upon a practice that might resemble the dual relationship of an interview. Indeed, as numerous science studies researchers have been at pains to argue, in the experimental sciences complex and arduous technical processes are devised to purify the encounter of its natural complexity (e.g., Latour 1993a). Regardless of whether—or rather, when and how— that process of purification may or may not be warranted,[15] the situations that concern the social sciences are rarely susceptible to purification. Heterogeneity, multiplicity, and historicity are not conditions one needs to get rid of, but constraints one must learn to inherit, for neither the objects of inquiry nor the situations they compose can come into matter without them (see Chap. 6).

Indeed, to the extent that situations are composed of disparate, individual, and collective objects with different interests, modes of mattering, and obligations, the risks of invention cannot be dissociated from the multiple, complex, and *noisy* patterns of relevance that inhere in such

---

[15] Indeed, to my mind the point is not to denounce work of purification as such. The process of purification that makes a laboratory experiment possible is, in Whitehead's (1955: 26) sense, a specialised mode of abstraction. And to abstract is not by definition 'wrong' or artificial, for abstraction expresses 'nature's mode of interaction'. The problem with purification as a specialised mode of abstraction appears when it exceeds the specific domain for which it may be relevant, and becomes an entire world-view, enforced generally. It is there that Whitehead's (1967b) notion of the 'fallacy of misplaced concreteness', that is, the confusion of an abstraction with concrete reality, makes itself felt. This is why Stengers (2000: 91) argues that 'the experimental event does not constitute a response without also posing a problem. […] [It] makes a difference, but it does not say for whom this difference will count'.

situations, for any relevant proposition must avoid subsuming the many versions of a problem under the purity of a unity, a concept or formulation capable of capturing them in a single mental fist. From an epistemological and methodological standpoint, the noise involved in such situations both complicates and contributes to the invention of problems that matter. On the side of complication, it does force a researcher oriented by the question of relevance to add to the risk of enabling objections to the pattern that inhabits a question in an encounter, the risk of the multiple definitions of a problem—'have I defined the problem in a way that enables all the versions put forth by the objects concerned with it to coexist without disqualifying each other?'.

What this may entail in practice will hopefully become clearer in the course of thinking with concrete encounters and discussing invention practically (see Chap. 4), but for the moment it might be worth noting that inheriting the heterogeneity and multiplicity of situations as a constraint upon invention is not about cultivating 'tolerance' or a simple 'relativity of opinions'. In contrast, if I suggest that addressing multiplicities may contribute to the achievement of relevance is because multiple encounters with different objects may also become a possible manner of actively producing objectivity in the sense defined above, that is, of inviting different versions of a problem to object to other senses of what matters. In this sense, the multiplicity of encounters involved in the development of social scientific problems is crucial for resisting the temptation to anticipate what matters for those to whom the question is posed.

## Conclusion: The Task of Cultivation

Thus, what the question of relevance demands is an active, practical and immanent mode of invention that, instead of summoning and indeed, subjecting the objects to the questions that are posed to them, may enable them to *object*, to make their obligations present so that the questions may seek to address their own sense of what matters. To be sure, the concrete actualisation of such a mode of invention has to be addressed in relation to the demands that each actual encounter needs to fulfil. For this reason, the next chapter will be an attempt to *think with encounters* and will have the purpose of actualising the possibility of such modes of invention by disclosing the fact that they have already been undertaken.

What the attention to the intellectual and technical requirements of invention in the social sciences makes available, however, is the beginning of an exploration that runs throughout this book. Namely, an interrogation that seeks not primarily a connection between epistemology and methodological guidelines, as if the former would be capable of providing the general principles that *ought to* be implemented, 'applied', in actual practices of inquiry regardless of the situation. What this speculative reconstruction pursues from different angles, what it seeks to cultivate, by contrast, is an interrogation into the relationship between modes of thought, modes of practice, and modes of experience—a question belonging to the cultivation of ethical sensibilities capable of developing another care of knowledge. Ethical sensibilities are felt orientations to the world that do not for that reason prescribe the terms of appropriate, adequate, or relevant comportment for all occasions. By contrast, they require a piecemeal process of cultivation sensitive to the particular perplexities that an encounter might generate, as well as to the possibilities that might inhere therein.

Thus, if Pickering's (1995) 'dance of agency' might be said to describe a mode of experimentation that might prevent the relative outside-ness of the object of inquiry from becoming part of the experimental apparatus, my sense is that what is required for an ethics of social inquiry is perhaps a different sort of dance. A dance in which actors are neither all-powerful nor created *ex nihilo*, but reciprocally transformed through the patterns of their often joined, often different, senses of relevance, as they become together in an *encounter*. The task is thus not to enforce a normative ethics of reality that be imposed upon the habits of thought and practice of a future social inquiry, but to create some of the tools required for an ethics that be cultivated *in* the process of learning how to think and know in an encounter. To that extent, what is at stake is the production of an image of inquiry that—as Deleuze (1994: 167) would put it—be ultimately an inquiry without image.

# 4

# Thinking With Encounters

## Introduction: What Is an Encounter?

In order to cultivate an ethics of adventure it is crucial that we disentangle the term from the more swashbuckling, personalistic accounts that have been given to it and which relate it directly with the figure of the 'hero'. By contrast, the kind of adventure I am attempting to characterise does not emanate from a heroic figure but from a meeting of heterogeneous bodies, objects, movements, questions, and senses of relevance. In other words, one does not wilfully decide to become an 'adventurer' and neither does one choose in what adventure one will embark on. Rather, one is given over to an adventure by virtue of an *encounter*. Indeed, as I will argue, it is out of the composition of a myriad of encounters that things come (in)to matter in specific and situated ways. It is thus only with encounters that adventures of relevance can be approached in a manner that is closer to their concrete and practical requirements.

Because it is found virtually everywhere, the term 'encounter' is—not unlike the term 'relevance'—one which oftentimes bears the danger of appearing intuitive and obvious. Thus, if one were to try to trace the term 'encounter' in the contemporary social science literature one would surely come across hundreds of articles and books the titles of which bear its presence. A closer look is likely to reveal, however, that many—if not most—of them contain no discussion of what an encounter is, or rather and more interestingly, what the implications of thinking about or with encounters might be. On the other hand, it is this intuitiveness of the encounter which may have the capacity, whenever the question 'what is an encounter?' or 'what does it mean to enter into an encounter and to produce feeling and thinking from it?' is raised, to force thought to change its habitual patterns and to situate us into the middle space of adventure. As Deleuze (1994: 139) powerfully affirmed, '[s]omething in the world forces us to think. This something is an object not of recognition but of a fundamental *encounter*'.

The notion of the encounter is a demanding one, for it already carries with it a particular understanding of relationality. As the term suggests, an en-counter is, in the most general sense, a meeting of heterogeneous elements. Thus, it designates, first and foremost, a mode of relationality characterised by the contingency of a coming into contact of various forms of mattering or patterns of relevance. But unlike some 'internalist' theories of relationality with which we have become familiar, to speak of an encounter allows us to resist the temptation to associate relational thinking with a general appreciation that would proclaim: 'everything is interconnected!' What it does instead is to force thought to wonder about when, how, in what manner and degree, and with what consequences, enduring things come to relate to and affect each other.

By 'internalist theories of relationality' I here mean the various propositions that pose relations as primary with respects to the objects they relate. In Karen Barad's formulation (2007: 140), such an account of relationality is expressed in the doctrine according to which 'relata do not preexist relations'. The notion of encounter, in my view, points to the limitations of such an account at the level of empirical objects. For if all relations among enduring things were constitutive of them, internal to their being, if everything was always already internally connected to everything else, indeed, if heterogenous beings were conceived *only* as effects of their internal relating, then there would be nothing to 'be met', and the very possibility of *encountering* an object would become an illusion of language (Savransky forthcoming).

To be sure, internalist theories of relationality are not uncommon in the structuralist and post-structuralist traditions that since the 1960s have pervaded the habits of thought and practice of the contemporary social sciences (Hunter 2006). In this sense, for example, and despite her groundbreaking work on the cultural processes of subjectivation, feminist theorist Judith Butler (1997: 119) once explicitly made the case that to describe the situation that constitutes the relation between a human subject and a set of regulative cultural norms as an 'encounter' is 'to take grammar at its word: there is a subject who encounters a set of skills to be learned, learns them or fails to learn them, and then and only then can it be said either to have mastered those skills or not.'

According to her theory of 'performativity'[1] and her reading of Louis Althusser's (1971)[2] famous essay on the hailing of the subject by authority, there is no subject prior to the incorporation of cultural rules and skills—the relations between the subject and the norm are entirely internal. They constitute the subject as such. Indeed they are not relations *between* subject and norms, because the subject herself is the effect of a process of normative inscription:

> To master a set of skills is not simply to accept a set of skills, but to reproduce them in and as one's own activity. This is not simply to act according to a set of rules, but to embody rules in the course of action and to reproduce those rules in embodied rituals of action. (Butler 1997: 119)

---

[1] I will discuss the question of 'performativity' in relation to the connections that inventions make in the next chapter.

[2] Interestingly, the title of a book that compiles the later writings of Althusser (2006), and which offers a very different 'Althusser' from the one that is normally associated with his 'Ideology and Ideological State Apparatuses', is no other than *Philosophy of the Encounter*. In this book, Althusser attempts to recover and make present for the Marxist tradition '*the existence of an almost completely unknown materialist tradition in the history of philosophy: the "materialism" of the rain, the swerve, the encounter, the take*' (Althusser 2006: 167, emphasis in original). Arguably, in her later works, Butler too has moved away from such an internalist position that precludes the encounter (for a wonderfully written example see for instance Butler 2005), although this has not prevented her followers from extending earlier arguments to the present.

Butler is right to say that, in the process of its own composition, the yet-to-be-formed subject cannot herself be the one who encounters cultural norms, for to suggest that would be to assume what demands to be explained. But this does not make the encounters that lead to the composition of a subject a mere grammatical illusion. Indeed, things other than the subject encounter each other and it is arguably out of such generative meetings, and not out of a smooth process of the internalisation of authority, that her notion of a subject may emerge (Savransky 2014a). As Deleuze (1994: 75) would ask: 'what organism is not made of elements and cases of repetition, of contemplated and contracted water, nitrogen, carbon, chlorides and sulphates, thereby intertwining all the habits of which it is composed?' In this way, the human subject can be thought as an emergent product of a myriad of encounters where modes of relevance, forces and habits become together—a form of organisation that emerges out of encounters between the habits of hydrogens, family names, bacteria, sexual and racial norms, conceptions of the self, carbons, political economy, proteins, and so on.

In this way, things come into matter, and they matter to each other. As I suggested in previous chapters, what allows for qualitative differences between things to be discerned is the specific trajectories and habits they inherit, the particular social order that each grouping enjoys. In other words, to think in terms of encounters is to address the becoming together of enduring objects of various natures. Interestingly, the name Whitehead (1978, 1967a) gives to these enduring beings that compose the world is that of 'societies'. As he puts it, '[a]n ordinary physical object, which has temporal endurance, is a society' (Whitehead 1978: 35). Thus, rocks, plants, human, and non-human animals are all societies.

Now, societies are not simply derivatives of some more primary set of relations. They are not mere epiphenomena. While they are indeed *composed*—that is, they emerge out of an organisation of composing elements[3]—they exist in their own right. A society, Whitehead (1967a: 203) would say, 'is its own reason.' And unlike their components, which are passing occasions that do not endure but only become and perish,

---

[3] Whitehead would call them 'actual entities' or 'actual occasions'.

a society 'enjoys a history expressing its changing reactions to changing circumstances' (1967a: 204):

> [i]t is evident from [the] description of the notion of a 'Society', as here employed, that a set of mutually contemporary occasions cannot form a complete society. For the genetic condition cannot be satisfied by such a set of contemporaries. Of course, a set of contemporaries may belong to a society. But the society, as such, must involve antecedents and subsequents. In other words, a society must exhibit the peculiar quality of endurance. The real actual things that endure are all societies. They are not actual occasions. (Whitehead 1967a: 204)

When addressing societies, thus, the notion of an encounter seems appropriate, for while societies are relational, they are not merely relational 'effects'. Whenever societies are concerned, 'relationality' means nothing if it does not succeed in turning our attention to the creative constraints through which concrete things come to matter and relate to each other.

In this way, for an encounter to happen two or more entities have to *meet*, that is, they have to pre-exist the encounter, even though they might certainly be affected by it and although something new—a *third entity*—might indeed emerge from it. The specific life-historical patterns of the many different societies that meet, or what Whitehead (1978) would call their particular 'routes of inheritance', simultaneously enable and constrain the manner the encounter takes. That is, things mutually pose their own obligations and negotiate how a novel thing may come into matter. Creative constraints are, thus, reciprocal forms of mattering that simultaneously limit and induce novelty.

As already hinted at by the discussion around the constitution of human subjects above, moreover, the creative, reciprocal constraints by which things come into matter in and for specific situations are certainly not restricted to encounters between humans, but go, as it were, *all the way down*. As Serres (2003: 61) puts it:

> 'Nature' inseminates itself with programmes. [...] To go with the physics of forces we require a general theory of marks, traces and signs to learn to remember like the world and to remember it, to write on and as it writes; things are also symbols. There is not just chemistry in chemistry: why does

an element react or not in the presence of another? Why then does it choose it in this way? What is the 'faculty' that makes it choose? Great masses write, molecules read. And, even more so than inert matter, living matter writes, reads, decides, chooses, reacts—one would have thought it long endowed with intentions. One hour of biochemistry quickly persuades one of the refined astuteness of proteins.

Conversely, the experience of a meeting of heterogeneous historical modes of mattering—of two or more humans; of a student and a book; of a child and a dog; of a wasp and an orchid, an anthropologist and a ghost; of two atoms, and so on—that constitutes an encounter becomes added to, and thus transforms, responds to, their respective routes, thereby inducing a transformation in each of the related elements. An encounter is not, then, just a coming together, but a *becoming* together. In this way, the encounter itself, when successful, can give way to a novel society—an emotion, a proposition, a child, for example—that might in its own turn come to enjoy a history and encounter other entities and milieus. Thus, societies encounter and become with each other. Because encounters are always concrete, they do not warrant generalist claims about the priority of either things or relations but force us to come to terms with the fact that 'just as the relations modify the natures of the relata, so the relata modify the nature of the relation' (Whitehead 1967a: 157). In other words, what is at stake in every concrete encounter and in the possibilities for novelty that it may open up is the way in which many routes of inheritance become together. That is, the particular *form* the encounter takes.

To the extent that inquiries can be thought as particular kinds of encounters through which multiple, heterogeneous habits of thought and feeling, and patterns of relevance, become together to produce problem-oriented propositions, the notion of an encounter prompts us to pay attention to what I, paraphrasing Michel Serres (Serres and Latour 1995: 127), would call an ethico-politics of prepositions in the process of social inquiry. Prepositions, as is well known, are those words that express the manner that a relation between two elements takes. Indeed, can it be that the social sciences have been, perhaps for too long, invested in knowing 'about'? In conducting experiments 'on'? In doing ethnographies 'of'? In speaking 'for'? In arguing 'against'? Might this attention to the prepositions that characterise the manner of social scientific encounters become a productive way of approaching the challenge of encountering objects in such a way that questions and their patterns of contrast be put at risk? What would it mean, for instance, to experiment *with*; to know *before* an object?

In this way, the possibility of cultivating a different care of knowledge that is made available by the question of relevance, that is, the question of how, in a given situation, things come to matter, may perhaps be approached in a more practical fashion: 'How to make this encounter fertile?' (Serres 2012: 166). Which modalities of encounter might become available in the process of wondering about how things come to matter? In this chapter I shall aim to experiment with some of these questions. Because of the contingent and concrete nature of encounters, however, such questions can hardly be experimented with in general, as a matter of pure abstract thinking. Thus, I must attempt to think *with* encounters.

## A Preliminary Note: Encounters All the Way Down (and Up)

In what follows I will discuss three concrete encounters drawn from published material by contemporary social researchers from very different geographical, disciplinary, and methodological backgrounds (namely, Despret 2004; Hetherington 2013; Motamedi-Fraser 2012). It would be too easy, and too unproductive, to select all those abundant encounters which belong to the sorts of inquiry animated by the ethics of estrangement that the adventure of relevance would attempt to resist; to speculate on their limitations and the reasons for their failures; to read them against themselves and to denounce them as irrelevant. To do so would silently transform this exercise in thinking with encounters into one of mobilising 'bad' examples.

In contrast, as I will discuss in more detail in Chap. 7, speculation also involves the taking of risks. In this case, that is the risk of thinking with those implausible, infrequent, yet actual encounters that 'exhibit the possibility of an approach by the very fact that they have already undertaken it' (Stengers 2011b: 313). In other words, the encounters explored in what follows have been selected, first and foremost, because in one way or another they testify to having taken risks that I have associated with the adventure of relevance. None of them is simply an empirical report, or a pure methodological reflection. Rather, each of them attests to having posed their own modes of guiding inquiries as a problem that demands to be developed.

Needless to say, my exploration will be necessarily partial, selective, and pragmatic. These three encounters are surely not the *only* ones that have posed the question of relevance as a problem to be developed. Moreover, in discussing these encounters and in relating them to the histories of the modes of inquiry to which they become a possible mutation, I will not be trying to characterise such histories and the complex varieties of, for example, 'experimentation' or 'ethnography', in any exhaustive way. Rather, I will do so only from the perspective of a speculative reconstruction that might nevertheless offer insights into the practical challenge posed by the question of relevance to a social science to come.

Having said that, I believe the selection does present its own advantages. First, the three encounters that I will attempt to think with belong to three different disciplines in the contemporary social sciences. While the first is clearly inscribed in the history of social psychology, the other two are closer to inquiries traditionally associated with the disciplines of anthropology, sociology and historiography. Thus, their co-presence in these pages prevents us from reducing the possibilities opened up by the adventure of relevance to one single discipline, be this sociology, anthropology, psychology, or another. The exploration of different disciplinary habits involved in what follows does not, however, have the ambition to endow the question of relevance with universal reach, but to make apparent the extent to which it might force those who are given over to its adventure, to *invent* a manner of dealing with the problems that demand to be dealt with.

Second, each of these encounters draws on very different research methods. The first one confronts us with the very controversial question of 'experimentation' in the contemporary social sciences, one that saw its 15 minutes of fame in the social psychology of the 1960s but which remains a not infrequent modality of inquiry in the knowledge-practices of economics and political science. The second encounter will prompt us to interrogate the practice of a much celebrated method in the so-called qualitative social sciences, namely, ethnography. Finally, the third method will not only raise questions about the encounter with an archive, but will also bring to the fore the challenges of encountering a kind of object that all social scientists, in some way or another, must learn to deal with, namely, words.

Such methodological heterogeneity will hopefully make apparent something I have suggested above. This is that the question of relevance does not by itself designate a particular method, nor aims at producing a methodological solution, conducive to facilitating the smooth and successful development of social scientific inquiries. In contrast, it involves a transformation at the level of the ethical sensibilities with which methods are identified—its job is not to provide solutions to research problems but to present *itself* as a problem that may force social scientists to hesitate, wonder, and invent. For this reason, relevance cannot operate under a rule of generalised applicability. The range of different modes of inquiry explored in what follows does not have as its aim the implicit suggestion that it can be 'applied' always, to any method, anywhere. By contrast, it always relates to *some* habits and *some* methods, *some*where. In other words, the challenges posed by the question of how, in a given situation, things come to matter will relate to the demands that the specificity of the encounter has to fulfil.

Finally, taking the risk of selecting encounters that show signs of having been given over to adventures of relevance implies that, unlike the typical exercises of 'debunking' by critical commentary, these cannot remain mere 'cases', convenient illustrations of an abstract argument. In contrast, I am here encountering each of them in their own specificity. Encounters go all the way down, and up, from proteins to the play of ideas. For this reason, what follows is not an attempt to 'apply' the more abstract arguments that precede this chapter to more 'mundane' situations. The explorations below will themselves bear the mark of an encounter—in discussing them, I emphasise certain elements, propose possible patterns of contrast, and also place certain demands upon them, and in turn, they obligate my thinking in unexpected ways, forcing me to adjust to *their* demands, and attempt to construct a sense of what, in each case, comes to matter. Indeed, they already have.

## Experimenting with Objects: Emotions, Social Psychology, and Multiple Objectors

Since their modern birth in the late nineteenth century, experimentation in the social sciences has become a much employed and debated mode of conducting inquiries and posing questions. Understood then—but still, perhaps surprisingly, today (see Webster and Sell 2007)—as the 'gold standard' of 'scientific' research, many disciplines, including sociology, economics, political science, and psychology turned to experimental methodologies to distinguish their modes of inquiry from the philosophical institutions from which most of its founding members proceeded. In this way, they began to shape new inquiries according to a model of scientific knowledge which, founded upon the modern bifurcation discussed in the previous chapter, placed the methods of other sciences like physics, chemistry, and biology as the best means for accessing the 'Really Real'. Despite their extended presence in many disciplines, it is arguably in psychology and, after the Second World War, in social psychology, that such modes of inquiry have enjoyed the most systematic and conspicuous history.

Most conventional histories of psychology associate the 'birth' of the discipline as a modern science with the inauguration, in 1879, of the first 'laboratory' for psychological research by the therefore proclaimed 'father' of Psychology, Wilhelm Wundt. This German philosopher and his students sought to develop a new empirical study of individual consciousness that drew on debates around the methodological opportunities afforded by 'introspection' and on the then recent innovations in nineteenth-century physiology. From its inception as a methodology in the social sciences, then, the aim of experiments was that of producing 'precise reports'. As Wundt (1983 cited in Danziger 1990: 209–210, emphasis added) himself put it, experimental arrangements '*force* introspection to give an answer to a precisely put question'.

Although Wundtian experiments generated much debate and opened up a prolific tradition of research in psychology, few of its defining characteristics have been preserved. Particularly, it was the testing of a 'precisely put question' through the manipulation of a situation—a feature arguably inherent to most laboratory experimentation—that remained a standard of experimental inquiry in post–World War II social psychology. This is not simply to claim that, of course, the nature and meaning of what 'experimentation' is has varied in the history of social sciences,[4] but that in the case of social psychology the particular changes in the aims and processes of producing experimental knowledge entailed a series of methodological, technical, ethical, and ontological assumptions that radically reshaped the practice of experimental inquiry and the way in which the nature of the object in question was to be conceived (Stam et al. 2000).

Indeed, while Wundt conceived of social and communal patterns, myths and symbolic systems as not susceptible to experimentation,[5] it was precisely the positivist individualism of post–World War II social psychology—the so-called fallacy of the group (Allport 1919) according to which only individuals were 'real'—that arguably forced a major reconceptualisation of experimental inquiries. Thus, in Wundt's laboratory, for instance, the roles of the one conducting the experiment and the one providing the source of psychological data were interchangeable. This suggests that the epistemic value of experimental data was one which was situated, that is, it depended on a particular interplay of actors, questions and responses that had to be collectively cultivated.[6] In this sense too, the experimenter and the participant were described as *Mitarbeiter* (co-workers) and participants were variously referred to in terms of the specific activities they were required to perform, such as 'the discriminator', 'the associator' or 'the reactor' (Danziger 1990: 32).

---

[4] As it also has in the natural sciences (see Hacking 1983). Indeed, even the notion of what constitutes a 'laboratory' has not remained stable (Guggenheim 2012).

[5] Wundt would strictly confine experimentation not only to the study of individual consciousness but also to the 'lower' dimensions of the latter, while 'higher' conscious process such as memory and language, as well as social and cultural patterns, would have to be studied in a different way. These latter dimensions belonged to what he was to term *Völkerpsychologie*, or Folk Psychology, which employed not experimental but ethnological methods.

[6] They were not only interchangeable but it was the role of the later called 'experimental subject' that was 'considered to require more psychological sophistication than the role of the experimenter' (Danziger 1990: 51). Proof of this is the fact that Wundt hardly ever acted as experimenter himself but did serve on many occasions as a source of psychological data for his students.

By the time the standardisation of experimental procedures in post–World War II social psychology came to dominate the modes of inquiry of the discipline (Stam et al. 2000), however, the division of labour became fixed, and the one acting as the source of psychological data acquired the now common name 'subject', a term which was used before the eighteenth century to describe 'a corpse used for purposes of anatomical dissection' (Danziger 1990: 53). Accordingly, the psychological data provided by the 'subject' was no longer conceived as having to be cultivated through training and experimental interplay, but was now regarded as an *abstract*, isolated, 'objective' datum of the individual mind.[7]

It is in this context that we find the famously controversial experiments by Solomon Ash, Philip Zimbardo, and Stanley Milgram that gave the discipline its much discussed—and disputed—reputation. Although perhaps not attracting as much media attention, this period of American experimental Social Psychology also saw the rise of a number of experiments on cognitive effects upon 'emotions', such as the one conducted by Schachter and Singer (1962), and in particular, the so-called Valins experiment (Valins 1966). It is the remaking of this latter experiment recounted by philosopher and psychologist Vinciane Despret (2004) that constitutes our first encounter.

The main aim underpinning Valins's experiments was the demonstration of an interrelation between cognition and emotion by showing that emotional states are influenced by cognitive cues taken both from the environment and from 'internal events', while they 'in turn arouse further cognitive activity in the form of attempts to identify the situation that precipitated them' (Valins 1966: 400). Thus, by means of an especially resourceful experiment illustrative of the aesthetics of experimentation that characterised American social psychology during the 1960s, Stuart Valins posed the question of whether the cognitive cues that influence emotional behaviour would still be effected if the 'internal event' which elicited them was 'fake'. That is, whether a bogus heartbeat would affect the degree of attractiveness of certain stimuli.

---

[7] This abstract conception of the psychological subject as a substitutable, universal data-source might account for the extended use of undergraduates in psychological experiments.

Valins (1966) thus devised an experiment in which 'volunteers'—actually, students for whom six hours of participation in experiments were a course requirement—were told that they would be part of a research project to test 'physiological reactions to sexually oriented stimuli' (1966: 401). The alleged 'physiological reactions'—which were actually a pre-recorded heartbeat—would be 'recorded', the subjects were told, during the screening of ten slides of half-nude women from the pages of *Playboy* magazine. The experimenter explained to the subjects that, while normally the procedure would take place in a centre for medical research which was better equipped, due to lack of available labs they had to use 'a fairly crude but adequate measure of heart rate':

> Here we are recording heart rate the way they used to do it 30 years ago. I will be taping this fairly sensitive microphone to your chest. It picks up each major heart sound which is amplified here, and initiates a signal on this signal tracer. This other microphone then picks up the signal and it is recorded on this tape recorder (the signal tracer, amplifier, and tape recorder were on a table next to the subject). [...] Unfortunately, this recording method makes it necessary to have audible sounds. [...] Since our procedure does not require concentration, it won't be too much of a problem and it is not likely to affect the results. All that you will be required to do is sit here and look at the slides. Just try to ignore the heart sounds. (Valins 1966: 402)

The experiment begins and the slides are shown sequentially. Some of them are accompanied by an increased heartbeat whereas for others the heartbeat remains normal. When the experiment comes to an end, the researcher interviews the subject and asks 'him' to rate the slides on a 100-point scale according to their appeal, ranging from 'Not at all' to 'Extremely' (403).[8] Which images do you prefer? And how much from 0 to 100? Such was the 'precisely put question' that Valins posed to his subjects. According to the statistics published by Valins, there was a positive

---

[8] As a matter of fact there are several interviews conducted and different ways of measuring the subject's preferences throughout different periods of time after the experiment. However, the other two measures make no qualitative difference to the initial question but were devised merely to test the long-standing effects of exposure to the experiment. Needless to say, the version of the experiment I am providing here is only a simplified summary.

correlation between the perceived increase in heart rate and the reported attractiveness of the images. The hypothesis was answered positively, and the experiment was deemed a success.

Despret's remaking of the experiment respected—despite some minor modifications—the original parameters and it initially obtained similar results. However, one alteration in the procedure makes present the possibility for a different mode of social inquiry that the question of how things matter opens up:

> Our final change was that we invited our subjects to come back ten days later so we could discuss with them how they felt about what we had asked them to do. Our second interview began with this question: 'In your opinion, what were we looking for?' (Despret 2004: 89)

What this additional question makes available in the remake of the experiment is precisely what Valins's version closed off. Indeed, while he did test his hypothesis, his precise question did not put the pattern of contrasts that the hypothesis made available at risk. In contrast, the question that he posed to the subjects of the study already included, implicitly, the pattern of contrasts created by the hypothesis that guided the study—should subjects prefer the pictures that coincided with the elevated heartbeat sound, this will mean, *necessarily*, that the heartbeat, as a cognitive cue, would be relevant for determining the emotional behaviour of the subject. Although the experiment was devised to 'deceive' the subjects of study so that what was asked would not be confused with what was expected,[9] the question—both in the first interview and in the follow-ups—still imposed a particular pattern of contrasts (yes/no) that was relevant to the hypothesis, yet not necessarily relevant to the participants. Valins's question circumscribed the question of relevance to the options created by the hypothesis—either false cues would be relevant factors in determining emotional behaviour, or they would not. Accordingly, the subjects actively incorporated the pattern generated by the question and 'reacted' to it, and to the rating of the pictures, appropriately.

---

[9] For a brief history of experimental deception in psychology see Herrera (1997).

In contrast, by inviting the subjects to provide their own versions of what mattered to them in participating in the experiment, the question posed by Despret crucially puts the pattern of contrasts that the experiment originally made available at risk. Interestingly, the responses to the question 'caused enormous surprise. [...] Each of the subjects we asked to help us explore our problem had a very exciting story to tell. And all of the stories were different!' (2004: 89–90). Instead of submitting to the pattern of contrasts made available by the experiment, '[e]ach had managed to connect his/her version of emotion to what the slide suggested' (2004: 90).

Thus, rather than seeking to falsify or confirm the initial hypothesis, Despret sought to explore the many 'versions' of how things—the participants, the instruments, the experimental situation itself—came to matter in different ways, and allowed the participants to propose relevant ways of reinventing the problem that concerned the experimental situation. In this sense, some suggested that the heartbeat—which nobody thought was their own!—was indeed a cue that prompted them to become more interested in the pictures; another said that he allowed 'the beat to touch him, take him in even, and that the heartbeat had "taken" the picture in as well' (2004: 90). Others, moreover, admitted to 'playing along' with what the experiment seemed to suggest. As she concludes the discussion of the results:

> With these declarations we had many versions of what the experience of 'being moved' might mean. Not one of them would have had the chance of enriching the version suggested by the slide if we had stuck to the classical process. Valins certainly can claim that emotion is not directly or merely dependent on the body, but his reasons for being able to confirm this—and the way in which his subjects actively contributed to the production of this version—continue to be definitively in the off-camera end of experimentation. Officially, all they caused was 'reaction'. They behaved like good subjects: they were willing to be taken hostage by a problem of which no one knew how far their interest in that problem went and how they themselves could construct it.

In this way, Despret invented a manner of encountering not an abstract, isolated and substitutable 'subject', but rather—reclaiming the terminology of early experimentation *à la* Wundt—multiple 'objectors'. That is, recalcitrant objects capable of resisting the pattern of contrasts that an inquiry makes available and of constructing multiple versions of how things came to matter in the experimental situation.

The preposition articulating the encounter is then crucially transformed, for the experiment is no longer one conducted *on* a subject by betting on the ignorance of the latter with respect to what is expected of her, but a mode of experimenting *with* an object, an objector, capable of making novel patterns of contrast available and, in so doing, of obligating the scientist to explore every version that the objects might suggest to her. The question of relevance thus, emerges in the process of negotiating the activity of experimentation by forcing the experiment itself *to invent*—to construct, with its objects, multiple versions of what matters.

In this way, rather than isolating the experience of emotional response and relating it to cognitive cues as if in a vacuum, the experiment becomes itself an ingredient in the experience it interrogates. To be sure, the experience of 'being moved' that Despret refers to is not independent from the situation that the experiment itself created. But this means neither that through the experiment Despret was able to reveal the contours of an experience in general, nor that her experiment *created* that experience out of thin air. The participants were moved by the experiment, but the latter did not determine *how* they would be moved. Rather, the experiment becomes *a* factor in the fact of that situated experience; it comes to matter in some degree and in some manner. Despret's question, which includes the experiment as a situated constraint upon the experience of the participants, constitutes thus a prepositional rearticulation for wondering about how the images, the fake heartbeat, the objects' own routes of inheritance, and the experimental setting itself come to matter in interconnected ways.

## Knowing Before the Field: Peasants, Responsibility, and How Beans Matter

To be sure, not all modes of inquiry in the social sciences have inherited the methodological individualism of experimentation, nor the demand to force a 'subject' to respond to a precisely put question by means of a controlled intervention upon the conditions in which the question is posed. In fact, although the sciences of the laboratory served as a model for the development of many social scientific practices, the naturalisms inherent in sciences like zoology, botany, and geology exerted a major influence in the becoming-modern of those social scientific modes of inquiry that were associated with 'the field' (see Kuklick 1997). Indeed, while the major early anthropological statements on other 'human cultural forms' emerged from data collected from missionaries' travels, it is the influence of the naturalist traditions of other field sciences that imposed the 'collection of empirical data by academically trained natural scientists' (Stocking 1983: 74) as a modern epistemic distinction. A distinction which, in turn, brought about the emergence of the practice that later came, for better or ill (Ingold 2008), to define the discipline of Anthropology to a large extent and that more recently has been extended beyond that discipline into other disciplinary spaces—the practice of ethnography.

Rather than the posing of a precisely put question, then, what was at stake in such naturalist modes of inquiry was the extensive and intensive study of limited areas—'field-work'—that would provide comprehensive insight into 'human nature'. As Gupta and Ferguson (1997: 6) put it: '[t]o do fieldwork was, in the beginning, to engage in a branch of natural history; the object to be studied, both intensively and in a limited area, was primitive humanity in its natural state'.

Due to the meeting of a humanistic naturalism and a modern, exotic fascination with the study of 'primitive cultures' in 'out-of-the-way places', nowhere else have the theme of 'adventure' and a particular ethico-politics of 'out-there-ness' and 'inside-ness' been more prominent and powerful than in the ethnographic tradition (Tsing 1993). Because it entails a leap into 'otherness', a delving into the intricacies of a situation and the developing of a feel for the field, the ethnographic mode of inquiry would seem to engender the danger of, as it were, making 'relevance' irrelevant. Has not the ethnographer already been cultivating, throughout the history of her practice, the adventure that the question of relevance opened up?

Initially, one might be tempted to submit to the assumption that inhabits such a question. However, to equate the adventure that relevance makes available to the one that has characterised the history of ethnography would be, I think, a mistake. For unlike the adventure that we have been tracing here, the ethnographic adventure has been definitely marked by the rise and fall of its 'heroes', and it has, moreover, taken a particularly 'manly' form. As Susan Sontag (1966: 74) sharply remarked in an essay on the work of French anthropologist and ethnographer Claude Lévi-Strauss entitled 'The anthropologist as "hero"', ethnographic anthropology 'is one of the rare intellectual vocations which do not demand a sacrifice of one's manhood. Courage, love of adventure, and physical hardiness—as well as brains—are called upon.'

Thus, despite the romantic and 'courageous' depictions of the empathic and other-loving ethnographer during the early generations of the practice, anthropologists and other social scientists have become, at least since the 1950s, acutely aware of the fact that the adventure of ethnography was not only manly but indeed, a white, modern, and colonial enterprise, 'enmeshed in a world of enduring and changing power inequalities, [in which] it continues to be implicated' (Clifford 1986: 9). Indeed, if Lévi-Strauss could be said to be the 'hero' of French Anthropology, then surely Bronislaw Malinowski did it for the British tradition. As George Stocking (1983: 71) interestingly notes, Malinowski's

> place as mythic culture hero of anthropological method was at once confirmed and irrevocably compromised by the publication of his field diaries [...], which revealed to a far-flung progeny of horrified Marlows that their Mistah Kurtz had secretly harbored passionately aggressive feelings towards the 'niggers' among whom he lived—when he was not withdrawing from the heart of darkness to share the white-skinned civilised brotherhood of local pearl fishers and traders.

In this way, the naturalist adventure which brought ethnography into being became, in its modern form, a tolerant conquest of 'living anachronisms' (Hindess 2008: 201) whose effect was not the cultivation of the heterogeneity and plurality of the world's many human natures—indeed, its *multinatures* (Viveiros de Castro 1998)—but the creation of a historically and geographically homogeneous space divided only by the drawing of two demarcations—the first, between 'us', modern, scientific adults, and 'them', pre-modern, fetishistic infants; the second, between 'us', humans of 'undeveloped' cultures and 'advanced civilisations', and on the other hand, nothing, bare nothingness, that is, the more-than-human world (Hindess 2008; Savransky 2012).

With the proliferation of post-colonial critiques of ethnography as a Eurocentric mode of inquiry and the later reflections on the writing of ethnographic narrative that were advanced in the context of the so-called reflexive turn (see Clifford and Marcus 1986) the politics and the care of ethnographic knowledge centred for more than two decades on questions of representation, the partiality of its modes of knowing, and the kinds of discourses that would or would not be appropriate to the writing of other cultures through reflexive engagements with fieldwork. Since then, however, ethnography has not only expanded widely throughout social science disciplines, but it has also been transformed in the process—by opening up the range of sites in which it may be conducted (e.g., Horst and Miller 2012), by including new modes of ethnographic engagement through the involvement of the senses (e.g., Pink 2009; Stoller 1989), by experimenting with novel forms of collaboration (e.g., Rabinow and Stavrianakis 2013), and so on.

As George E. Marcus (2012a, b) has recently argued, current innovations in ethnographic inquiry testify not so much to the 'crisis of representation' that characterised the concerns with discourse and reflexivity of the 1980s and 1990s, but to a 'crisis of reception' in relation to its outsides. A crisis which, crucially, forces ethnography not just to continue experimenting with different tropes and stylistic writing strategies as it had been doing in previous decades, but also to practically create new constraints for producing fieldwork (Faubion and Marcus 2009). In this sense, the prepositional modality that the notion of the encounter makes felt also problematises the constraints through which a problematic field may be inquired. It forces us to wonder about the manner in which the ethnographer situates herself in relation to the field and the many entangled modes of mattering by which they are brought into being.

It is thus that I encounter Kregg Hetherington's (2013) ethnographic account of his fieldwork in rural Paraguay. Hetherington was in the process of producing an ethnography *of* peasant activism along the turbulent east of Paraguay's expanding soybean frontier. Concerned with issues of poverty, property, and politics, he initially constructed the scientific problem as laying 'in a new agrarian structure developing in rural Paraguay, [whereas] the beans were merely incidental, easily replaced by something else, like canola or corn' (66). But, one night, after having moved into Antonio's house—a local leader in the peasant activist movement—Hetherington was confronted by the former with an objection that would obligate him to hesitate and wonder about his mode of encountering the field; an objection which would, moreover, 'redefine [their] relationship' (65). As he relates it,

> [h]e [Antonio] had been telling me the story of a friend who, while working for a nearby soybean farmer, had contracted a mysterious illness that had made him suddenly swell up and die. Upset by the story, he launched into a rant about soybeans until he was almost shouting above the din of rain on the roof. 'You come back in two or three years,' Antonio said. 'We're all going to be dead. All of the children are going to die. There's no future left for us. It's the soybeans that are killing us.' He went on for some time like this, telling similar stories about soybeans and death, and I realized, with some discomfort, that he really meant it. Then, after a brief hesitation, he turned to me and asked, 'What do you think of what I just said?' I had a lot more difficulty responding to this question than I like to admit. (2013: 65)

After this encounter—which was followed by a second one, with Andrés, a business consultant who while reading the newspaper commented mockingly, '"So now your campesinos are afraid of soy!"' (2013: 66)—Hetherington's ethnographic inquiry was forced to initiate a process of metamorphosis that would prompt him to cross the two demarcations that the history of ethnography had delineated and which, he realised, had themselves become built into the pattern of contrasts with which he initially posed questions to the field. He no longer could define the problem as he had heretofore, nor could his ethnography be simply one *of* peasant activism:

> Until this point, I had approached ethnography as an extended discussion with humans about humans, and I was less interested in beans than I was with what Antonio said about them. Which meant that it wasn't much of a conversation with humans either. To be blunt, Antonio kept pointing at the beans, and I kept looking at *him*. I instinctively translated his state-

ments about the nature of beans into social phenomena: I was comfortable saying that this was a figure of speech, a kind of political rhetoric, or even to claims that this is what Antonio believed, all of which explicitly framed 'la soja mata' (soy kills) as data for social analysis, rather than analysis itself worthy of response. (2013: 67)

It is precisely the need to articulate a *response* to the obligation posed by his 'informants', an obligation which forced him to wonder about and learn how to come to terms with the situated mattering of beans instead of reducing them to products of human representation—that is, to affirm soybeans as a situated presence *that matters*, in some degree and manner—which prompted him to an adventure that was doubly risky. First, he had to take the risk of crossing the abyss that had historically made the more-than-human world irrelevant to ethnographic inquiry. Second, he took the risk of becoming responsible, which is to say, of *inventing a manner of responding* to the situation he was studying.

In other words, the encounters with Antonio and Andrés provoked him into a different prepositional mode of conducting ethnographic research—it was not, it could no longer be an ethnography of peasants, and neither could it turn into a post-humanist study of multispecies entanglements (Haraway 2008), even though such worldly entanglements were certainly at stake. That soybeans kill was certainly no cause for celebrating their relevance, even though they were, in fact, relevant—'that nagging thing, not an object or instrument of some malevolent agency, but a thing that exceeds such explanations' (Hetherington 2013: 74).

Sitting uncomfortably with his established habits of posing questions, Hetherington's encounter with the field forces us to interrogate the ethico-politics of propositions in play. For the encounter prompted him to know not *about*, not even and only *from* the field, as if he could 'become' another peasant in the fight against soybeans, and neither was he working *with* the peasants in what could be misread as a kind of participatory action research.[10] In contrast, he was, I propose, knowing

---

[10] As he himself argues, not only was he 'a foreigner to the situation that gives rise to killer beans' (2013: 72) but also, the demands—but also the suspicions—placed upon him certainly addressed him as an 'expert' of some kind, a position he had to learn how to enact responsibly.

*before* the field, that is, producing propositions and articulating responses *in the presence of* all the entities, human and other-than-human, that constituted the situation in which he was entangled. He was making the problematic togetherness of the heterogeneous modes of mattering that composed the situation constitute the very *risk* of invention. As Hetherington (2013: 72) argues:

> An ethnography in response to Antonio can be formulated in one of two ways. On the one hand, it can do what I initially did: participate in reestablishing the priority of frames of reference by disqualifying the talk of killer beans as, at best, a figure of speech not meant to be taken literally or, at worst, a mistaken reading of the situation caused by a restricted understanding of what was going on (what Andrés would call 'ignorance'). On the other hand, it can itself be formulated very much from within the situation, as a *proposition* addressed to campesinos as the creators of killer beans. [...] It is therefore appropriate that the response I offer here, the proposition I am formulating after so much hesitation of my own, did not initially present itself in representational form but, rather, as situated interventions that arise from both conversations with campesinos and much exposure to soybeans.

His response not only involved the production of a piece of ethnographic writing but, in addition, he himself became involved in the attempt to articulate a proposition that assigned relevance and responsibility to soybeans so that it would effectively make them legally responsible too, so that it would bring them '*before* the law'. Hetherington's proposition sought to make the relevance of killer beans felt not only in the making of social scientific knowledge, but also, and crucially for the peasants, in the making of the law.

By producing knowledge *before* the field he and the peasants initiated a process that involved both the tradition of Western anthropological reasoning and the Supreme Court of Paraguay in an attempt to push both of them beyond the habitual patterns of contrasts that would allow them to disqualify the peasant's obligation ("soy beans kill!") as a pre-modern, animistic belief. As a result, the process opened up the possibility of a worldly reconceptualisation of the relationship between soy producers, peasants, beans, and the law; the human and the more-than-human world; a reconceptualisation that has made a major difference in the rural political economy of eastern Paraguay (2013: 76).

Because the adventure of relevance to which Hetherington was given over proved to be in many ways a success, one might feel tempted to ascribe to him the position of the true 'hero' who devoted his inventive inquiry to work *for* the sake of the peasants. However, I would be wary of giving in to such a temptation. For his success is not that of the *resolution of a situation* by the empowerment of the peasants' capacity to act and to make the presence of killer beans relevant to Anthropology and to Paraguay's law.

In contrast, by producing knowledge *before* the field, that is, in the presence of all the heterogeneous entities that brought it into existence, what he managed to cultivate was a proposition that would reinvent the problem that concerned the situation. His inventive practice thus consisted in developing the problem in particular ways so that the many beings with which it was concerned could be articulated. As Hetherington (2013: 80) notes, '"[l]a soja mata" [soy kills] didn't become a matter of undisputed fact, but it was also not easily disqualified. Instead it became a serious proposition in a wider dialogue of actions and responses'. Unlike heroes who, since the Greek tradition, always bear with them the promise of immortality, the success of this proposition is one which provides no guarantees, and it does not prevent the emergence of new forms of disqualification: 'I wonder, in fact, if the greater danger for campesinos in this new position isn't the temptation to use disqualification themselves' (2013: 80).

## Knowing in the Midst of Words: Social Science, Interpretation, and the Risk of Telling

As is well known, the decades of the 1960s and the 1970s saw the rise of a number of criticisms and attacks on the neo-positivism that prevailed in the social sciences of previous years, criticisms which problematised the sheer possibility of any unmediated access to an outside world and increasingly came to emphasise the socially constructed and discursive nature of reality. In Chap. 3 we have already explored some of the epistemological dimensions of social constructivism in relation to notions of objectivity and the making of social scientific knowledge. It suggested that Science creates the phenomena which they claim to study. The epistemological position it made available was not however its only effect. The slogan *'everything's a text'*, inherited from the deconstructionist tradition initiated by Jacques Derrida (1976, 2001) and the rise of poststructuralism in France more generally,[11] expressed the emphasis on the discursive production of the world through practices of speech and writing and thus also operated at a methodological level, by opening up a myriad of interpretative studies and modes of inquiry into the oral and written practices of meaning-making.

Thus, in disciplines such as psychology, anthropology, sociology, and political science—to name but a few—interpretative studies of words and their combinations in narrative and discursive patterns of language in use, rather than individual consciousnesses or social practices per se, became privileged materials of social scientific inquiry (for influential examples in the vast literature see Whetherell and Potter 1987; White 1973; Clifford and Marcus 1986). Such a turn to language and meaning produced a mode of inquiry which saw words as the very *stuff* of which the world is made. To the extent that this was thought to be the case, moreover, words were read not as referring to an outside to which they would relate, but only to other words in an endless play of signification and *différance* in which one interpretation would follow another ad infinitum. As Derrida (2001: 351) urged the 'human sciences' in quoting Michel de Montaigne, if everything *is*, or can be read as, a text, then '[w]e need to interpret interpretations more than to interpret things'. Rabinow and Sullivan (1987: 6, for a more recent account, see Becker 2007) made a comparable statement in an early reader on the interpretive turn in social science:

---

[11] Michel Foucault would normally be also included in such a list, but I am reluctant to do so. Indeed, although a certain reading of his work (particularly of *The Archeology of Knowledge* [2002]) was immensely influential for a variety of modes of discourse studies, his own notion of 'discourse' was, in a strict sense, hardly reducible to the linguistic. There are others who could be included in this list too, such as Roland Barthes, John Austin, and Ludwig Wittgenstein.

interpretation begins from the postulate that the web of meaning constitutes human existence to such an extent that it cannot ever be meaningfully reduced to constitutively prior speech acts, dyadic relations, or any predefined elements. Intentionality and empathy are rather seen as dependent on the prior existence of the shared world of meaning within which the subjects of human discourse constitute themselves.

Knowledge about worlds was thus replaced with an interpretation of *words*, their patterns and webs of meaning in action. Moreover, insofar as interpretation was seen as unlimited, it became relatively unconstrained as a practice—because words and texts are made of and refer to nothing more than other words and texts, to other webs of meaning, semiosis is an open-ended process which entails no risks. No interpretation can, in any strict sense, 'fail', for it is the interpretation of the text which brings the text into existence.[12]

To be sure, the proliferation of studies in the social sciences that, during those decades, proudly admitted their inheritance to the so-called linguistic turn has by now diminished in number and strength, and the concept of 'discourse' is perhaps no longer capable of capturing the empirical imagination of contemporary social scientists quite in the way that it used to. Not surprisingly, the laissez-faire attitude of interpretation associated with such a practice, once very much celebrated by researchers, is now seen as lacking 'accountability' in relation to the relative outsides to which the knowledge-practices of the social scientists relate (e.g., Rabinow & Marcus 2008).

Indeed, while many—if not most—social scientists still feel compelled to add *scare* quotes to 'reality', the anxiety over issues of language and representation is now perceived, by some, as a malaise of the past. Not only have critics of the linguistic turn argued that not everything is a text, but, through the kind of pendular movements that often characterise the dynamic intellectual investments of the social sciences, theorists and

---

[12] While the notion of unlimited semiosis was initially proposed by C.S. Peirce, other semioticians like Umberto Eco (1992: 24) disagree with the deconstructionist reading according to which 'the text is only a picnic where the author brings the words and the readers bring the sense.' 'Even if that were true', Eco argues, 'the words brought by the author are a rather embarrassing bunch of material evidence that the reader cannot pass over in silence, or in noise.'

practitioners have also encouraged others to move *beyond* language into the study of the material dimensions of experience—practices, bodies, affects, emotions, and so on (see for instance Blackman 2012; Massumi 2002; Schatzki et al. 2001, among many others).

While these may generally be welcomed moves, there still remains the question of what manners of encountering words are made available in a world that, while decisively not entirely *made of* them, still includes them as specific elements in its own process of becoming. Indeed, even if 'ethnography' may have become a new preferred methodology in many contemporary social sciences concerned with the study of practices, 'discursive' modes of inquiry still abound in social research, and 'words' are still the main *material* in which the inventions of social scientific knowledge-practices are crafted. Moreover, the need to think about the specificity of words and their patterns becomes particularly pressing, for example, in *historical* social scientific modes of inquiry, where words—in official textual records, in written testimonies, in works of fiction, in inscribed objects–, often in incomplete form, that is, as traces and threads of another present, remain, both empirically and in principle, crucial objects of encounter (see Ginzburg 2012).[13]

The question, or questions, I think, could be posed thus: in a world which is neither the self-evident world that allowed social scientists to use words to describe reality 'as it really is', nor a world exclusively *made of words*, how may words come (in)to matter? What *kinds* of relations might allow for an encounter with words to become fertile? Rather than articulate an abstract response to these questions, I will attempt to experiment with them by encountering the recent adventure of sociologist Mariam Motamedi-Fraser (2012) with archives and words. As she describes it (2012: 85), 'this project came out of a series of unlikely coincidences and strange encounters' which *perhaps* began—because, as Motamedi-Fraser argues, it is never easy to determine when or where a project begins—when she came across two references to a story called '*Irradiant*, written by a tribesman from Lorestan in World War II

---

[13] For a discussion of the effects of the linguistic turn in the historical social sciences see the edited collection by Attridge et al. (1989). See also Clark (2004).

occupied Iran' (2012: 86).[14] Such encounter prompted her to trace the story to the Bodleian Library in Oxford, England.

From the outset, however, the *Irradiant* archive was recalcitrant to being traced:

> The Bodleian Library took some time to find the Irradiant archive because it did not, until I asked to read it, have a permanent shelf-mark. Indeed it did not have a permanent shelf-mark until I kept reading it. […] I began by creating a rough catalogue of the contents for my own use […], which was sometimes a disorienting experience, early on, because the materials were often transferred overnight, over a series of nights, into renumbered acid-free boxes and, in the process, slightly reorganized. That feeling of delirium, in the morning, on finding new boxes, and finding things, or not being able to find things in them. (2012: 87)

Indeed, it was the very objection posed by the elusive materiality of the archive, its recalcitrance to being catalogued, and the difficulties, both institutional and material, associated with its conservation, which served as an initial creative constraint for the encounter, so that she began an attempt at cataloguing it while it 'transformed [her] from reader into sometime-archivist' (2012: 87). To be sure, as she realised soon enough, archives are not just made of words either, but are complex physical objects of paper, clips, binders, variously shaped boxes, ink, and rust that are themselves in a continuous process of transformation (Rao 2008).

But the adventure to which this sociologist was given over cannot in any way be reduced to one that might have taken her from an encounter with words, that is, with the story of *Irradiant*, to a material ethnography of the archive. Although the awareness of the archive's materiality, indeed, of *the story's* materiality, contributed to her cultivation of a different kind of 'attentiveness to the materials, the kind of attentiveness that often does not produce immediate (or even any) results, and that takes time' (Motamedi-Fraser 2012: 89), it was also the specificity of words and their heterogeneity that obligated her to transform the mode in which she might encounter them, to open up the ethico-politics

---

[14] '[A]nd let it be said', Motamedi-Fraser (2012: 87) notes, 'that references to *Irradiant* in the English-speaking world are rare'.

of prepositions that articulated her practice, and to be transformed by words in the process. As she put it:

> I was 'handling' a lot of words, written in many kinds of texts; I was thinking about how words are, and could be, generated and generative, manipulated and manipulative; I was reading and writing about a writer, and how he came to write a novel in a third language; I was experimenting with writing myself, and with two different languages; I was not doing much else. (2012: 96–97)

Indeed, many words, in many texts, in various languages, and with many different natures: factual, fictive, truthful, artful. Motamedi-Fraser was encountering words, she was not just producing knowledge *about them*, interpreting them, as if they were 'necessarily bound to language and literacy' (2012: 97). As she notes, even when she at first tried to produce knowledge about them, to *tell a story* of them, to ask them the question that most habits of telling seem to require, namely, *what kind of story can I tell about you?* she failed to receive a response, for the proliferation of materials and words of many different kinds and natures—'the excess of them even' (2012: 89)—amid which she found herself, '[suggested] to me that these materials do not want to tell; or at least, that they are not for telling about; and certainly, that they will not be told' (2012: 89).

This excess of words that objected to make itself *told*, to become the object of yet another 'interpretation', open up the possibility of a different way of articulating an encounter, one that is not about the interpretive creation *of* stories about stories, but rather one which requires a different manner of relating to words, of attending to their obligations and of wondering about how *those* words matter. In Mariam Motamedi-Fraser's encounter with the words of the *Irradiant* archive, the putting at risk of the question *what kind of story can I tell about you?* forced her to become attentive and responsive to the risk of words that object to being told about, and to invent ways to 'lure those materials and methods into posing their own problems' (2012: 85). If the words could not be told *about*, if telling was not relevant to the encounter with them, she had to invent a manner of learning how they came to matter—a manner that required 'living there for a while', *in the midst of words*, 'without knowing what it will yield, if it yields anything at all' (2012: 89).

Her adventure did yield, however, a form of writing, and a product, a book, that is not for that reason a mere 'interpretation' of what she read. Because the many and multiple words of the archive refused to be told, Motamedi-Fraser could not just simply trace the story of *Irradiant* by writing *about it*, as the habitual manners of the sociologist would dictate. Indeed, it was this obligation to inhabit the archive, to live, feel, read, and know *in the midst of* the many words that compose it, that forced her to embark on a different kind of adventure. An adventure which, she wonders, might perhaps constitute a form of *sociological failure* (2012: 90), so long as the success of sociological propositions is reduced to *telling about society*, and to do so *either* by means of facts *or* by means of fictions (cf. Becker 2007). Indeed, the words of the Irradiant archive objected to the two patterns of contrast generated by the implicit question of 'what kind of story can I tell about you?' First, they resisted the pattern that immediately assumes that it matters that 'some' story be told. Second, they objected to the pattern created by the notion of a 'kind' of story, that generates an array of relevant options concerning the many pre-established genres that normally dictate the types of stories that may be told in general. A contrast that suggests that it matters to the story that it be one pre-established *kind* of story rather than another. In this sense, the words that Motamedi-Fraser (2012: 93) encountered objected to the very distinction of kinds that would separate factual from fictive stories—they 'mostly refuse to identify themselves as clearly one or the other (regardless of the author's intentions or of the disciplinary, professional, institutional, legal, and commercial processes by which a text comes to be constituted as, say, a work of history).'

This objection took at least two entangled forms. First, *Irradiant* is itself a story, 'believed by some to be an epic account of an ancient Mithraic or possibly pre-Zoroastrian religion in Iran'(2012: 86), and by others to be a 'literary hoax' (2012: 88). Second, the archive did not only contain the story of *Irradiant*. Or rather, it contained much more of the story than any number of words populating the manuscript. There were also letters, 'factual' documents, and other papers and objects that related the temporary disappearance of the manuscript and which made apparent the multiple relationships between the (hi)story of *Irradiant*, the 1953 coup in Iran, and the involvement by Britain and America in its unfolding. Indeed, the historical nature of the stories belonged to

> a period of Iranian history when the relations between facts, truths and fictions were used and abused by some Iranians and especially by the British and the Americans. Or, more accurately, a period when many of the scales and perspectives by which realities are constituted were purposefully or inadvertently rendered inoperative. (2012: 93–94)

Thus, because the words in the midst of which she risked knowing objected to the pattern of contrasts that the question *'what kind of story can I tell about you?'* generates, that is, the assumption that it matters that some story be told, and that it matters whether the story is a work of fact or fiction, a third objection made itself felt. Namely, an objection to the assumption that it matters that there be a distinction between the one being told and the one doing the telling. Obligated by these three objections, the adventure materialised—always provisionally—in a book that does not, indeed, cannot *tell about society*, but develops the activity of 'storying' as a problem for the story, for her, and for the reader, to be developed.

Thus, what is produced by this encounter with words, one which cannot rest comfortably in the practice of interpreting them freely, but which involves the risk of inventing in the midst of them, of putting at risk the pattern of contrasts that the question *what kind of story can I tell about you?* generates, is not the *elimination* of all contrasts between teller and told, fact and fiction. Indeed, the elimination of a contrast has no other effect than mere anaesthesia, an indifference to what may come to matter. Instead of eliminating the contrasts that were objected to by the objects, the encounter has intensified the complexities of patterns. It has transformed the distinction between truth and fiction, teller and told, by dramatising their problematic relationship as one which is not mutually exclusive but rather, as historian Carlo Ginzburg (2012) has proposed, constituted by risky and reciprocal borrowings. Wondering about how those words of different kinds, languages, and materialities, situated by archives that not only contained them but were part of them, came (in)to *matter* in specific ways, allowed for the problematic togetherness of 'fact' and 'fiction', teller and told, story and history, to be felt.

## Conclusion: Cultivating Perplexity

The point of this chapter has been neither to 'demonstrate' a purported application of the arguments of preceding chapters to more concrete situations, nor to inductively draw from such situations general prescriptions for the conduct of inquiry. Rather, it has been to make perceptible, and by the same token, to cultivate from a different angle than heretofore explored, the real possibilities from which this speculative inquiry into the question of relevance in contemporary social science emerges. In this sense, while the encounters explored in this chapter have forced this text itself to invent, to propose possible prepositional modalities that might help us disclose the intricacies of their developments, it would be a mistake to read them as examples, that is, as *exemplars* of the kinds of procedures that all experimenters, all ethnographers and all readers should implement and follow.

Knowing *with*, *before*, and *in the midst of* objects are propositions whose sense comes into existence by and depends on the encounter with each of these concrete practices, and thus do not 'exemplify'—they do not create a new norm for articulating modes of inquiry, and they do not allow us to legislate, in advance, what pattern of contrasts will make the obligations posed by the object of an encounter felt. Encounters like these remain improbable, perhaps even implausible, certainly infrequent in comparison to the hundreds of other existent and published research articles to which they nevertheless relate by way of contrast. But it is precisely their actuality, the fact that they have been undertaken, regardless of how improbable or implausible they may seem, that makes them felt as real *possibilities*.

Some may object to the attempt to think with and construct propositions from such rare encounters. I believe, on the other hand, that as James (1956: 299–300, emphasis in original) once put it, it is easier to attend to 'the accredited and orderly facts of every science' than to the 'dust-cloud of exceptional observations, of occurrences minute and irregular and seldom met with'. And while 'the charm' of most sciences is to present themselves according to their regular, conformal models this charm has the effect of making 'a different scheme unimaginable. No alternative, whether to whole or parts, can any longer be conceived as possible.' Thus James reminds us that anyone 'will renovate his science who will steadily look after the irregular phenomena. And when the science is renewed, its new formulas often have the more of the voice of the exceptions in them than of what were supposed to be the rules.'

For sure, such exceptional encounters do not teach us *what to do*, they do not yet afford the proclamation of new rules, nor do they guarantee what might happen to that which they bring into existence, and to the many other existences with which these novelties might, in turn, come to relate. This latter question, which I have associated with the concept of 'connections', will be the concern of the next chapter.

By itself, then, an encounter does not offer solutions without, at the same time, becoming problematic: it 'moves the soul, "perplexes" it —in other words, forces it to pose a problem' (Deleuze 1994: 140). Indeed, the problematic lesson our encounter with these three encounters poses is that the perplexity that may ensue from them does not dictate the terms in which the perplexed might respond. In other words, the perplexity induced by an encounter, one that might induce not paralysis or retreat into old habits, but the adventure of inventing a manner of making that encounter fertile, also requires careful attentiveness, wondering, and imagination. It is what, paraphrasing Dewey (1998), I would call a 'cultivated perplexity', for these encounters make present the difficult, patient, and uncertain process that is required to transform the habits with which inquiries are conducted so that an encounter may *become* endowed with the capacity to transform them, to put the patterns of contrast that initial questions generate, and to change the manner in which the relationships between researcher and researched are experienced such that a proposition that matters may be invented.

# 5

# Modes of Connection

## Introduction: Knowledge and Its Effects

Whenever an encounter succeeds in becoming fertile, it does not only induce a transformation of the elements that are brought into delicate contact by it. A successful encounter also fosters the invention of propositions that may in turn come to matter in relation to, and beyond, the situation with which a problem is concerned. In this sense, the knowledge-practices of the contemporary social sciences must also be thought as potential factors in the process of mattering of inventions that will become added to—thereby changing the composition of—the worlds with which they relate. In other words, that which is brought into existence by the encounter will come to enjoy a history of its own and will thus come itself to affect the many other existences and 'outsides' to which it may become connected. Thus, cultivating an ethics of adventure also requires attention to the *mode of becoming* that connects the world that a set of practices inherit to the world that those practices may come to affect. With this in mind, we must now turn our attention to the question of *connections*. The question, that is, of the many differences that the novelty brought into being by the encounter might make to the 'outsides' which it may affect. It is this attempt to think with and through the question of the *effects* of what a practice of social inquiry might succeed—or fail—in cultivating that will constitute the aim of the present chapter.

To pose the question of how to think through the effects that social scientific inventions might or might not be able to set in motion confronts us again with the assumptions of some of the contemporary demands for relevance explored in Chap. 2. For the ways in which the notion of relevance is often mobilised would seem to imply a certain scepticism, a sense of suspicion, concerning the possible effects and the 'societal implications' of knowledge-making in the contemporary social sciences.

Indeed, it seems difficult, if not impossible, to understand the nature and stakes of recent debates around the so-called crisis of the contemporary social sciences without drawing attention to what the crisis itself seems to put into question—namely, the fact that the knowledge produced by the social sciences establishes a connection to the world, that doing social science makes a difference beyond the academy. For in the many forms of research audit in universities and other higher education institutions, relevance tends to become coupled—confusingly, as I have argued above—with notions of 'impact' and 'engagement', suggesting that the manner in which it concerns knowledge-production is of the order of an effect upon a wider public that might—should!—be measured by 'outputs' capable of exhibiting 'obvious, direct and auditable real-world effects' (Flinders 2013: 153). Alarmingly, then, the procedural language of audit systems and novel forms of scientific governance designates 'relevance' as that operator which questions, sceptically and from the point of view of a logic of accountability, the effects of scientific knowledge-production upon scientific and more-than-scientific worlds (Nowotny et al. 2001).

To be sure, what does and what does not constitute proof of a 'real-world effect' is itself a matter of heated debate and scholarship (see Burrows 2012; Flinders 2013; Strathern 2000, among others). Aside from the problematic definition of what is conceived by such demands as a 'real-world effect', however, the sheer concern with the wider implications of social scientific knowledge-production has infected the moral economy of such sciences beyond mere calculative aims, forcing social scientists to interrogate their practices in challenging ways. They have prompted many researchers not only to contest the rationalities that pervade the definitions of what effects count and how, but also to raise the much more interesting—albeit quite possibly less obvious, direct, and auditable—question of how to think about the differences that knowledge makes.

Conversely, such a concern has a clear resonance with the anxiety that seems to run through and between the lines of some of the calls for new forms of public social science. Despite the fact that they aim to construct more of a moral and political project than simply an instrumental response to the demands of audit systems, the debates around public social science discussed earlier seem, from this point of view, to actively incorporate the pattern of contrasts that such demands generate. Indeed, in identifying the 'crisis' of social scientific knowledge with the practical and communicational difficulties of engaging in a conversation with multiple publics, they seem to take at least two elements for granted. First, they accept the way the problem of relevance is defined—'relevance is something that is added by way of impact'. Second, in reducing the achievement of relevance to a matter of communicating the findings produced by the more 'professional' strands of the disciplines, in attempting to define the problem as the difficulty of making publics 'listen' and 'understand' science, they seem to take for granted that the 'solution' can also be reduced to more and better public engagement.

As I have argued above, such a conception of relevance imagines it as a mere subjective judgement of worth, rather than situating it as an aspect of the world. Furthermore, it seems to exclude the 'real world', that is, the world of socio-material, naturalcultural modes of mattering that compose actuality, from the very definition of what constitutes a 'real-world effect'. Indeed, unless one were, *a priori*, to arbitrarily exclude scientific knowledge-practices from the set of human practices that since the industrial revolution are seen to have progressively acquired a tectonic force, the proposition of the Capitalocene forces us to cast the question of the effects of knowledge-practices under a different light. That is, no longer from a position of suspicion and scepticism—'does knowledge *really* matter? does it *actually* have an effect upon the world?'—but with a careful attention to the multiple and immanent productions of value-actuality that different modes of connection make possible. Rather than cast doubts upon the efficacy of human practices for making connections, the Capitalocene forces us to care for the kind of connections that they make.

In this sense, a different tradition of thinking in the social sciences and the humanities might seem, at least at first sight, better equipped for allowing us to explore such questions. This is the tradition that, in various ways and as a response to the widespread positivist claim that the social sciences merely 'mirror' or 'reflect' the real, has argued for the 'performativity' of knowledge-making—it has affirmed that knowledge does not simply reflect a pre-existing real but performs, enacts, or constructs the real through its own theories, practices, methods, and propositions. In contrast to those who doubt whether the social sciences produce effects, and to those who think that public communication might secure the taking hold of effects, for this tradition the efficacy of social scientific inventions is presupposed. Indeed, what could be more effective than having 'reality' itself as an effect?

In what follows, I will revisit recent debates around the performativity of knowledge-making in order to explore both its valuable lessons and some of its limitations. As I will argue below, insofar as most—if not all—of its versions suggest that knowledge-practices are not just effective but *constitutive* of reality, the logic of performativity presents a promising but ultimately inadequate approach to the question of connections. For it ends up presupposing that which it seeks to explain, namely, the question of how, in certain circumstances, scientific propositions might take hold.

After discussing such approaches and their limitations, I suggest that the question of the efficacy of knowledge-production requires a more nuanced and textured understanding of the interactions between scientific inventions and the different *milieus* to which they might come to connect. In so doing, I will attempt to propose a different understanding of efficacy that might provide us with a more nuanced interrogation of what might be at stake in the question of connections. As will become clear, however, my intention is not to so much to replace performativity with some alternative theory, but to make present the extent to which the achievement of a successful connection between an invention and its milieus is, as it were, *beyond theory*.

## From Performativity to Connections

Although 'performativity' has become a widely employed term in some strands of the social sciences and humanities, it might be worth, for reasons that will become apparent in what follows, revisiting the tradition of performativity from its earlier stages and following its development. While a certain logic of performativity could be traced back to the early American pragmatists, or indeed to the sophists (Cassin 2014), the notion itself was coined by English philosopher of language John L. Austin in his 1955 William James Lectures at Harvard University and later published in his famous *How to Do Things with Words* (1975). In these lectures, Austin sought to problematise the assumption, commonly held by analytic philosophers, that all a linguistic utterance could do was to reflect some state of affairs, to state a pre-existing fact of the world. The immediate implication of this 'constative' understanding of language, as Austin called it, was that insofar as utterances state facts, all statements could be judged as to their truth or falsity with regards to the reality of the stated fact. Yet, Austin (1975: 5) contested, there are utterances that 'do not "describe" or "report" or state anything at all, are not "true or false"; [...] the uttering of the sentence is, or is a part of, the doing of an action'. Such utterances, which *perform an act* rather than state a fact, he called them 'performatives'.

'I declare you husband and wife', 'I name this ship the *Queen Elizabeth*', 'I promise that…'—such utterances have become famous examples of performatives, whereby what the utterance accomplishes is not a statement that could be said to correspond truly or falsely to a pre-existent state of affairs, but an *act* that, at least in these examples, creates its own reality: the consummation of a marriage, the naming of a boat, the enunciation of a promise. According to Austin, however, to call the force of such acts 'performative' is hardly specific enough. Indeed, all of the aforementioned examples are characteristic of a particular kind of performative act which Austin (1975: 116) termed 'illocutionary':

> [t]he illocutionary act 'takes effect' in certain ways, as distinguished from producing consequences in the sense of bringing about states of affairs in the 'normal' way, i.e. changes in the natural course of events. Thus 'I name this ship the *Queen Elizabeth*' has the effect of naming or christening the ship; then certain subsequent acts such as referring to it as the *Generalissimo Stalin* will be out of order.

According to Austin, then, an illocutionary act is its own effect. It brings that which the utterance claims into being. This specification is important. For, as we will see shortly, it is this sense of the performative, the sense of a conventional claim which brings that which it names into existence, of *an act that is constitutive of that which it speaks*, that—on the face of it—has been taken up more emphatically by some contemporary social scientists to account for the effects of knowledge-practices.

Before addressing this issue, however, we should attempt to distinguish this illocutionary effect from another type of performative which Austin termed 'perlocutionary'. As he puts it, '[s]aying something will often, or even normally, produce certain consequential effects upon the feelings, thoughts, or actions of the audience, or of the speaker, or of other persons [...] We shall call the performance of an act of this kind the performance of a "perlocutionary act", and the act performed, [...] a "perlocution"' (1975: 107). As this passage makes explicit, then, performatives may not just have the effect of bringing into being that which is performed but also of producing a *consequence*, of affecting an ongoing course of events.

The logic of performativity invites thus an attention to the effects that certain claims bear upon reality. It is this kind of attention, expanded beyond the strict linguistic phenomena that were Austin's original concern, that has attracted the interests of many scholars in the humanities and the social sciences in order to account for the processes, both semiotic and material, through which humans and nonhumans produce and transform reality.

Arguably, one of the first thinkers to successfully expand and reshape the logic of the performative in the humanities and the social sciences has been feminist philosopher Judith Butler. Ever since her famous *Gender Trouble* (1990), Butler has put forth an understanding of gender and sex formations not as expressions of an inward nature, but as thoroughly *performative* acts. Unlike Austin, however, for whom the efficacy of a performative depended largely upon the intentions of the speaker, Butler was interested, as we already saw in the previous chapter, in understanding the formation of the gendered and sexualised speaking subject *itself* as the effect of a performative operation. By supplementing Austin's work with Derrida's (1992) reading of the former, Butler situates the efficacy of the performative not in a theory of subjective intentionality, which would require a preformed, 'natural', subject constituted before language and culture, but in a theory of iterability. That is, a subjectivity which is not the originary *cause* of its own sexualised and gendered being, but the performative *effect* of a process of citation of cultural norms that regulate gender and sex.

In a different context and somewhat more recently, some social scientists have notably incorporated a logic of performativity to account for the effects that knowledge-practices, both within and outside the social sciences, induce upon, or rather, within, reality. In this sense, for instance, Thomas Osborne and Nikolas Rose (1999: 370) have sketched a brief history of the emergence of 'public opinion' as an effect, after the Second World War, of the theoretical, methodological, and technical procedures of statistical polling thereby advancing the contention that '[t]he social sciences have brought, and can bring, many new phenomena into existence. The social sciences can and do create phenomena.'

Similarly, in their co-authored article titled 'Enacting the Social', John Law and John Urry (2004, see also Law 2004) have made an explicit case that the social sciences 'are performative. By this we mean that they have effects; they make differences; *they enact realities*; and they can help to bring into being what they also discover' (2004: 392, emphasis added). In their view, thus, reality is 'produced with considerable effort, and it is much easier to produce some realities than others' but ultimately 'the world we know in social science is both real and it is produced' (2004: 396).

Moreover, in what has been perhaps the most prolific recent debate around performativity in and by the social sciences (see the edited volumes by Callon 1998 and MacKenzie et al. 2007), Michel Callon (1998) sets out to contest a widespread assumption held by economists regarding the failures of economic theory. Namely, the assumption that the failures of economic theory in addressing the realities of markets, that is, economic realities, can be explained by arguing that in striving to abstract and generalise its knowledge-claims, economics has become too detached from its object of study. 'The matter,' Callon (1998: 1–2) argues, 'is not so simple':

> [s]aying that economics has failed by neglecting to develop a theory of real markets and their multiple modes of functioning, amounts to admitting that there does exist a thing—the economy—which a science—economics—has taken as its object of analysis. The point of view that I have adopted [...] is radically different. It consists in maintaining that economics, in the broad sense of the term, performs, shapes and formats the economy, rather than observing how it functions.

This is perhaps the clearest example of the sort of illocutionary logic of performativity that has pervaded the approach to the effects of knowledge-making in the social sciences. Indeed, Callon's argument suggests that the economy is not that in relation to which the science of economics poses questions and makes 'claims' that are to be assessed as to their truth or falsity. The economy is, by contrast, *the product of those 'claims'*. 'Claims' here are to be conceived broadly. More specifically, Callon's argument suggests that both economic theories and what he calls 'calculative agencies'—economic inventions, technological devices, practices such as marketing and accountancy, as well as the many technologies of 'metrology' (MacKenzie 2004: 305)—rather than the linguistic statements of a few economists, actively bring the economy into being.

Although there are some evident similarities, it is important to note at this point that, unlike the arguments put forth by social constructivists that were discussed in Chap. 3, for whom to speak of the 'social construction of reality' was often mobilised as a denunciatory argument, revealing the hidden, human, and conventional nature of scientific knowledge-claims (Hacking 1999), arguments for the performativity of knowledge adopt a less humanist and more of a productivist tone. Rather than focus on linguistic and social conventions, in these works, the emphasis is rather on the orchestration of the many human and non-human, semiotic, and material, agencies—that is technologies, instruments, methods, modes of calculation, and so on—that together enact realities into being. And instead of employing 'construction' as a critique of realist claims, they often seek to affirm very 'real' effects that knowledge-making produces. Thus, in an important sense, 'construction', 'performance', 'enactment', 'production', and so on are not terms that would seek merely to debunk the realistic claims of scientific theories, methods, and claims but to draw attention to how those scientific constructions, *quite literally*, bring realities into existence.

'Quite literally' is, however, a misleading expression. Indeed, it is often unclear what is meant by the process whereby reality is said to be 'produced', 'enacted', 'constructed', 'brought into being', and so on by the social sciences. While in many cases these authors draw rhetorical force by relying on the illocutionary dimension of performatives—and 'bringing reality into being' is surely the most emblematic phraseology—oftentimes such contentions are, as it were, *appeased*, in one and the same argument, by statements that would suggest that rather than full-blown illocutionary effects, the sort of efficacy associated with social scientific inventions could be likened to perlocutionary effects. That is, that inventions have consequences upon a world of phenomena, entities, and relations which are however not entirely of their own making.

For example, although Osborne and Rose (1999) make the explicit claim that the social sciences create the phenomena which they purport to describe, they also argue that they 'have played a *significant role* in making up our world, and the kinds of persons, phenomena and entities that inhabit it' (1999: 368, emphasis added). Does this mean that they create only certain phenomena but not others? Or that the phenomena that they do create are not, or at least not immediately, constitutive of 'our world'? Or that the social sciences are not the only factors in the production of phenomena? If so, how do the different factors interact in the composition of the world? Is the question of efficacy and 'real-world effects' then displaced onto how a phenomenon created by the social sciences comes to make up our world?

Not dissimilarly, while Law and Urry (2004: 392) argue for a view that suggests that the social sciences 'enact realities', that they bring them into being, at some other point in the article they also affirm that '[the social sciences] (help to) *make* social realities and social worlds' (2004: 390, emphasis in original). The introduction of the term 'social' here is rather puzzling—is it, as someone like John Searle (1996) has argued, that *only* 'social reality' is constructed? The rest of the article and indeed the rest of their work seems to suggest—rightly, I think—that any clear-cut distinction between 'social' and 'non-social' reality does not hold. How shall we interpret, moreover, the use of the parenthesis when Law and Urry claim that the social sciences (help to) make reality?

Again, while Callon (1998: 2) and his colleagues put forth the radically illocutionary argument that 'economics, in the broad sense of the term, performs, shapes and formats the economy', he also concedes that, by and large, 'perlocution is actually more fundamental and in any case more general than illocution' (Callon 2007: 164). Thus, the 'performativity' of economics is to be understood through a process of 'framing' and 'overflowing' whereby a certain economic theory, model, or assemblage of calculative agencies 'frames' the market in particular ways while also necessarily leaving other relations and effects out of its calculations—what economists usually refer to as 'externalities'. What explains the constative failure of economics, Callon argues (1998: 17), is thus not that economic models are false or inaccurate in their framing, but that 'total framing' is by necessity impossible. 'Any frame is necessarily subject to overflowing'. But why, one may wonder, would there be failures—*misfires*, in Austinian terminology—if the reality which is said to exceed any framing is nothing but the effect of the frame itself? How can a reality that is nothing but the effect of a model object to the latter and put it at risk?

I raise these questions neither with the aim of analytically deconstructing these arguments nor of suggesting that the questions I identify in them can be solved simply by claiming, in the same analytical tone, that one should write clearly, or to remain faithful to Austin's original formulations. I believe in none of those analytical procedures, nor share their ethical and political commitments. Rather, I am convinced, with Butler (2007: 153), that 'it matters whether we think we are building a reality or making certain things happen.' While arguments for the performativity of knowledge sometimes read as a celebration of scientific efficacy and as a final blow to anybody who might still wonder whether there is something 'out there' in relation to which social science attempts to pose questions and produce propositions, I raise these questions in the hope that they can make felt the *difficulty* inherent in thinking about the relations between scientific inventions and their effects. My aim is, as Haraway (2012) would put it, to 'stay with the trouble'.

I fear that if one were to be committed to the illocutionary sense of performativity, to conceive of the effects of social scientific inventions as none other than single-handedly producing the reality for which they make themselves true, as being the very *sources of* reality, then 'reality' itself would become rather impoverished. Indeed, in such accounts of performativity the efficacy of inventions is always already presupposed because, to put it bluntly, illocutionary effects are all-mighty.[1] They not only make certain things happen; they are also said to produce the very *worlds* in and for which certain things happen.

Nevertheless, if as Haraway (1991: 198) once put it, 'the world is not raw material for humanization', then neither can it be a mere receptacle for whatever social scientific practices make to inhabit it. If questions of efficacy *matter*, then, it is precisely because sometimes the making of a difference is achieved, and sometimes it is not. Or more precisely, because even though differences may always be produced, they are *not* always differences that matter. In other words, a failure, however partial, however relative, to achieve a certain effect, matters as much as a success does.

Now, while Callon affirms that framing is always partially unsuccessful, and while Butler's account of performativity is certainly attentive to the possibility—or rather, the necessity—of failure, the logic of repetition that they deem essential to understanding the efficacy of performativity only views such failures as *constitutive*: 'performativity *never* fully achieves its effect, and so in this sense "fails" *all the time*; its failure is what *necessitates* its reiterative temporality, and we cannot think iterability without failure' (Butler 2007: 153, emphasis added). This account however is not easily reconciled with the fact that 'performativity' in the Derridarian, and indeed, in Butler's reading, is defined not as a single act but already

---

[1] When taken far enough, the logic of performativity even manages to turn failures into successes, as exemplified by Donald MacKenzie's (2004: 306) notion of 'counterperformativity', which involves the successful accomplishment of a self-undermining effect.

as a *series* of iterations. What is it, then, that fails? And when? If failure is *always* part and parcel of performativity, why does it matter when it succeeds? In this sense, as Paul du Gay (2007: 174) interestingly suggests, while this view subordinates empirical failures to theoretically congenital ones, the explanatory power of performative arguments still depends upon a more nuanced—yet theoretically under-explored—set of empirical possibilities: that *sometimes* inventions produce certain effects, and *sometimes* they do not.

This difficulty in giving an account of the empirical possibilities of failure or success poses, moreover, an additional problem. Because it either presupposes efficacy or its failure as necessary, the logic of performativity that understands knowledge as a *source of reality* does not appear to be particularly well equipped for addressing the contemporary demands upon the social sciences to account for the differences they make. From this point of view, such demands can only be thought either as a badly thought question or as the effect of naturalisation of something that in fact would not be possible without social scientific inventions.

In this sense, for instance, one might be tempted to argue that the procedures through which 'relevance' and 'impact' are measured are heirs of a tradition of sampling and statistical reasoning that is itself one of the many 'impacts' of mathematical and social scientific inventions. Nevertheless, to dismiss the concern for the effects of social scientific inventions in this way does not make the potential threats to the futures of contemporary social sciences any less pervasive, and it precludes the possibility of extracting from its interstices potentially powerful propositions for engaging it.

Thus, although illocutionary effects are both possible and actual, and Austin's examples are clear indications of their actuality, abstracting from them a maxim that could become a generalised theory of the effects that social scientific inventions induce seems to diminish, rather than enhance, their capacity to force our thinking in productive ways. For whenever that to which an invention connects is thought of as the effect of the invention itself, performativity becomes a preformism 'that regards the real as simply the realisation of the possible' (Bell 2008: 402). As Vikki Bell (2007) has argued, in order to avoid this, performativity needs to be complemented with, and problematised by, a consideration of the intrinsic, creative, differentiating capacities of the world to organise and individuate itself. As she puts it:

> [i]f processes in the world can self-organize and emerge so as to surprise us, such that matter cannot be said to imitate forms according to laws [...] the operations of a social apparatus of normalization cannot be considered to constitute matter, nor to control the processes at stake. (Bell 2007: 110–111)

Thus, as both critics and proponents of performativity often implicitly and—less often—explicitly suggest, the effects of scientific inventions might be better understood by recourse to a process that is more akin to what Austin would call a 'perlocution'. In contrast to illocutionary effects, the notion of a perlocutionary effect requires that we conceive of the relationship between an invention and a milieu as something other than a unilateral creation of the latter by the former.

As I mentioned above, perlocutions do not belong to the grand operation of reality-making *tout court*, but rather to the more modest logic of connection-making: making a difference, introducing a novelty which might be capable of acting as a vector in the transformation and/or sustenance of the becoming of an ongoing process of events. In this sense, the inventions produced by knowledge-practices are neither coextensive with, nor the source of, reality as such or in general, but become *factors in* the sustenance and transformation, in the cultivation or decay, of the worlds with which they connect.

Such a move from 'reality-making' to 'connection-making' is however not yet a solution to the problem of effects but an alternative way of developing the problem. In order to do that, we need to attend to two interrelated questions that, although they will not find final answers in the course of this chapter, might open up a different sensibility for approaching the question of the effects of knowledge-making upon the world, a sensibility that is perhaps more modest and curious. First, the question of the efficacy of inventions requires a more nuanced and textured exploration of the interrelations between inventions, efficacies, and milieus—how and in what circumstances does a social scientific invention produce what effects? Second, we have to interrogate the question of how to think about different *modes* of connection. In other words, we need to raise questions that inquire not only into the question of efficacy as matter of degree—that is, that treat efficacies as something to be quantified—but also into the manners in which inventions and their consequences come (in)to matter.

## On the Efficacy of Inventions: Knowledge and Its Milieu

As Austin (1975: 8) himself claimed at the beginning of his lectures, the production of the performative may be one, or even the 'leading incident in the performance of the act […], but it is far from being usually, even if it is ever, the *sole* thing necessary if the act is to be deemed to have been performed.' To pose, rather than presuppose, the question of the efficacy of inventions is thus to induce a mode of interrogation that the tradition of performativity after Austin has either taken for granted or addressed only in terms of general 'conditions'. Thus, while Callon deems 'overflowing' a necessary dimension of the making of economies, and Derrida and Butler posed iterability as a condition for the efficacy of a performative—and its paradoxical, constitutive failure—Pierre Bourdieu (1992) famously argued that the conditions for the efficacy of an act were to be thought of in terms of social fields and symbolic power: who, in a certain social field, has a power to say what and with what effect.

But to think of efficacy in terms of conditions is to address both the invention and its coming to matter as abstractions divested of any specificity, whereas the problem of efficacy cannot be dissociated from the always specific, fragile, and situated modes of connection that may take hold. The question is thus not how 'knowledge', in general, relates to 'the world', in general. Those are abstractions which might help us think—or not—but which in any case should not be confused with the concreteness of *this* invention and how it might come to relate to *that* part of the world to which it might connect. 'Conditions', by contrast, designate what needs to be met, in general, so that an effect might be possible. As Stengers (2011d: 49) argues, to speak of 'conditions' is to emphatically dissociate the production of knowledge from its adventure: 'conditions are supposed to answer a fundamentally anonymous problem, which anyone could raise, the answer to which will therefore be valid in principle for anyone.'

To counter such an anonymous mode of thinking, Stengers proposes that we think in terms of 'requisites' or requirements, which 'for their part, are immanent to the problem raised; they are "what this problem needs for a solution to be given to it"' (2011d: 49). What thinking of efficacy in terms of requisites makes present, thus, is the question of when, in what circumstances, and how, a scientific invention may acquire a capacity to come into matter. It is to suggest that effects do not take hold either by themselves or in a vacuum but do so only in relation to a *milieu*.

Taking into account the 'milieu', which is to say, the specific patterns of relevance that constitute a space of interdependencies in relation to which connections may take hold, involves entertaining the thought that the world is not only open and dynamic, but that it is also plural, that there is a relative outside to every milieu, and that these interactions between milieus may have a bearing upon the success of a connection. Wondering about the milieu is to affirm that it matters *to what* social scientific inventions become connected—that inventions do have consequences, but they do not control the process through which such consequences take hold. In this way, the notion of 'milieu' also raises the question of how to characterise the various *modes of connection* that may be established between an invention and the milieus with which it connects. Namely, not only whether or not an invention succeeds in coming into matter but, again, the situated question of *how* it comes to matter in and with a particular milieu.

Thus, approaching efficacy through milieus allows us to entertain the question of the effects of a social scientific invention ecologically, as the question of how different parts of the world come to relate to each other in specific and potentially novel ways. Thinking ecologically, however, does not necessarily entail a disguised reintroduction of a notion that Michel Serres (1995) has taught us to distrust, namely, the notion of 'environment'. For while an 'environment' requires the postulation of a centre *around which* other existences may come to be situated and sustained, a milieu[2] designates 'a pure system of relations without supports'

---

[2] Which in French simultaneously denotes the 'medium', the 'surrounding', and the 'middle' (Massumi in Deleuze and Guattari 1987: xvii).

(Canguilhem 2008: 103). It is a space of complex interdependencies without centre that is constituted by the diverse patterns of relevance, problems, and solutions that the things that compose it propose to each other.

For this reason, whereas the 'environment' presupposes a static relation between that which is placed at the centre and those other existences that surround it, the relationship between an entity and its milieu is crucially dynamic. It is, in Georges Canguilhem's (2008: 113) words, 'a debate'—a fragile, precarious, and metastable negotiation between elements that are brought into contact. In this way, even though not all may experience them in the same way, none of the elements concerning a milieu are exempt from the consequences that will bear upon it, for the milieu itself is nothing but a 'certain number of combined, overall effects bearing on all who live in it' (Foucault 2007: 21).

Constituting nothing but a system of relations without support, one should not look for an underlying substance capable of expressing the essence of a milieu. The milieu is, by contrast, thoroughly *problematic*—it comes to matter only through situations that put the question of the togetherness of things as a problem to be developed. Thus, just as what happens between subjects and objects, and between encounters and connections, the difference between a thing and its milieu is never absolute but *relative*, both in the sense that a thing also acts as a milieu of its components, and in the sense that their existences are mutually sustained or transformed by the ways in which they matter to each other. As Deleuze and Guattari (1987: 313) put it:

> [e]very milieu is vibratory, in other words, a block of space-time constituted by the periodic repetition of the component. Thus the living thing has an exterior milieu of materials, an interior milieu of composing elements and composed substances, an intermediary milieu of membranes and limits, and an annexed milieu of energy sources and actions-perceptions.

The relationship between a thing and its milieu can thus be conceived as a process of transitioning between the one and the many—the synthesis of a one from the many that constitute its interior milieu, or its milieu of emergence (or, the encounter), and the addition of the one as a novel component to the many that constitute its exterior milieu (or, its connections). As Whitehead (1978: 21) has famously argued: '[t]he novel entity is at once the togetherness of the "many" which it finds, and also it is one among the disjunctive "many" which it leaves; it is a novel entity, disjunctively among the many entities which it synthesizes. The many become one, and are increased by one.'

Thus, unlike a 'condition', which by its very ambition of anonymous generality must remain causally stable, the mutual requirements that emerge between an invention and its milieu create a space for thinking in terms of complex, dynamic, circulating, and emergent understandings of causality, where a partial effect from the point of view of one process becomes a partial cause from the point of view of another (Foucault 2007). In this sense, François Jullien's (1995, 2004) work on the concept of 'efficacy'—or *shi*— in Chinese culture[3] might provide us with a cue for exploring the question of connections in a more textured, demanding, and modest manner.

As he argues, in contrast to Western traditions of model-making which involve setting up the conditions for a means–end relationship whereby what is at stake is the intrusion of an idea, 'however arbitrary or forced', into the realm of fact (Jullien 2004: 32), efficacy depends not on abstract, general conditions and goals, but on immanent and always shifting *dispositional determinations* of reality (Jullien 1995: 61). A disposition designates the reciprocal and dynamic connections between the invention and its interior and exterior milieus. In fact, for Jullien, if efficacy depends on something it is on the very degree of dynamism which the relations between milieus may attain:

> a disposition is effective by virtue of its renewability; it is a tool. To say that *shi* [efficacy], as a strategic tool, must be as mobile as water [...] means more than merely saying that the ability to adapt is necessary or purely a matter of common sense. What is involved is the deeper intuition that a particular disposition loses its potentiality when it becomes inflexible (or static).

---

[3] Although Jullien is not too widely read in the anglophone world, it is important to specify the kind of reading of Chinese culture and thought that he constructs, and, accordingly, the mode in which his work will be taken up here. Jullien's approach to China is not exactly that of a conventional sinologist, but of one who works 'at once as a philologist and a philosopher' moving between hermetic sinology and a non-simplistic comparativism 'toward the elaboration of a theory' (1995: 19). Although the contrasts drawn in his work oftentimes seem to convey a considerable amount of Occidentalism (particularly in Jullien 2004), one should bear in mind that their task is neither simply to *compare*, nor to celebrate Chinese thinking *per se*, but to articulate, by means of a 'tentative entrée' (1995: 20), propositions for the transformation of our Western habits of thought. It is following this constructive, speculative gesture that I draw upon his work.

Thus, in this account, efficacy emanates from the shifting movements that are instituted between an invention and its milieu. What a disposition of reality progressively generates, then, is a potential, or as Jullien (1995) calls it, a 'propensity', for certain effects to take hold. Unlike the production of a performative, which is more or less arbitrary and whose success depends either on the intention of the actor, on her symbolic capital, or on the historical iteration of the act, the art of establishing an efficacious connection is that of *cultivating the propensity emanating from a disposition of reality*, to the maximum effect possible (Jullien 1995: 15).

Let us explore this art in the midst of the process of invention I have been sketching in previous chapters. First, there is the crucial question of the encounter as an interior milieu for an invention, or a milieu of emergence. That is, the relationship between the actual world that a process of inquiry inherits, the many routes of inheritance of the entities that meet, and the proposition that may come into matter through the becoming together of the many patterns of relevance involved in the encounter. To this extent, and insofar as dispositions are dynamic and shifting, there is much that the practice of inquiry itself is responsible for in contributing to the particular modality by which the encounter is articulated. For this reason, I think 'propensity' here should not be read as involving an image of nature as a static reservoir of possibilities, an image that would reinstate the figure of the 'neutral' scientist that the more conservative versions of positivism may have tried to enforce. If propensities are 'natural', then nature is precisely that which is reshaped in the articulation of particular dispositions. The manner of a disposition, how an encounter is articulated, is thus a crucial factor in the cultivating of efficacy. We find a resonant formulation to this effect in Whitehead (1978: 85, emphasis in original), when he argues that,

> [t]he breath of feeling which creates a new individual fact has an origination not wholly traceable to the mere data. It conforms to the data, in that it feels the data. But the *how* of feeling, though it is germane to the data, is not fully determined by the data. The relevant feeling is not settled [...] by the data about which the feeling is concerned.[4]

---

[4] By now, the reader might have noticed that I have, whenever possible, tried to confine textual quotations of Whitehead's work to passages that do not require much explanation of technical vocabulary. This one, however, demands a note. For although it has clear aesthetic connotations,

The objects of an encounter may object, but they do not simply *impose* a pre-existing propensity, and they do not dictate the terms or manner in which the encounter might become fertile. As I argued in Chap. 4, the perplexity induced by an encounter such that it may launch the inquiry into an adventure is not merely a gift that might sometimes obtain, but it requires a task of cultivation. And scientific habits and practices are certainly responsible for what they cultivate. Cultivation does not, on the other hand, designate an all-powerful social scientist that can single-handedly bring about an effect. Indeed, the efficacy of a proposition is not dependent upon the mastery that the social scientist may claim over the process of invention itself or over an act of communication and 'public engagement' that might be said to follow. This is an adventure without a hero, whereby the encounter itself, and not those who might imagine themselves as eliciting it, becomes endowed with the power of relaying its own propensity.

An essay by Emmanuel Didier (2007) provides us with an interesting example of this process of cultivating a propensity emanating from a particular disposition of reality. His encounter is with the practices of the first agricultural statistics produced by the United States government during the first half of the twentieth century. As Didier (2007: 302) summarises the process, statistics could not be said to 'perform' nature or the economy for they too *require* an encounter with farming-related objects that precede them. This however does not mean that statistics merely 'reflect', innocently or without any degree of responsibility, the reality of those objects. By contrast, 'they transform those objects by establishing relations between them, thereby actualizing some of their previously nonexistent characteristics.'

Didier (2007: 302) notes that such an understanding forces one to resist the temptation to explain the process in terms of conditions, for 'the problem is not only one of a stable mold (the conditions) that would shape the iron in fusion (the theory, the model, or the statistics).' Instead, the problem concerns the particular elements that the statistician will

---

the term 'feeling' here does not denote a human psychological operation but a metaphysical one. As Halewood (2011): 32) suggests, for Whitehead '[a] stone feels the warmth of the sun. A tree feels the strength of the wind.'

attend to, 'how precisely he or she will use these resources, and what specific relations he or she will find between them.' As he suggests, '[t]hat things exist prior to their description is unquestionable, but those things look much more like a set of resources for action than like an unchanging and determining condition' (Didier 2007: 302).

In Didier's account, statistical reasoning and techniques certainly *do* something, and their actions are not determined by the objects whose possible relations they actualise, although those objects are certainly *there*, present, making their obligations felt. On the other hand, that they *do* something does not imply that the action they perform is that of creating those objects. To express or cultivate a potential is not to generate it *ex-nihilo*. It is a potential born of a disposition of elements, and it is this disposition 'which is new and surprising.' Thus, unlike arguments for the performativity of knowlegde, which often seem to involve the image of a 'sudden occurrence following an explosion produced by the waving of some magic wand' (2007: 303), what is at stake is rather that which 'oozes from at least two elements when we find a way to put them together' (2007: 302).

Didier's nuanced account of the attentive and creative role of statistics has strong resonances with what I have called 'invention'. What both of them make present is that, in being caught up in an encounter, the challenge is that of experimenting with modes of inquiry that may be capable of discerning and negotiating the patterns of relevance emanating from the process in which social scientists, objects of inquiry, methods, instruments, technologies, and questions partake. As we saw in the previous chapter, such a process cannot be determined in advance, by a pre-established procedure that could guarantee a certain degree of efficacy, but requires piecemeal, progressive adjustments that relate to the specific demands that the encounter has to fulfil. Thus, like relevance itself, the success of invention belongs to what, in Chap. 6, I will refer to as an 'event'.

Nevertheless, once an invention has been brought into being, once the many become one, there remains the question of how the latter might come to relate, whether it will endure in, and what kind of difference it will make, to the milieus to which it connects. And such a question cannot be answered unilaterally, by looking only at the invented proposition itself. In other words, one cannot provide an adequate account of the efficacy of social scientific inventions—or anything else, as far as I can imagine—without including in the account an attention to the way in which the milieu itself *experiences* the invention; without coming to terms with the fact that both invention and milieu *participate in their own becoming together*. As Whitehead (1967b: 94) phrases it,

> [t]hat which endures is limited, obstructive, intolerant, infecting its environment with its own aspects. But it is not self-sufficient. The aspects of all things enter into its very nature. It is only itself as drawing together into its own limitation the larger whole in which it finds itself. Conversely, it is only itself by lending its aspects to this same environment in which it finds itself.

Indeed, for an invention to endure, for it to survive as a factor and fact in reality, more is required than its mere coming into existence. Between itself and its milieu there is a connection whereby the invention, as a factor in the becoming of its milieu, stubbornly affirms its own mode of relevance. At the same time, the milieu entertains its own sense of how the invention may matter to it, inheriting the former in its own manner, so that whenever a connection succeeds, invention and milieu exchange some of their properties. *Pace* the illocutionary logic of performativity, an invention does not by itself bring its milieu into being but finds itself 'both dominating the milieu and accommodating itself to it' (Canguilhem 2008: 113). The one is added to the many and the many become one, not by the deliberate waving of a magic wand but through the process of an immanent debate, a co-adaptation of values whereby the milieu *feels* the invention and the invention the milieu, that a transformation of *both* might take hold in a way that cannot be fully anticipated. As Whitehead (1955: 86) suggests in his *Symbolism*,

> [i]t is the transformation of this potentiality into real concrete fact which is an act of experience. But in transformation from potentiality to actual fact inhibitions, intensifications, directions of attention toward, directions of attention away from, emotional outcomes, purposes, and other elements of experience may arise.

Paying attention to the possible transformations of experiences involved in connections invites, I think, a less aggrandised and more textured appreciation of the question of the efficacy of knowledge. Relatedly, it also raises historically situated questions as to the many modalities in which inventions and milieus may have become connected, and the consequences they have entailed. It also raises speculative questions, to be entertained but never dispelled in advance, concerning the manners in which propositions yet to be articulated or yet to be connected may come to matter for possible milieus and vice versa—what are the temporalities of actual connections? How are certain inventions experienced by their milieus, and how are the milieus experienced by those inventions? How are the intensifying and inhibiting effects of a connection distributed? What are the unexpected outcomes?

I will not provide definitive answers to such questions. In fact, I *could not* provide them even if I tried, for what such questions make present is that connections cannot be explained through abstract principles and do not submit to the 'conditions' that a general theory of effects might force upon them. By contrast, they require attention to the specific *modes* of connection that might obtain, or fail to obtain, between certain inventions and their milieus. A mode of attending not to whether knowledge has certain effects or not, but to *how* its efficacy is actually achieved—to what degree, in which manner, with what consequences, at what price, and in the name of what (Savransky 2014b). Such an attention must ultimately be historically, empirically grounded in actual connections. In the next section, thus, I will attempt to experiment with the some of these questions by drawing, however briefly, on a historically situated connection to illustrate some of the possible complexities involved. To be sure, it is not my purpose in what follows to pre-empt such questions from finding other empirical responses. My only aim, by contrast, is to attempt to open up or intensify the possibility of an interrogation that our current habits might make difficult to explore.

## Modes of Connection: Matters of Belief, Partial Efficacies, Circulating Effects

In order to open up an exploration of the diverse modes that connections may take, I will briefly draw on a historical connection that, because of its unstable, ambivalent, and problematic character, might help us illustrate the complexities associated with such processes and the limitations of approaching questions concerning the efficacy of knowledge either with scepticism or with an inflationary optimism. The connection in question concerns a non-secular—or non-Christian—chapter in the biography of the Western, secularised invention of 'matters of belief'.

Although the term 'belief' has, to be sure, a very long past, with its origins in Vedic and Latin languages, for a long time it was inextricably connected to practices that embodied 'the promise or the trust in the objectivity of some gesture' (Certeau 1985: 195). By contrast, its current meaning as 'a representation capable or not of enjoying an individual or collective assent (of the type: "I believe in it" or "we do not believe in it")' (Certeau 1985: 196) dates, according to Michel de Certeau (1992), only to the seventeenth century. A time when a series of transformations of the relations between the theological, the social and the epistemological dimensions that composed the Christian, Western milieu (Asad 1993)—transformations associated with the rise of modern science but also with the emergence of so-called natural religion—reinvented 'belief', alongside with the notion of 'religion', into a discrete realm of experience thereby turning it into an intellectual object, distinct from the complex economy of practices it entangled (Certeau 1985).

While this reinvention surely predates the modern birth of the social sciences, it is one which has continuously been cultivated within Western milieus. Moreover, the so-called founding fathers of the social sciences, including thinkers like Marx, Durkheim, Weber, Frazer, and others, crucially contributed to cultivating it while reinventing it, again, as a 'universal' problem of empirical, *social* inquiry. So have many sociologists, anthropologists, and historians *of* 'religion'—and not only of religion—to this day (Asad 1993). Bifurcating the world into those who 'know' and those who 'believe', matters of belief became not only what was to be expelled from the practice of science, but also, and simultaneously, what a specialised science, a science of the social, would make a privileged object of scientific knowledge—a practice of 'knowing' what others 'believe'.

In this way, 'religion' was carved out as a discrete realm of reality to be understood as a matter of belief, 'a matter of symbolic meanings linked to ideas of general order' (Asad 1993: 42), and beliefs were, in turn, taken as symbols of a 'deeper' meaning concerning society. As Certeau (1992: 138) put it, many social scientists 'spontaneously take their task to be the need to determine what a field delineated as "religious" can teach them about society [...]. What they place under the rubric of "society" is not one of the poles of a confrontation with religion but, rather, the axis of reference, the obvious model of all possible intelligibility, the current postulate of all historical comprehension.'

At this point, one might be tempted to denounce the very invention of 'belief' as an all-too-modern artifice that remains inadequate to the study of *any* experience whatsoever, including Christian, Western experiences. For although God is *now*, for many Christians, a private matter of belief indeed, 'He' too once performed miracles and intervened publicly and materially in the world 'He' had created (Certeau 1992). Of course, it would be a blatant gesture of 'presentism' to attempt to connect the modern experience of 'belief' to the Christian West *before* the event of the invention of matters of belief and the correlative desacralisation of society had taken place. It would certainly be a mistake to attempt to connect 'belief', that is, to a time when Western inquiries were not concerned with what others believed in but with discovering the innumerable wonders and marvels that, literally, *populated* the Western world with divine presence (see Daston and Park 2003).

As Sanjay Seth (2004: 89) has suggested, however, 'the procedures and categories and protocols of the present are themselves (sometimes) connected to the past that is being objectified.' Thus, while in the middle ages the milieu that I have here sketchily termed the 'Christian West' did experience the relevance of witches—to the point of burning them—and of a God that could make direct interventions upon human affairs, it then was the same milieu that underwent a transformation of how those beings came to matter, and turned both witches and Gods—and indeed many other-than-human beings—into matters of believing, or not, in them. In this way, even though the Christian, Western milieu inhabited by witches and God can be seen as part of the West's past and perhaps not of its present, it 'is (seen as) part of the *same* past that then gave up belief in witches, and that withdrew from God his agency in history. That is, this was part of the same past that subsequently disenchanted and desacralized the world [...], and engaged in rational practices like writing history' (2004: 89, emphasis added).

In other words, to the extent that the invention of 'matters of belief' is connected to the transformation of a particular milieu that has in turn sustained the invention while becoming together with it, 'belief' is not to be completely rejected but rather affirmed as a historically and geographically specific mode of experience. Indeed, the point is not to denounce 'belief' as an abstraction that may occlude or prevent the experience of a Christian, Western world pregnant with divine presence. Rather, and so far as the Christian West is concerned, 'belief' has succeeded in establishing a connection with the milieu and has thus come to matter as a fact to be encountered. In other words, for many in the West, beliefs do matter.[5]

Such affirmation is not necessarily warranted, however, when the question concerns the mode of connection between matters of belief and other milieus that do not share the same history. Indeed, a different problem emerges when we interrogate the attempts made by government administrators, educators, policy makers, and social scientists to connect such a modern, Christian, and Western invention to milieus with which it had not experienced any such 'debate'. To claim that 'matters of belief' may have become a possible element of a modern, Christian and Western experience is not the same as taking it to be a self-evident, abstract, and universal factor capable of connecting to, and explaining the experiences of, others for whom that connection has not been experienced—of accounting for the ways in which other-than-human beings *matter everywhere, always*.

In this way, in his *Subject Lessons: The Western Education of Colonial India*, Seth (2007) describes the problematic modes of connection of the Christian invention of 'matters of belief' as it was exported to Hinduism in colonial India through practices of Western education. Ironically, secular education in government schools and colleges was introduced in India with the aim of shaping the character of the Indian subject *without interfering* with their religious beliefs (Seth 2007: 49). The problem was, however, that while government officials and educators presupposed that 'secular

---

[5] Including, of course, those who vociferously and righteously claim that they only believe in 'Science', and those that anxiously insist they do not believe in anything.

education' meant leaving religious beliefs out of classrooms, they also assumed by the same token that Hindu gods came to matter and were animated, like in the Christian tradition, as a set of compartmentalised beliefs experienced by human subjects. Before colonialism, however—and to a large extent, also after colonialism—Hindus *did not believe in gods*. Rather, '[t]he numerous deities of Hinduism are co-present with humans, and highly visible; they exist as spirits, ghosts, and in the form of those numerous idols that so offended the sensibility of their rulers' (Seth 2007: 64). And they could not be just set aside into a private affair, for 'these obstreperous deities infect [their] life, pervade it, even invade and take it over, independently of [their] likes and dislikes' (Nandy 2001: 127–128).

Thus, as Seth explains it, the mode of connection of matters of belief, conceived as a universal proposition for inquiring into and dealing with any 'religion', including Hinduism, entailed a transformation of the manner in which the many Hindu gods came to matter in and for the Indian milieu.[6] By attempting to transform the pattern of relevance of these gods into a matter of Hindus believing or not in them, one of the consequences of the connection was that of intellectually bifurcating Hinduism into two forms. On the one hand, a 'high' or 'classical' form which transformed Hindu polytheism into a 'more-or-less monotheistic creed, with the profusion of Hindu gods representing different aspects of one God' (Seth 2007: 62). On the other, a 'primitive, even "animist" popular Hinduism, swarming with gods and spirits and idols' (2007: 63). As Seth (2007: 63) argues, such a connection was partly efficacious, in that

> [s]ome Hindus also came to reinterpret and redefine their religion in ways influenced by western accounts and critiques of it. In the course of the nineteenth century movements of religious reform such as the Brahmo Samaj and the Arya Samaj sought to reform or redefine Hinduism (often by claiming that popular, 'superstitious' forms represented a degradation of an original Hinduism, or 'survivals' of the religious beliefs of the pre-Aryan inhabitants of India). The result was that the riotous pantheon of gods was downgraded, and Hinduism emerged, like other 'proper' religions, as a philosophy and a set of coherent beliefs to which its adherents subscribed.

---

[6] Indian—and not Hindu—because as Ashis Nandy (2001: 126) argues, 'these gods and goddesses not only populate the Hindu world but regularly visit and occasionally poach on territories outside it.'

Thus, matters of belief did infect the Hindu and Indian milieus in a manner that Bonaventura de Sourza Santos (2009) has aptly termed 'orthopaedic'. Orthopaedics, in this sense, can be thought as a *mode of connection* whose effect takes hold 'by reducing the existential problems to analytical and conceptual markers that are strange to them' (Santos 2009: 110)—by connecting matters of belief to a milieu for which believes did not matter, thereby exorcising its deities and effectively desacralising the more-than-human world that did matter to it (Savransky 2012). But in the case of Hinduism, the success of connection was only *partial*. For despite the exportation of Western education, 'for the vast majority of Hindus, then and even today', Seth (2007: 63) argues, 'their religious practice was not an expression of their religious belief. […] Hindus did not in fact "believe" in their religion, and it was not beliefs that constituted Hinduism'.

Now, from the point of view of an illocutionary logic of performativity this partial efficacy of the invention of matters of belief might be deemed a full-blown failure. For if we take such a logic seriously, we have to acknowledge that the invention of 'matters of belief' did not succeed, in spite of its influence in bifurcating Hinduism intellectually, in bringing a new Hinduism 'into being'. The most that can be said, I think, is that it succeeded, as a 'perlocutionary' effect, in *partially* affecting the milieu with which it was made to connect.[7] This is not to say that it did not make certain—quite interesting—things happen. To the contrary, the mode of connection it established was indeed complex and suffused with unexpected consequences.

For those—rather few—Hindus for whom the connection was indeed efficacious and thus came to experience Hinduism as a matter of belief, the reported consequence was, largely and for some time, an experience of 'moral crisis'. One characterised precisely by the 'inconsistencies' of a yet incomplete transition to 'secular values' that made them, in the eyes of the British as in their own, susceptible to 'impiety, dissolute behav-

---

[7] This is arguably the case for the 'Christian West' too, even in spite of the efficacious connection of 'religion' and 'belief', and despite so-called secularisation theories which prophesied the erosion of everything 'sacred' in an increasingly 'modernised', Western milieu (see Bruce 1992). In fact, some affirm that the West is witnessing an expansion of the sacred that, as Vásquez and Marquardt's (2000) example of the apparition of the Virgin Mary on the facade of the building of the Financial Corporation of Clearwater (Florida) makes manifest, can sometimes take trenchant, if humorous, forms.

iour, bad manners, conceit, immorality, and a decline in respect for elders and for "authority" more generally' (Seth 2007: 57). As Seth (2007: 75) discusses,

> [t]he discourse of moral decline arose because it was felt by many that the knowledge disseminated through schools and universities had produced an unexpected effect: educated Indians had been plunged into a moral crisis, no longer fully able to believe in the moral code derived from the own religion and worldview, without yet being in a position to embrace the rationality and morality corresponding to the new world of colonial civil society.

Overestimating the scope of the diagnosis, such a concern was commonplace among British Indian government officials and administrators, Church missionaries and educators, who regarded the 'moral decline' brought about by their own Western invention as a serious danger to British rule and East India Company profits (Seth 2007: 48). The scope of the diagnosis was overstated however, because, to be sure, the very experience of a 'moral crisis' due to an incomplete transition between beliefs systems and moral codes presupposed that an efficacious connection had taken place when, in fact, it had not. In other words, for there to be an 'inconsistency' of beliefs, there first had to be beliefs—beliefs had to matter. And they did come to matter, but only for some.

Thus, 'moral crisis' was not just a *possible* corrosive effect of the orthopaedic connection of 'matters of belief' to Hinduism that could be remedied, as some Church missionaries might have wished, by imparting not only secular education but also the word of (the Christian) God.[8] It was itself *the mode* in which the effects of the connection took hold. As Seth (2007: 77) puts it, '[o]nly those for whom the categories of mind, belief, the indivisible self, and the like had become meaningful could characterize their experience (or that of others) in terms of crisis and inconsistency.' The many others that were described as subject to such

---

[8] As this phrase suggests, they might have wished an *addition* of Christian teachings *to* secular education rather than a replacement of one by the other, because 'missionaries and government officials alike shared the belief that modern science was a solvent of Indian religious beliefs, which in their view mingled a false theology with fantastical and nonsensical explanations of the world and its functioning' (Seth 2007: 49).

a moral crisis but for whom matters of belief were never as efficacious were 'quite unaware that they were' in any such crisis (2007: 75), because in fact, they hardly could be. For them, it was not that the mismatch between secular and Hindu moral beliefs did not matter or was seen as unproblematic. Rather, *beliefs* as such did not matter, and hence no crisis could ensue from what did not matter—or equally, from what did not exist.

Nevertheless, this partial failure of the connection between matters of belief and Hindu/Indian milieus did not necessarily make those for whom the invention was inefficacious less well equipped to manage the practical demands of educational life under colonial rule. Instead, they would experience and engage Western education in a way that met the practical demands of passing examinations, but which was otherwise set entirely in their own terms—treating education as a mere instrumental affair for accessing government jobs; using techniques of rote learning instead of developing forms of 'understanding'; producing 'keys' and 'made-easies' instead of studying from the actual textbooks; and so forth (Seth 2007: 17–46).

Indeed, this was not only a way of resisting the taking hold of effects. It was also a way of infecting these very effects with the milieu's own patterns of relevance such that 'a circular link is produced between effects and causes, since an effect from one point of view will be a cause from another' (Foucault 2007: 21). Thus, although the aim of the introduction of Western education in colonial India was to shape the character of the Indian subject by forcing it to abandon 'religious beliefs' and instead embrace and develop a 'taste for literature and science' (Seth 2007: 17), the techniques of rote learning, or cramming, employed by many students '[were] seen to be closely connected with an indigenous pedagogy' which thus infected government schools with 'old methods, simply applying them to new materials' (Seth 2007: 32). They were altering the very inventions that were meant to alter them. Who was the effect of what and who was, in fact, learning what? In the process of connections, efficacies were only partial, effects became causes, and causes became captured by effects.

Much more could be discussed in relation to Seth's fascinating account of the Western education of colonial India, but I hope this summary incursion already makes perceptible some of the possible questions and problematics that an interrogation into modes of connection, rather than the sceptical quantification of the efficacy of knowledge or its aggrandising celebration, might be capable of yielding. What it might also make perceptible, I think, is that to speak of 'connections' and to inquire into their actual modalities of taking hold is to imagine a different world, and different ways of taking care of it, to that assumed by those who distrust that social scientific inventions make any differences as well as by those who celebrate, perhaps in excess, the differences they make.

## Conclusion: A World of Connections

As I have argued throughout this chapter, the effects of inventions are not that of bringing entire realities into being, but of producing subtle, piecemeal transformations in ongoing courses of events. Their efficacy, moreover, can be established neither by means of a theory capable of explaining and justifying the success of a connection in advance, nor by the designation of a set of abstract and general conditions that may assure, under 'the right circumstances', that certain effects will take hold. Efforts can and must be made, and one is certainly responsible for paying due attention to the obligation that objects pose, for putting the patterns of contrast that a question generates at risk. But the requirements of an effect are always immanent to the concrete connection at stake.

Insofar as it depends upon the debate established between the invention and its milieus, the success of infecting the lives of those an invention may come to address and of being able to transform them and be transformed by them, of becoming *interesting*, as Stengers (1997: 83) would put it, cannot be promised. It can, however, be approached with the care that every cultivation of possibilities demands. The question of connections, thus, allows us to think the problem of how inventions come to matter, and how they endure in existence, in terms of a process of becoming together of patterns of relevance. A process whose success depends not only upon invention alone but upon the modes of exchange between the invention and the milieus to which it connects.

Now, to claim that social scientific inventions are not in and of themselves capable of making certain effects take hold is not so much to make a claim about the nature of those inventions as it is to make one about the world in which inventions come to matter. Because if social constructivism dwelled in a world that was raw material for humanisation and the illocutionary optimism inherent in some theories of performativity tends to live in one that is a passive receptacle of our socio-material fancies, connections presuppose a world whose destiny is neither fixed, determined in advance, nor entirely susceptible to what an invention might seek to make of it.

By contrast, to think in terms of connections is to inhabit a fundamentally unfinished world organised by numerous, diverse, and changing milieus. A world requiring both invention and a singular attention to how things, in different milieus, come to matter. Thinking in terms of connections forces us to come to terms with a world of *events*, of things that matter, void of foundations yet full of partial stories and efficacies, unexpected consequences and intrusions, out of which novelties sometimes may and do emerge.

As I shall argue in the next chapter, however, an event is nobody's creature, it can never be traced back to an author that could be said to have brought that partial story into being. If, as James (1996: 130–131) put it in his *Some Problems of Philosophy*, 'we ourselves are constantly adding to the connections of things, organising labor-unions, establishing postal, consular, mercantile, railroad, telegraph, colonial, and other systems that bind us and things together in ever wider reticulations', this 'we' must not designate any stable identity defined in advance—be that 'we humans', 'we westerners', 'we men', 'we social scientists', not even 'we humans-plus-technology'—but must itself refer to the very *achievement* of a connection, a form of problematic togetherness of all those who, for better or ill, have experienced, and still experience, its becoming.

# 6

# An Ethics of Adventure

## Introduction: The Transformation of the Possible

As I have argued in previous chapters, the speculative reconstruction of the contemporary social sciences that the question of relevance makes possible involves not the proposition of a different job description of their many practices but a possible transformation of the *ethical sensibilities* that inform them. Indeed, even though I have tried to articulate the implications of this question within an argumentative complex that I believe resonates with some characteristic lines of inquiry of certain versions of contemporary social science, my sense is that the mode of operation of this project is not that of arguing itself through such a complex, of presenting itself as a proposition that demands to be entertained because it be necessarily 'truer' or 'better articulated', or because it could be said to be more 'persuasive'. To be sure, argumentation and persuasion are crucial tools, but as William James (1956) intuited more than a century ago, their efficacy is not merely 'rational'—reasons are felt. Put differently, they work not merely by presenting a thought, but by provoking thinking and feeling. Thus, if this reconstruction might become capable of affecting the practices with which it engages, its ultimate aim is that of inducing a transformation of the *ethos* with which such practices are identified, of prompting them to 'feather and launch the arrow of the question another way, from another departure point, toward something else' (Cortázar 2011: 43).

As I have argued, the question of relevance proposes a different image of practice that is none other than an inquiry without image—an inquiry whose ethos is that of cultivating, *in* the very process of thinking and learning how to know, sensibilities that may allow it to become singularly sensitive to the demands that an encounter has to fulfil. I have provisionally called that ethic an 'adventure', for its coming about is never one that could be secured or guaranteed either by means of epistemological formalisms or by strict methodological prescriptions. Rather, an adventure is characterised by an investment in the *possibility*, not of providing a solution to a pre-existing problem, but of an invention that matters for those concerned.

After the detailed explorations carried out throughout the preceding chapters, we might now be in a position to pursue the challenge of providing a more general characterisation of such an ethics. In order to do that, in this chapter I will suggest that we need to come to terms with a notion that has made repeated appearances throughout these pages but whose definition has remained, until now, not sufficiently specified. Namely, the notion of event. The aim of this book, I suggested, is to provide a response, however partial, to the question of what might be required for contemporary social scientific practices to take up 'relevance' as an event that concerns the coming to matter of the situated facts and patterns that organise and relate humans, other-than-humans, relationships, ideas, feelings, and so on in ways that matter for those with which a problematic situation might be concerned. As I have suggested, moreover, the possible success of an adventure belongs neither to the order of a form of scientific or technical mastery that would endow the social scientist with a right to establish what the relevant questions may be, nor to a matter of mere empathy for those to whom questions are posed. Rather, it constitutes, in its own right, an achievement that cannot be secured in advance but towards which inquiries may strive to work. In this sense, I shall argue in what follows that, ultimately, taking the question of relevance seriously involves orienting knowledge-practices by, and towards, events.

Briefly put, an event is the effect of something that happens, a transformation induced by an occurrence. However, it is not to be confounded either with the happening itself—which might instead receive the name of an 'accident' or an 'incident'—, or with the many different ways in which it might be experienced or inherited by the milieus with which it might connect. For the event 'subsists or inheres' as an incorporeal effect in the actions and passions of bodies and their practices (Deleuze 2004: 7): '[t]he event has a different nature than the actions and passions of the body. But it *results* from them' (2004: 108, emphasis in original). Thus, the event is not what occurs but a novelty introduced *in* that which occurs, and as Michel de Certeau (1997: 17) famously put it, '[n]ovelty remains opaque'. In this sense, the event is not the bearer of its own signification and it does not dictate the terms in which its heirs will interpret it (Stengers 2000). It testifies less to what it is than to the multiplicity of responses it generates.

Because it is not simply an accident that happens, but both an opening and an achievement that emerges from and within that which happens, an event cannot be said to occur *in* time, as if time and space could precede it. Rather, it is that which marks time by throwing it 'out of joint' (Deleuze 1994: 89), producing a caesura, a difference between a before and an after. Betraying all predictions based upon probabilistic calculations or on the plausibility of a historical narrative that would privilege a regular and continuous temporality from past to present, from present to future, the event is, in short, *the transformation of the possible*. As Deleuze (2007: 234) has phrased it, '[t]he possible does not pre-exist, it is created by the event'. For 'the event is itself a splitting off from, or a breaking with causality; it is a bifurcation, a deviation with respect to laws, an unstable condition which opens up a new field of the possible' (2007: 233).

Thus, events synthesise time and space on and for each occasion, throwing them out of joint and transforming the distributions of what is, and what is not, possible. In this sense, the names that certain political events often acquire seem to silently transmit this wisdom about the relationship of the event to time and historicity—it is not only that things happened in May 1968, on 9 September 2011, or on 15 May 2011—although of course a myriad of accidents and incidents happened on those dates—but rather that *they* happened, May 1968, 9–11 and

15-M, as events that demand to be inherited. 'This experience happened. It is impregnable; it *cannot be taken away*. But what does it mean for us?' (Certeau 1997: 13, emphasis in original).

Indeed, because the event is creative of time rather than contained by it, because it presupposes not a chronology but a veritable poetics of time, its own temporality can never be the present as such. Instead, 'an event is always what has happened or what is about to happen, but never that which is happening' (Deleuze 2004: 10). Thus, no one can proclaim an event in the present nor assign oneself authorship over it.[1] From its own point of view, the event, as a becoming, conjoins future and past, active and passive, more and less, too much and not enough, the already and the yet to come. As Deleuze (2004: 3, emphasis added) suggests with reference to events in Carroll's *Alice' Adventures in Wonderland*:

> [w]hen I say 'Alice becomes larger,' I mean that she *becomes* larger than she was. By the same token, however, she becomes smaller than she is now. Certainly, she *is* not bigger and smaller at the same time. She is larger now; she was smaller before. But it is at the same time that one becomes.

Conceived of as a wrinkle on the surface of history, the event could be regarded as the incorporeal backbone of the processual world in which I have situated this inquiry into the knowledge-practices of the contemporary social sciences. For it affirms a world that is both sustained and transformed as its many heterogeneous actors intervene in it, 'even though it is replete with neither divine providence nor ready susceptibility to human mastery' (Connolly 2011: 6). In other words, it inhabits a world without foundations, in the sense that its foundations are always being created anew with every event (Brown and Stenner 2009).[2]

For this reason, it should come as no surprise that the social sciences have traditionally sustained a rather conflictive relationship with the

---

[1] Another way of saying this is that the present is nothing but the transition between events (See Chap. 7).

[2] This is not to be taken to mean that history is erased with every event, or that the actual world poses no constraints on how the future might be shaped. What this means is that the continuity of history, or indeed, of any experience for that matter, is not a given, but itself an achievement—a process whereby events conform to previous events. In Whitehead's (1978: 35) words, 'there is a becoming of continuity but no continuity of becoming'.

concept of event. In this sense, although it could be said to constitute the very conundrum of historiographical inquiry, historians have rarely addressed the event as a problematic concept to be developed theoretically in any deliberate fashion (Dosse 2010; Sahlins 2005; Sewell 2005). Moreover, those who have not simply taken it for granted, 'have spent', in the words of Marshall Sahlins (2005: 294), 'a lot of waking hours puzzling over events in order to invent all those ways of putting them down.' Embracing an ethics of estrangement that would invite social scientists to search for regularities and law-abiding patterns of historical and social processes in order to *explain* the would-be 'apparent' nature of experiences, the social sciences have for a long time experienced and been oriented by what might be called, in the words of one if its strongest detractors, 'a horror of the event' (Braudel 1982: 28).

Thus, members of the *Annales* School initiated by Fernand Braudel and Lucien Febvre regarded what they called 'evenemential history' as a whimsical endeavour that is overtaken by the capricious, dramatic, and 'delusive smoke' of the instant (Braudel 1982: 27). In contrast, they proposed that in order for historiography to become truly 'scientific' and even endowed with mathematical rigour (1982: 42), historiography had to abandon its fascination with events and focus on the very long time span patterns of the *longue durée*:

> [t]o go from the short time span, to one less short, and then to the long view (which, if it exists, must surely be the wise man's time span); and having got there, to think about everything new afresh and to reconstruct everything around one: a historian could hardly not be tempted by such a prospect. (1982: 77–78)

What is involved in the notion of the *longue durée* is thus a teleological temporality that attributes the causes of events to abstract, transhistorical processes or laws that, moreover, may lead to some other historical state in the future. From this point of view, events are nothing but epiphenomenal instances of deeper, enduring, more-than-historical patterns of order.[3]

---

[3] At most, the only event that such a form of historiography does take seriously—for some reason—is an inaugural, cosmic-like event such as, say, 'capitalism', which *ipso facto* becomes the subsequent determining cause of everything that follows (Sewell 2005).

This transhistorical explanatory character of the *longue durée* testifies to its debt to the notion of 'structure', as the latter was developed particularly by the Structuralist tradition of Claude Lévi-Strauss (1963) and which, after the Second World War, pervaded the social sciences—at least in Europe—as a whole.[4] Drawing on a combination of lessons from the work of Ferdinand de Saussure and Émile Durkheim, this immensely influential school became equally dismissive of the event, thereby becoming a crucial actor in the 'evolution of a more and more immobile history' (Dosse 2010:67. my own translation). For structuralists, the task was to do away with the event—and indeed, whenever possible, with history altogether—by searching for the universal laws unconsciously governing social and cultural phenomena:

> In anthropology as in linguistics, therefore, it is not comparison that supports generalization, but the other way around. If, as we believe to be the case, the unconscious activity of the mind consists in imposing forms upon content, and if these forms are fundamentally all the same for all minds—ancient and modern, primitive and civilized (as the study of symbolic function, expressed in language, so strikingly indicates)—it is necessary and sufficient to grasp the unconscious structure underlying each institution and each custom, in order to obtain a principle of interpretation valid for other institutions and other customs, provided of course that the analysis is carried far enough. (Lévi-Strauss 1963: 21)

As various scholars have attested, even if today not many researchers would claim without caveats to be orthodox structuralists or historians of the *longue durée*, such 'horror of the event' still pervades the *ethos* of many contemporary social scientific practices and conceptualisations. For instance, William Sewell (2005) has shown how such teleological and structural conceptions of temporality still remain at work in much of contemporary historical sociology, including the work of Immanuel Wallerstein and Charles Tilly, among others.

A similar case could arguably be made about many social science readings of the work of Michel Foucault which, despite its emphasis on a form of effective history that would deal 'with events in terms of their

---

[4] In fact, in his *On History*, Braudel (1982: 31) himself explicitly acknowledges his debt to Lévi-Strauss, arguing that 'for better or ill, [structure] dominates the problems of the *longue durée*'.

most unique characteristics, their most acute manifestations' (Foucault 1984b: 88); despite the fact that among the aims of his genealogical project was that of 'restor[ing] to discourse its character as an event' (Foucault 1981: 66); despite his radically eventful archaeology, as François Dosse (2010) has called it, the contemporary social sciences have not hesitated in turning the curious and unique events that interested Foucault into a critical theory of neo/liberalism *tout court*, and they have not hesitated to turn 'discourse' into a general theory, an *approach* even, to the relationship between power and subjectivity (Savransky 2014a).

Thus, to restore the event to the world that a social science would have to learn to come to terms with involves a profound shift in its habits of thought and practice, one which we have been exploring through different problematics in preceding chapters and which might now be confronted directly. First, it is necessary that we pause and consider some of the specificities and requirements that such the concept of event might demand. As I will show in the next section, by articulating a processual world, the event becomes the site where history and metaphysics join hands, forcing our thought to pragmatically move between the general and the singular, the ordinary and the exceptional.

Second, I will suggest that it is out of the double temporality that characterises events, out of their subsistence as that which has happened and that which is about to happen, that emerges a double ethical challenge for a social scientific practice that could be said to constitute a veritable *adventure*—that of learning to become situated between the event as a fact–that–matters which demands to be inherited, and that of learning to become exposed to an event as a possibility of the coming in(to) matter of a different world to come. I shall explore these two temporal and ethical dimensions of the event in subsequent sections of this chapter.

## Between the Ordinary and the Exceptional: A Pragmatics of the Event?

In throwing time out of joint, the event becomes the site where history and metaphysics meet—histories matter. Time and space become abstractions that do not explain but *are to be explained* by the becomings of always contingent and changing events. Both generated by, and generative of, naturalcultural histories, events are, in a sense, the very *pulse* of reality, which is also to say, of what comes in(to) matter. In this way, in *The Concept of Nature* (2004: 14–15), Whitehead proposes that 'the immediate fact for awareness is the whole occurrence of nature. It is nature as an event present for sense-awareness, and essentially passing. There is no holding nature still and looking at it.'

To conceive of events as the very pulse of the real bears the consequence that, from the point of view of a metaphysics of the event, no legitimate scope can determine the latter's status, for the world is itself a process of concatenation, of comings into matter of time and space. No sunset repeats itself twice. The importance of this metaphysical dimension lies in the implication that no one can be endowed with the right to set a threshold above which one can declare an event, and below which one must remain silent. As Stengers (2000: 67) argues, the event 'has neither a privileged representative nor legitimate scope. The scope of the event is part of its effects, of the problem posed in the future it creates.'

That said, from the point of view of the way in which the concept of the event may be capable of orienting social scientific practices, and to that extent, of pointing towards those comings to matter that may contribute to the inquiry of a problematic situation, the celebration that '*all is event!*' should be approached with care, for its implications might otherwise become counterproductive. In other words, although such may be indeed the case from the standpoint of a dispassionate consideration of the nature of things—thus remaining a potent critique of modern scientific materialism—we should be careful not to extend the affirmation of the ubiquity of events into an all encompassing abstraction that, instead of enabling the event to stop our thinking from turning around in circles (Stengers 2000), may inhibit our capacity to care for those differences that make a difference.

Specifically, the implications of such an undifferentiated and celebratory claim may give rise to at least two different positions that risk losing sight of the pragmatic force of such a concept. The first might receive the name of the 'banalisation of the event'. If we rested in the comfort of such a celebration, if events of varying scope and consequences were to constitute the very effects of a 'whatever happens', if no role could be found for them other than sustaining the ordinary succession of things, then what practical difference does the notion of 'event' itself make? And how might it be able to prompt, rather than paralyse, practices of inquiry? Indeed, if we stop at the affirmation that everything whatsoever is an event, then why would events matter anyway? What would it mean to claim that May 1968 was an event—in contrast to, say, June 1968? In this way, the banalisation of the event operates by multiplying differences to the point of a general indifference to what may come to matter.

The second perilous implication of overemphasising the ubiquity of events belongs not to the danger of downplaying the differences they create but, in contrast, to a certain attitude that I would call a 'cynicism of the event'. Indeed, if we take an undifferentiated approach to the becoming of events that suggests that everything is an event and, *ergo*, that whatever someone or something does constitutes an event, then we might run the risk of reducing the event to the actions of a wilful author. In this way, the event becomes prey of the very ethics of estrangement it might otherwise be capable of challenging. The cynicism of the event becomes perceptible, for example, in the discourse of certain sociological approaches that, in adopting a social constructivist position, would argue that an event is nothing other than whatever the media present as such (for a classic text see Nora 1972, more recently Bensa and Fassin 2002). As Pierre Nora (1972: 162. my translation) has classically phrased it:

> The mass media have from now on the monopoly over history. In our contemporary societies, it is through them and through them only that the event strikes upon us, and it cannot escape us. It is not enough, however, to say that they stick to reality, in the sense that they would become part of it and of us in restoring to it its immediate presence [...]. The press, the radio, images, are not simply the means of relatively independent events, but their very condition of existence.

The cynicism of the event is paradoxical for it at once affirms the ubiquity of events yet confounds their heirs with their authors, reducing the event to its retrospective recognition produced by actors and practices. In other words, all is event, yet there is nothing new under the sun, nothing new has in fact come to matter. To warn against an epistemology of events, or a 'sociology of events' in a social constructivist sense, however, is not to suggest that the coming of events is in any sense *otherworldly*, that events come from a beyond that concerns no one and that requires nothing. The emergence of an event does require a milieu, even a milieu characterised by dimensions one could call 'social', but it cannot be *explained by* it as if the event were the product of a choice. Indeed, as Stengers (1997: 216–217) puts it,

> to combine the notions of event and choice implies that no instance—whether political, ethical, of the mass media, or technical—can be said to be the 'author' of this choice. Because in this case, it is much rather the event itself that has decided the manner in which these instances will be articulated. Many accounts enable one to follow the history that has led to this choice, its hesitations, and the relationships of forces involved in them. No account can have the status of explanation, conferring a logically deducible character to the event, without falling into the classic trap of giving to the reasons that one discovers a posteriori the power of making it occur, when, in other instances, they would have had no such power [.]

Insofar as the event marks a difference and an opening, whoever speaks in its name, even if with the purpose of denying it, of swearing that nothing, in fact, has come to matter, is already situated by the event, becoming its inescapable heir. For this reason, and as will become clearer in the coming sections, allowing for the event to orient social scientific practices in order to cultivate a different care of knowledge does not involve a process of turning those practices around the true or correct explanation of the former, nor of claiming authority over its production, but of inventing ways of inheriting and remaining open to it, of exploring the possibilities it creates.

In any case, then, it would seem that there is a tension between metaphysical and historiographical approaches to events. For the former, as we have seen, events constitute the very pulse of the real thereby providing an image of a world of becoming that exists only insofar as it differentiates itself. For the latter, if the event is to matter, it must constitute an intense and rare achievement, a shift in the order of things, an unpredictable opening onto a future that is more than a mere prolongation from the past. From the point of view of history, the event is something that 'stands out against a background of uniformity; it is a difference, a thing we could not know a priori' and that cannot be reduced to its cause (Veyne 1984: 5).

Such an apparent tension is not, however, insurmountable. Affirming the significance of certain historical—and as we will see, scientific—events and inheriting the difference they create, does not necessarily presuppose a world where processes of differentiation and creativity are, by definition, rare. The distinction between one approach and the other belongs rather to the particular trajectory from which events are discerned. In other words, to affirm that events *matter* is not to immediately provide an answer to the question of *how they matter*. While the metaphysician approaches the question of events from the point of view of a consideration of the general nature of things, of the cosmos itself as being both universe and event, the historian approaches the event from the situated perspective of the pasts and futures an event creates, from the transition it sets into motion, and from a particular genealogy of other events. In this latter view, an event is discerned for its significance with regards to a trajectory of events whose specific characters are otherwise not disclosed in that immediate discernment, except insofar as a relationship between them is established (Whitehead 2004: 52).

Thus, the ordinary and the exceptional are not necessarily antithetical notions but they presuppose each other reciprocally. To put it another way, although the possible difference between events is only a matter of degree and not of substance, from the point of a situated inquiry, it is that matter of degree that matters. For instance, the transformation effected in the world of a child who has just learned to walk constitutes an event within a particular genealogy which corresponds, say, to the child's biography. Times and spaces both shrink and expand, allowing her for the possibility of reaching previously unattainable objects, and confronting her with a future the temporal and spatial dimensions of which are much larger than previously imagined. In parallel, the Second World War can be said to constitute an event where, '[f]or the first time, reason, science and technology went beyond the deadly laws of life. War for the sake of war prevailed over the struggle for life. The Bomb beat Darwin' (Serres 2013: 14).

To be sure, to say that both of these cases constitute events in their own right is not to attempt to flatten out their important differences. Thus, their respective scopes and capacities for propagation or the horizon that defines the limit of their respective situations, may vary greatly. So much so that, while from the point of view of a genealogy of war and death the significance of the event of a child learning to walk might be rather negligible, to the biography of a child who has to learn to inherit a culture of science, technology, war and death, the transformation of possibilities effected by the Second World War still matter.[5]

What also varies in this comparison is the degree of novelty each event introduces. As Michel Serres (2013: 2) proposes with the humour of a geometrical formulation, insofar as events are always at the same time achievements and openings, their novelty 'is proportional to the length of the preceding era concluded by the event.' Differences of scope and novelty notwithstanding, both events suppose, from their own point of view, that is, from the point of view of the situated genealogies to which each of them belong, an asymmetry between cause and effect, and thus, the creation of a radical difference between a before and an after that involves a change in the order of things. In other words, if an event can be said to be a wrinkle on the surface of history, it is only on condition that histories themselves be conceived of as entirely composed of wrinkly surfaces.

The importance of this difference between the general and the exceptional in the becoming of events lies in that it enables an attention to the radical contingency and novelty of events in relation to others without thereby denying the thoroughly *eventful* character of reality. Thus, in order to approach the question of the event so that it may be capable of orienting the ethics of inquiry of the contemporary social sciences, what is required is neither a metaphysics nor a historiography, but a *pragmatics* of events. To speak of a pragmatics of events is, therefore, to approach them in terms of the differences that situated novelties create, of the specific manners in which events come to matter, of the problems they will pose to their heirs, and of the many ways in which events are inherited, thereby propagating their effects.

---

[5] Interestingly, in the latter genealogy, a child learning to walk might perhaps be conceptualised as what Paul Veyne (1984: 19) would call a 'non-event'. A non-event is not the absence of an event but 'an event not yet recognized as such—the history of territories, of mentalities, of madness, or of the search of security through the ages.'

Constituting modes of inquiry whose risk is that of coming to terms with a world of contingent, complex, and unpredictable changes in the order of things, adventures are situated by the double temporality of the event, that is, by what has happened and towards what might happen. They are both heirs of the multiple series of events that compose the historical world they must invent a manner of encountering, and they can also, potentially, become involved in the transformation of the possible by producing inventions that matter. As the 'horror of the event' makes perceptible, however, the ethics of estrangement that could be said to characterise much of contemporary social scientific knowledge-practices does not contribute to cultivating modes of inquiry that be particularly sensitive to an eventful world. Rather, it fosters an ethos by which the epistemic merit of its practices and propositions is often understood *against* such sensitivity—the less constrained by events, the more 'scientific'.

Thus, in the following sections of this chapter I will attempt to begin to sketch what such a process of pragmatic attunement to events might entail. In order to better account for the double temporality of events, I will address this challenge in turns, asking first what might be required for a social scientific practice to be situated *by* what has happened, and second, what it would mean to orient such practices *towards* what might happen. It must be noted, however, that such a partition has the only purpose of approaching this difficult question slowly and with as much clarity as possible. For the fact remains that both dimensions of the orientations discussed in what follows are to be understood not only as mutually compatible, but as reciprocally articulated, so that there cannot be one without the other.

## Children of the Event: Towards an Ethics of Inheritance

From historiography to sociology, the modern ethics of discovering—or perhaps, of un-covering—the unconscious or underlying laws governing cultural, social, and historical patterns turned the event into a monster that anyone who would take pride in calling herself a 'social scientist' should combat. To confine the 'horror of the event' to the search for structural laws, however, would not only be inaccurate but would risk inciting a false sense of comfort about the present of social scientific practices. The danger such confining poses is that of prompting us to think that this fear of events belongs to an infancy the contemporary social sciences have now outgrown. Indeed, a critic may argue, they no longer aspire to such a quest for the laws of the social but have become more modest in their ambitions, seeking to provide meaningful interpretations, and probable or plausible explanations of phenomena which nevertheless cannot, by right, gain the status of immobile laws. The critic may rebut that the reign of structuralism has given way to a so-called post-structuralism which has claimed, by contrast, to foreground the significance of 'contingencies' in the becomings of history and, by so doing, has placed the horror of the event in the recent past, one defined by a mix of innocence and hubris which contemporary knowledge-practices have amply overcome.

But even if the notion of social or cultural 'law' might no longer have the rhetorical or the epistemic force it once had, even when it has come to be looked upon with suspicion, as a term of abuse, by those contemporary social scientists who have—for better or ill—been affected by critiques of Enlightened thought, even so, this does not automatically push practices of social inquiry 'beyond' this horror that once explicitly characterised their relationship to heterogeneous, historical events. Indeed, my sense is that whenever the social sciences see their task as providing explanatory 'conditions' or 'contexts' for the becomings of events *in general*, it is not ludicrous to assume that the experience of horror induced by the novelty of an event still haunts their inquiries.

In this sense, for instance, the social constructivist positions discussed in Chap. 3 provide a good example, for in approaching experimental scientific inventions from the point of view of their micro- and macro-social conditions, their studies effectively sought to dispel the contingent and rare achievement that makes of a scientific invention an event. To be sure, to contest the becoming of an event by 'uncovering' its social conditions is to suggest that the event was in fact made *possible* by those conditions. The event, however, is just what betrays its own conditions of possibility. It is not what *is made* possible, but what *makes* the possible. Thus, it cannot be explained by general conditions ascribed to it a posteriori.

To be oriented by past events, by the contingency, and irreversibility of that which has happened, is not to approach them with the aim of explaining them away, nor of restoring to them the rightful sense of belonging to an epoch for which they might simply constitute examples. Insofar as relevance belongs, as I have suggested, to an event of a coming to matter, to suggest that events matter might be rightly seen as a tautology. Logical considerations notwithstanding, it seems like a tautology worth incurring into: events matter; they cannot be taken away. As is part of the tacit wisdom of many historians, to be oriented by past events, in contrast, is to invent a manner of inheriting them, to affirm that it is never those who come after it that situate the event within a context or a set of historical, social, economic, and cultural conditions, but that it is the difference the event creates that has already *situated them* as children of the event.

To attempt to inherit an event, to dare become children of the event, then, is to affirm that it is the latter that poses a problem, and it is this problem posed that transforms one into a researcher, into a developer of problems. Not the other way around. As Stengers and Pignarre (2011: 4) phrase it while daring to inherit and prolong a cry—Another World Is Possible!—that the event of the World Social Forum made resonate, becoming children of the event involves 'not being born again into innocence, but daring to inhabit the possible as such'. Rather than becoming the event's spokesperson, it requires us to become 'obliged by something that constrains us to abandon the precautions that befit authors', those precautions that, anxiously raising concerns about the legitimacy of the event in question, would force us to reduce the experience of being overtaken by the problem an event poses—one that forces us to think, imagine, and make a different future—to a mere private affair.

It is because part of what is at stake in becoming children of the event is daring to affirm that which shocks us into thinking and feeling instead of explaining it away, because it requires a process learning to honour that which throws us into an adventure, that we must resist the temptation to assume that only 'legitimised' events, those that tend to become privileged representatives of the differences they can make, have the capacity of situating us as their heirs, of moving us into thinking and inquiring.

I thus want to explore the process of becoming the child of an event through an unusual example. This is the thesis, put forth by cultural and literary studies scholar Harold Bloom (1997, 1999), that the work of Shakespeare constitutes an aesthetic event that has not only shaped what he terms the 'western canon', but whose effects extend far beyond the realm of aesthetics, involving a radical transformation of the possible ways of becoming a self, a psycho-social mutation of Western subjectivity that he polemically calls 'the invention of the human' (1999: 4):

> The idea of Western character, of the self as a moral agent, has many sources: Homer and Plato, Aristotle and Sophocles, the Bible and St. Augustine, Dante and Kant, and all you might care to add. Personality, in our sense, is a Shakespearean invention, and is not only Shakespeare's greatest originality but also the authentic cause of his perpetual pervasiveness. Insofar as we ourselves value, and deplore, our own personalities, we are the heirs of Falstaff and of Hamlet, and of all the other persons who throng Shakespeare's theater of what might be called the colors of the spirit.

Writing against a version of the ethics of estrangement that he calls, after Nietzsche, the *School of Resentment*—which in his account refers primarily to the proliferation of post-structuralist and 'postmodern' traditions in cultural and literary studies—and who, in his view, 'insists upon a Shakespeare culture-bound by history and society' (1997: xv), he argues that no approach that seeks to explain the Shakespearean event, or the 'Shakespearean difference', in terms of Western culture and dominance, in terms of gender, class, discourse, or colonialism will be able to provide a satisfactory answer to the question: 'Why Shakespeare?'.[6] As he expresses it in his always provocative tone,

> [a]llegorizing or ironizing Shakespeare by privileging cultural anthropology or theatrical history or religion or psychoanalysis or politics or Foucault or Marx or feminism works only in limited ways. You are likely, if you are

---

[6] It should be noted that 'Shakespeare' here names the event of the work itself and not the author, of whom we know close to nothing (Bloom 1999: 718). Indeed, the difference between the former and the latter is the very difference between a pragmatics of the event and a theory of genius. Although a reading of Bloom certainly makes both readings possible—and I am emphatically interested in the former rather than the latter—it is not at all clear to me what his own position on the matter is, considering that he has dedicated yet another monumental book to the question and history of *Genius* (2003).

shrewd, to achieve Shakespearean insights into your favorite hobbyhorse, but you are rather less likely to achieve Freudian or Marxist or feminist insight into Shakespeare. His universality will defeat you, his plays know more than you do, and your knowingness consequently will be in danger of dwindling into ignorance. (Bloom 1999: 718–719)

This is not to be taken to mean that to cultivate anthropological, theatrical, religious, psychoanalytic, Marxist, feminist, or Foucauldian modes of thinking is by definition a doomed exercise. To be sure, each of these traditions of thinking and feeling may provide crucial instruments for orienting attention and forms of care for what has come to matter that others may have neglected, for generating questions that may open an inquiry, and for learning to discern and identify possibilities emerging from it. But insofar as we remain Shakespeare's children (Bloom 1999: 726), insofar as we are 'monumentally over-influenced by him', it is in vain to mobilise such traditions in order 'to historicise or politicise him', to reduce the event to an example of what we already know: 'Shakespeare will not allow you to bury him, or escape him, or replace him' (Bloom 1997: xviii).

Here it is not a matter of judging whether there is such a thing as a Shakespearean event. Surely, such a proposition cannot be dispelled simply by saying that literature is, by definition, incapable of an event that is more-than-literary. What might the meaning of what we call *poetry* be if not that of an aesthetic invention that never confines itself to language? What interests me here however is the ethical exercise involved, the attempt to read Shakespeare's plays from the point of view of the children of the event, from the point of view of the problematic future—literary, cultural, political, psycho-social—that it created, and for which it came to matter. My view is that such an exercise orients scientific and interpretive practices away from an ethics of estrangement, which ultimately restores to history an inescapable character of continuity, to what I would call an *ethics of inheritance*, which confronts the event not with the question of what has made it possible, but with the question of what it has generated, of the way it has come to matter for those that have become, in one way or another, concerned with it. As Deleuze (2004: 169) phrases it in a particularly stoic form: '[e]ither ethics makes no sense at all, or this is what it means and has nothing else to say: not to be unworthy of what happens to us.'

An ethics of inheritance does not however imply resignation,[7] and it is emphatically *not* to be confused with a moral mandate that would dictate: 'Thou shalt not historicise'. That events cannot be reduced to social, cultural, economic, or psychological causes does not mean that such factors do not constitute a milieu of emergence for the becoming of events, nor that events have no history. Conversely, to relate the history of an event is not *necessarily* to reduce it to the factors that constitute its breeding ground. As historian of science Lorraine Daston (2009: 812–813) argues in relation to the historicising of scientific categories and events,

> to historicise the category of fact, objectivity, or proof is not thereby to debunk it, no more than to write the history of the special theory of relativity thereby undermines it. This is a point perhaps made more easily in ethics than epistemology; the fact that the judicial ban on torture arose in a specific historical context carries no weight arguments concerning its moral validity. Analogously, the fact that scientific objectivity arose in a specific historical context neither supports nor undercuts its epistemological validity. 'If historical, then relative' is a non sequitur. Why then do so many philosophers (as well as scientists, sociologists, and yes, historians) nonetheless believe it follows?

The answer to this question is that narrating the history of an event is not to reduce it to its historical conditions *so long as* those conditions are *not* endowed with the power of explaining the event away. In other words, so long as it is the event itself that is seen as situating its own past, and not the other way around.[8] As William Sewell (2005: 101) argues, '[e]vents must be assumed to be capable of changing not only the balance of causal forces operating but the very logic by which consequences follow from occurrences or circumstances' (2005: 101).

---

[7] For it 'is highly probable', Deleuze (2004: 170) suggests, 'that resignation is only one more figure of *ressentiment*, since *ressentiment* has many figures.'

[8] To the extent that history and event, as I have shown above, implicate each other reciprocally, to attempt to explain away an event by historicising it is something of a paradoxical operation. For although it mobilises historicism as a method, thereby suggesting that everything has a history, it implicitly shares the metaphysical assumptions of those it seeks to 'debunk', namely, that only that which has no history is, in a complete sense, true and real.

In this way, insofar as events are discerned within a genealogy or trajectory of other events, one of the first requirements of a social science oriented by an ethics of inheritance is the assumption that any given event always maintains a relationship to other events that form its trajectories of becoming and with respect to which it matters. This does not mean that events directly and actively *cause* and *are caused* by each other, but it does mean that they are not entirely independent from each other, maintaining what are to be thought of more in terms of relationships of resonance, or what Deleuze (2004) would describe in terms of 'quasi-causality'.

Furthermore, a social science oriented by events would have to refrain from presuming to know in advance what might be capable of constituting a possible force in history. Again, the singularity of an event affords no confinement within a pre-existent set of conditions of possibility. Thus, to approach what has happened as *de jure* an effect of social, or cultural, or economic, or technological forces is ultimately incompatible with the question of how the mattering of an event might be capable of situating its heirs in multiple ways. As Harold Bloom's thesis makes perceptible, *aesthetics* might indeed be capable of a transformation of possibilities with a scope that radically exceeds its specific domain. This does not mean, however, that the 'social' can *never* be a force of history because it would itself *always be* the effect of something else (cf. Latour 2005), but rather, that whether or not the 'social' constitutes a factor in the becoming of an event is a problem that cannot be solved by recourse to principles. It is, in other words, a question of inquiry that is never dissociated from the way in which an event is being inherited.

Finally, to cultivate an ethics of inheritance is to abandon any pretension of historical finality, and to assume that, as Sewell (2005: 102) puts it, 'contingency is global, that it characterizes not only the surface but the core or the depths of social relations. Contingent, unexpected, and inherently unpredictable events [...] can and do alter the most apparently durable trends of history.' Sewell also notes, of course, that this is not to deny the existence of enduring historical patterns of order, or that one can do away with capitalism, the global division of labour, or sexual inequality by the waving of a magic wand, as is if history was 'a tale told by an idiot.' What it does mean, however, is that history 'displays both stubborn durabilities and sudden breaks, and even the most radical historical ruptures are interlaced with remarkable continuities.'

In other words, insofar as events always force us to sway between the ordinary and the exceptional, between message and noise, by breaking with an order of things and instituting novel distributions of what is and what is not possible, they constitute not only a protest against the rationalisms that would always seek to restitute to the world an immobile order, but also a warning to those who, in the name of radical contingency or chaos, would proclaim that there never is any order. Rather, orders are incessantly being constructed and transformed by the becoming of events.

As intimated above, an ethics of inheritance is only one of the two reciprocally implicated dimensions of the relationship between events and social scientific adventures. For to affirm the power of events to shape the history of which a practice might become an heir has also a more speculative dimension. Namely, that other, unexpected events might happen in the future. Thus, an adventure is nothing other than a process of articulating, in practice, an ethics of inheritance with what we might call an ethics of exposure. An exposure, that is, to the possibility, however unlikely or implausible, of an event to come. It is thus to this dimension that we must now direct our attention.

## The Lure of the Event and the Ethics of Exposure

The poem by Julio Cortázar that has uninterruptedly inspired these pages could be read, I argued in the introduction to the book, as a plea for scientific knowledges to abandon the immobile comfort of their observatories where galaxies are grasped in a mental fist and the journey of eels is embalmed in a nomenclature that presents it as the expectable, indeed, logical consequence of a neuroendocrine process. The plea was not merely a protest against science *tout court*, but an invitation to a different science, one that would step out into the open, wander in the night, not with the aim of searching as if knowing what it will find, of acquiring 'mental satisfactions or submitting a not yet colonized nature to another turn of the screw', but of opening 'toward another understanding'. An opening 'to another sense that in turns opens us' (Cortázar 2011: 49). It is this stepping out into the open, this adventure, that prompts us not only to strive to inherit that which has happened but, equally and at the same time, to become oriented towards events that *might* happen, and which might happen 'with the suddenness of cats or the bath overflowing while we answer the phone'. As the poem suggests, however, such events tend to happen to those who step out into the open while carrying 'the cat in their pocket' (Cortázar 2011: 57). To those, that is, who allow the event to become a lure that might guide their practices towards cultivating the possibility of its actualisation. But what does it mean to be lured by the possibility of an event?

This is surely a difficult question, especially in a scientific culture that demands that events be defined in advance of the actual research process, in advance of posing the question of relevance, and that demands that they be anticipated in such a way that they might always be promised to constitute exceptional events, groundbreaking discoveries, and transformative innovations (Strathern 2000; Fraser 2009). But it is also difficult to the extent that the social sciences have become prone to think about everything, including not only humans and other-than-humans but also their own inventions, in terms of actions and effects. And the difficulty has to do with the fact that while the event is indeed an effect, it cannot in a strict sense be *effected*, either 'performatively' or otherwise. Deleuze (Deleuze and Parnett 2006: 48) interestingly expresses this paradox when he asks,

> How could an event not be effected by bodies, since it depends on a state and on a compound of bodies as its causes, since it is produced by bodies, the breaths and qualities which are interpenetrating here and now? But how could the event be exhausted by its effectuation, since, as effect, it differs in nature from its cause, since it acts itself as a quasi-cause which skims over bodies, which traverses and traces a surface, object of a counter-effectuation or of an eternal truth?

Thus, an event is something that might happen but not something that can be *made to happen*. In contrast, its happening is always the result of an unexpected and complex constellation of bodies and its mixtures, and can never be contained within the bounds of an explanation that could hold the event still by reducing it to its cause, in order to capture it in a mental fist, or worse, to embalm it. In other words, to will an event is not to produce events at will—orienting social scientific practices towards the possibility of an event is certainly not to suggest that everybody should, or even could, go about creating, making, and proclaiming events—be that the event of a discovery, of an accomplished 'impact', of yet another intellectual 'turn', or any other.

Indeed, to the extent that an event can be thought of as an effect, the latter resembles less an act than an achievement—namely, a delicate, difficult, and rare realisation that *can be* attained by a mingling of bodies and other events, but whose success cannot be ascribed to any single author and is never guaranteed. 'Any event is a fog of a million droplets' (Deleuze and Parnett 2006: 48). What this implies, then, is that the becoming of an event always requires a delicate configuration of multiple entities, practices, and trajectories of which scientific practices are only one element among many. It is arguably for this reason that, in the case of the experimental sciences, Isabelle Stengers (2000: 68–69, emphasis added) describes the scientific practices of experimental replicability not as that which conveys a certain phenomenon with the authority of an immobile law, but as the effect of an event that reveals its own breeding ground so that it can possibly be experienced again:

> What scientists know, as I am trying to singularize them—thus excluding the systematic producers of artifacts 'in the name of science' or 'in the name of objectivity'—what their tradition tells them, is that the foundation has already given way to diverse reprises, that the soils have been occupied, that is, that the event can be repeated. No procedure, however rational it might be, and no submission to criteria, whatever it may be, can guarantee this repetition. But the repetition would not find the terrain where it could be produced were not the scientists *acting with a view towards its production*.

In other words, what any scientist *learns*, be it experimental or social, hard or soft, is not the correct formal and methodological procedures for the unlimited production of events. It is never about becoming a *master* of the event, capable of producing it at will so long as the right kinds of instruments and mechanisms are in place. In contrast, what is

## 6 An Ethics of Adventure

at stake is a mode of practice and inquiry that forces those who are lured by the possibility of learning anything at all to situate themselves in the middle so as to expose themselves, their questions and their patterns of contrast, to the buzzing multiplicities that in becoming together in a delicate and always fragile constellation *might* achieve the production of a difference that matters, which is to say of an event. This is why one cannot emphasise enough the importance of social scientific practices to be defined not by their methods, nor by the theories they support, but by the risks they take. For the event marks the limit of risk. It is the limit that—for those encounters who have succeeded in becoming articulated in such a way that a proposition that matters could be invented—marks the difference between a before and an after. In other words, it provides the signal that something has indeed been learned. To become exposed, to put oneself at risk is, thus, what any adventure requires, and it is what opens up the *possibility*, but never the promise, that something might be learned:

> Depart. Go out. Allow yourself to be seduced one day. Become many, brave the outside world, split off somewhere else. These are the first three foreign things, the three varieties of alterity, the three initial means of being exposed. For there is no learning without exposure, often dangerous, to the other. I will never again know what I am, where I am, from where I'm from, where I'm going, through where to pass. I am exposed to others, to foreign things. (Serres 1997: 8)

As I have shown in previous chapters, to become exposed is not simply a critique of what has been termed the 'ivory tower', nor can it be equated with a celebration of just any form of inquiry that calls itself 'empirical'. Empirical research does not, in and of itself, guarantee that an encounter might become articulated in a manner that allows for a proposition that matters to be invented.

In contrast, to be lured by the possibility of an event, to work with a view towards a possible invention requires, first and foremost, that one encounters situations and objects of inquiry without a predefined conception of what is naturally or culturally possible. Indeed, insofar as the event is that which, by introducing a novelty in the world, makes a difference that transforms the possible, to encounter a situation with a predefined sense of what that situation is capable of is to mobilise the notion of 'the possible' as that which sets the ultimate limits to what might become relevant in that situation. It is, in order words, to reduce the possible to the known and to silently prophesy the death of the event.[9] This is precisely what the question of relevance seeks to resist. Indeed, to orient an inquiry not towards the production of a solution to a pre-existent problem but towards the question of 'how is it, here, that things matter?' is to expose such a mode of inquiry to an unknown, and thus, to be lured by the emergence of a different order of the possible.

Relatedly, and insofar as I am not advocating a form of inquiry that, in presupposing a conceptual *tabula rasa*, might confuse ignorance with innocence, to become exposed is also to allow that one's questions, one's manner of defining a problem, one's sense of what matters, might be mistaken. To believe that one could be mistaken is not simply a good antidote against dogmatism—although it should be noted, this is not minor either—and it is not simply to suggest that, indeed, part of the risk of a social scientific inquiry is that it may fail to produce what it might have expected, and that it may even fail to produce anything that an institution or a funding body might find worthwhile (See Chap. 5). Crucially, entertaining the possibility of being mistaken is also to affirm that taking the question of relevance seriously matters, that working towards the invention of a proposition that matters is indeed worth the trouble.

It is here, I believe, that William James' (1956: 17–19) empiricist distinction between the passions of 'knowing the truth' and that of 'avoiding error' profoundly resonates with an inquiry oriented by an ethics of exposure, which is also to say, oriented towards events. Indeed, to the extent that many contemporary social sciences have—not entirely without reasons—become suspicious of the very concept of truth—and some in fact, are suspicious of reality as such—and afraid of its normative political consequences, much critical scholarship today seems to revolve

---

[9] It is arguably for this reason that Henri Bergson (see especially his 'The Possible and The Real' in Bergson 2007) and, later, Gilles Deleuze, are generally critical—although not always, as this chapter shows—of the notion of 'the possible' and argue instead for a concept of 'the virtual'. Needless to say, the way in which I have been employing the notion of the possible here is closer to their use of the term 'virtual.'

around the avoidance of error, and operates by *analysing*, which is to say, by undoing, the operations of those who, in risking a truth, confuse it with their own unacknowledged habits or desires. But as Michel Serres (1997: 79) argued, '[o]ne exposes oneself when one makes, one imposes oneself when one unmakes. When one unmakes, one is never wrong, in effect. I know of no better way to be always right.'

To be sure, I am not suggesting that such critical operations come to a halt, for critique is not just an intellectual tool but it is also, after all, a thing of this world (Boland 2013).[10] Conversely, neither am I suggesting here that we resort to a transcendental notion of truth that might, yet again, restore to social scientific practices the modern dream of discovering eternal, unconscious laws of the social. To my mind, both such propositions have the same effect—that of working towards the stabilisation of the possible.

In contrast, in a world of events, errors are not such 'solemn things. In a world where we are so certain to incur them in spite of all our caution, a certain lightness of heart seems healthier that his excessive nervousness on their behalf' (James 1956: 19). They are the necessary steps of any inquiry that is oriented by an ethics of exposure. Similarly, to seek the truth, as James proposes we do, does not require that we abide by a transcendental notion of truth that could deliver the timeless predicates of reality. Indeed, in a world of events concrete truths perhaps need not be predicates which, for their part, are always entangled with the many modes of inheriting an event. Perhaps concrete truths resemble less a 'what' than a 'that', a 'variation of interest' (Whitehead 1968: 11), the experience that something has happened, that something has come to matter, that a different order of possibilities has been opened up, and that such an event cannot be undone, despite all the critical procedures and exercises in estrangement that we might put into play in seeking its dissolution. It is with the possibility of such an experience that I want to associate the event as that which might happen, and it is *towards* such experiences that inquiries in the social sciences could be oriented.

---

[10] And I shall have more to say about such critical operations in the next chapter.

## Conclusion: Transitional Knowledge

To cultivate a mode of inquiry that be oriented by events, between events, and with a view to their possibility is, ultimately, the task that the question of relevance requires. A task that, as I have suggested, supposes a transformation of some of the ethical sensibilities that may inform inquiry while *simultaneously* forcing us to reconsider the nature of that process we call 'knowledge' in a world where regularities are not a given but rare and complex achievements. In a sense, some of the sensibilities that I have sought to cultivate in this and previous chapters—exposure, inheritance, obligation, wonder, hesitation, the possible, and so on— could be interpreted as a 'return' to a certain care of knowledge and care of the world that have, since the rise of Enlightened thought, become rather disreputable (Daston and Park 2003).

But, just like events, sensibilities do not simply 'return' either, and we do not return to them. Indeed, if the notion of the event teaches us anything, then at the very least it makes evident that there is no such thing as 'returning', unless that which returns is difference itself (Deleuze 1994). To attempt to cultivate, in these pages, a different set of sensibilities does not mark a 'return' to a pre-modern or medieval care of knowledge whereby sensibilities such as exposure and wonder were conceived of as the effects of divine intervention, just as Deleuze's reclaiming of the event through a reading of Stoic philosophy does not, in and of itself, foster a return to stoicism. Thus, such attempts should not be confused with a nostalgic lament that regrets, like Max Weber (2009), the modern scientific 'disenchantment' of the world. For such a lament accepts the very Enlightened disjunction that opposes scientific knowledge to the perplexities induced by the transformations of the possible.

In contrast, to turn that disjunction into a possible conjunction, as a possible social science might do, is simultaneously to suggest that the production of knowledge cannot be equated with the 'true' definition of essences and substances that confuses the question of how things come to matter in specific and situated ways with the question of how they have always been and how they will always be. It cannot be reduced to the construction of systems of correspondences, static differences, and immobile relationships. It is also to suggest that producing knowledge cannot be reduced to a celebration of chaos, ontological incoherence, elusiveness, or mess (cf. Law 2004), even though learning to deal with those aspects of the world might often be required.

As Michel Serres (1982: 73) argues, '[t]he only systems, instances, and substances come from our lack of knowledge. The system is nonknowledge. The other side of knowledge. One side of nonknowledge is chaos; the other, system. Knowledge forms a bridge between the two banks. Knowledge as such is a space of transformation.' Indeed, to resist the disjunction between knowledge and the transformation of the possible is to approach practices of knowledge-making not from the point of view of what they succeed in holding still, but from the standpoint of the transitions their adventures achieve, between those events that have come to compose a situation and constitute our present, and those that generate an opening towards a different world to come.

# 7

# For Speculative Experimentation

## Introduction: 'The Latest Theory Is That Theory Doesn't Matter'

Throughout this book, I have sought to contribute to a philosophical outlook that could be resolutely termed 'empiricist', a radical form of empiricism that I have associated in different ways with thinkers such as William James, John Dewey, A.N. Whitehead, Gilles Deleuze, and Isabelle Stengers, among others. As I have argued, one of the defining features of radical empiricism is, to be sure, its commitment to the priority of experience. Indeed, a commitment to *experiences* of all natures and manners, as means of feeling, knowing, and thinking the world and the relationship that our practices sustain in and with it. It was James (2003: 22) himself who expressed such a commitment in a form that could almost be read as a maxim. 'To be radical', he proposed, 'an empiricism must neither admit into its constructions any element that is not directly experienced, nor exclude from them any element that is directly experienced'. As we have seen, what is given in experience is certainly more than just discrete things in isolation, as classical empiricism would otherwise have it. Experience also includes the many relations and modes of togetherness by which things come to matter.

Thus, I have sought to explore the problematising character of 'relevance' in relation to the ways in which the practices of contemporary social science *experience* and may come to 'know' the worlds they encounter, while revisiting what 'knowledge' as a process and a form of relating to the world might entail. At the same time, I have attempted to propose certain instruments for a different care of knowledge by which such modes of experiencing might remain open to the situated question and negotiations of how things matter, to what degree, and in what manner.

To the extent that certain versions of the Aristotelian clear-cut distinction between *theoria* and *praxis* still have some purchase on the ways in which contemporary social scientific inquiries are understood, organised, funded, and alas, experienced, a sceptical reader might still retain a feeling of suspicion regarding the very nature of my exploration. Indeed, for all the discussions around relevance, around practical encounters, adventures, objections, wonder, hesitation, events, this exploration might, in her view, remain just another 'theoretical' exercise. It might thus fail to live up to its own commitments. The sceptical reader might then ask: '*if experience is primary and practices are crucial to it, why do "theory"? why does theory matter anyway?*' Surely, one could easily dismiss the question by undermining the very distinction that underpins it. One could simply reply that 'theory' and 'practice', 'theoretical' and 'empirical' inquiry, are not in fact two distinct activities or forms of knowledge. One could argue, as it has been done by many authors in various ways, that theorising— or more plainly, thinking—is in fact a practice too. A practice that has less to do with the image of 'The Thinker' conveyed by Rodin's famous sculpture of a solitary man in reclusion from the world,[1] and more to do with a difficult articulation of an array of encounters between humans, a more-than-human world, ideas, discipline, creativity, and events.[2]

---

[1] Or perhaps it is *just* like Rodin's *Thinker*, given that he wrote that '[w]hat makes my Thinker think is that he thinks not only with his brain, with his knitted brow, his distended nostrils, and compressed lips, but with every muscle of his arms, back, and legs, with his clenched fist and gripping toes' (cited in Caso and Sanders 1977: 133). I am thankful to Kane Race for bringing this illuminating passage to my attention.

[2] There are numerous versions of this argument and even some empirical studies on what sort of practice thinking might be (for a historico-philosophical study of ancient philosophy as a spiritual exercise see Hadot 1995, on intellectual invention in science and culture see Schlanger 1983, for a

To be sure, one might certainly be 'right' to suggest that this is the case, and I am prone to agree that any simple distinction between 'theory' and 'practice' ought to be problematised. Nevertheless, to bypass the question by suggesting that it is simply unfounded and thus, that it itself does not matter, is to presuppose that what makes a question 'relevant', even a sceptical one, is a logical or intellectual justification whose legitimacy could easily be judged in advance. If my attempt at taking the question of relevance seriously has had any degree of success, I would hope that it—almost—goes without saying that this is not the case.

Thus, although from the 1960s to the 1980s the social sciences and humanities saw an expansion of 'theory' within anglophone universities, there are good historical and intellectual reasons for taking such a sceptical question very seriously today. For, as historian Ian Hunter (2006, 2007) has rightly argued and as I will discuss below, while what is commonly known as 'theory'—or rather 'Theory', with a capital 'T'—has constituted a very heterogeneous intellectual event that defies unification, it can perhaps be best understood as the renewal of a certain ethos which radicalises the exercise in estrangement and that, more specifically, may be characterised by an attitude of suspicion about, perhaps even disdain for, the positive knowledges produced by the empirical sciences. Moreover, as I will show in the next section, some of the recent attacks on 'Theory', particularly in the contemporary social sciences, can be seen as a set of empiricist responses to such a disdain for experience, by calling for a provincialised return to 'the empirical' (see for instance Adkins and Lury 2009; Boltanski 2011; Latour 2004).

In this sense, if the social sciences and the humanities can be said to be undergoing a crisis that, as I suggested in Chap. 2, is expressed through various demands for relevance that threaten their intellectual and institutional *futures*, for the past fifteen years there has been a growing, generalised sense—of concern, for some; of celebration, for others—that 'theory' has *already failed* to meet those demands, that its time is up, that it has run out of steam, and that perhaps we might all be better off

---

discussion of 'conceptual practices' in science and mathematics see for instance Pickering 1995, for a recent attempt at empirically studying social theory as a practice see Heilbron 2011).

without it (see for instance Eagleton 2003; Elliot and Attridge 2011; Latour 2004; Mitchell 2004; Patai and Corral 2005).

On 11–12 April 2003, for example, the then editors of *Critical Inquiry*, a University of Chicago-based journal that has to this date been at the forefront of theoretical work and debates in the humanities and the social sciences, invited the members of the journal's editorial board to a public meeting in Chicago. The aim of the meeting was to discuss 'the future of the journal and of the interdisciplinary field of criticism and theory it addresses' (Mitchell 2004: 324). Prior to their attendance, each of the participants was asked to write a short statement in response to a series of questions which testify to the climate of concern mentioned above. Some of the questions read:

> What, in your view, would be the desirable future of critical inquiry in the coming century? If you were able to dictate the agenda for theory and criticism in research and educational institutions, and in the public sphere, what would you imagine is the ideal structure of feeling and thought to inform critical practice? And, above all, what steps do you think need to be taken in the present moment to move toward this desirable future? What, in short, is to be done? (reproduced in Mitchell 2004: 330)

Interestingly, the public event on the question of the futures of 'Theory' and the demands for relevance that it faced managed to attract the attention of major US newspapers including the *New York Times*, and the *Boston Globe* (Mitchell 2004). Despite the variegated statements produced by the long list of distinguished scholars that participated in the symposium, however, the *New York Times* sentenced the event with a headline that read: 'The Latest Theory Is That Theory Doesn't Matter' (Eakin 2003, April 11).

Thus, the question of the role of theory today and of its place within the radical empiricism in relation to which I have developed this work is one that cannot go unexamined. To be sure, the scope of such questions amply exceeds any response I can and shall risk giving within the bounds of this chapter. Furthermore, even if my response was to constitute a whole book instead of a chapter, it can never be, nor pretend to be, a final response capable of single-handedly settling the stakes of the debate.

Thus, in this chapter I will attempt to explore some aspects of these questions with the aim of articulating a plea for the possibility and the role of a certain mode theoretical activity today. The hope is that it might, first, provide a partial response to the questions posed by my imaginary—yet possibly quite real—sceptical reader, and second, make a contribution, however modest and partial, to the ongoing debate on the future of theorising in the contemporary social sciences and the humanities.

In so doing, I will propose a particular *mode* of theorising or thinking that differs in important respects from the *ethos* that has been associated with the moment of 'Theory' emerging from the work of structuralist and post-structuralist thinkers in France towards the end of the 1960s and that made its way into anglophone universities in subsequent years (Hunter 2006). What I will attempt to propose is another type of intellectual exercise, one I want to associate with a practice of 'speculation', indeed, with what I will refer to as a kind of *speculative experimentation*.

As I will argue, instead of turning the ethics of estrangement into an exercise of mobilising thinking, or theory, to suspect experience and the empirical, speculative experimentation, as its name suggests, always begins from the facts of experience and seeks to return to them, albeit in a transformed way—transformed, that is, by the imaginative leap involved in the invention of concepts that seek to inhabit the possible. To engage in speculative experimentation, I suggest, is to engage experience insofar as it is yet to be constructed, as itself transitioning between what is and what might be. In this way, engaging in forms of speculative experimentation might offer us the possibility of a radical empiricist theorising characterised, first and foremost, by turning theorising itself into an adventure.

Thus, while what we commonly associate with 'Theory' constitutes an intellectual operation committed to the production of critical diagnoses of the present such that its time is always the 'now' (Lauretis 2004), the business of speculative experimentation is, as Whitehead (1958: 82) once put it, 'to make thought creative of the future'. It is crucially characterised by the wager that the future might be more than a mere continuation from the present, by the investment in the possibility that our propositions might find a response from the world as it transitions into the not-yet, allowing it to actualise a different mode of becoming. A mode of becoming that may enable practices, in turn, to move from another departure point, towards somewhere else.

In order to understand the stakes of the wager involved in speculative experimentation we first have to explore some of the reasons for the so-called demise of 'Theory' in the contemporary social sciences and the humanities and its relation to a certain revival of empiricism, so that we can extract from its interstices constraints and propositions that may allow us to devise a different relationship to, and a different role for, the practice of theorising. I will thus turn to this thorny question in what follows, and then come back to the question of speculation in subsequent sections of the chapter.

## Theory's Thousand Tiny Deaths: Social Theory, Experience, and the Ethics of Thought

That what we once knew as 'Theory' is dead seems nowadays to be both a generalised concern and a new common knowledge within certain strands of the contemporary social sciences, and indeed, of the humanities. Claims that we are situated 'after Theory' are shared both by critics of so-called Theory and by those who seek to expand novel forms of theoretical inquiry into the future. As soon as one—prompted by a feeling of curiosity or mourning, or a mix of both—attempts to explore the reasons for its demise, however, it becomes very difficult to define why it died, who or what killed it, whether its death is something to be grieved or celebrated, or whether it has in fact died at all.

Indeed, it has been argued that 'Theory' was too philosophical and not specific enough to survive in the disciplines it nevertheless affected (Patai and Corral 2005); that it was 'so wilfully obscure' (Eagleton 2003: 77); that it operated analytically, by being always right (Latour 2004); that it was not philosophical enough (Osborne 2011); that it turned the social sciences and the humanities into a politics by other means (Jacoby 2005); that it was too logocentric, ignoring every other aspect of human existence (Wellek 2005); that it infused the humanities with political purchase (Butler et al. 2000); that it killed 'Man' and 'The Author' through its various anti-humanisms (Clairborne Park 2005); that it was incapable of thinking beyond the presence of Man and its humanity on earth (Colebrook 2014); that it constituted the incorporation of culture itself into the productive advance of late capitalism (Jameson 1990); that it is the capitalist culture of war that now literally deploys 'Theory' and its concepts (Massumi 2011); *that 'Theory' is long dead*; that it 'has never been more alive and well' (Wolfe 2011: 34).

Part of the reason for 'Theory's' thousand tiny deaths and resurrections, surely, has to do with the fact that its historical trajectories differ considerably, depending on whether the focus is on the past and future of literary studies, art theory, or of, say, sociology. But also, and relatedly, what accounts for the multiplicity of death and (re)birth certificates is that in each of them 'Theory' tends to mean something slightly different. Although there seems to be some loose consensus that 'Theory' refers to the influence in anglophone universities of a series of authors and works broadly associated with French structuralism and post-structuralism such as Claude Lévi-Strauss, Louis Althusser, Jacques Derrida, Jacques Lacan, Michel Foucault, Roland Barthes, Jean-François Lyotard, and so on, some commentators also refer to the critical traditions ensuing from the Frankfurt School and the social theory of Pierre Bourdieu (Boltanski 2011), and yet others include thinkers from very different philosophical outlooks such as Richard Rorty (Jacoby 2005), who is also presented elsewhere as an exemplary 'anti-theorist' (Eagleton 2003).

This also applies to the question of what the object and the correct language of so-called Theory might be. As Ian Hunter (2006: 78) has noted, '[o]ne of the most striking features of recent discussions of the moment of theory in the humanities is the lack of even approximate agreement about what the object of such theory might be and about the language in which it has been or should be conducted.' So how can we approach the question 'what is 'Theory'?' in a way that it might allow us to confront its predicament and to rearticulate a different mode of theorising? Hunter (2006, 2007) himself offers what I believe to be a helpful approach to this question, one that resonates with the definition of 'contemporary social science' provided in the introduction to the book. In trying to lay the grounds for a 'history of "Theory"', he argues that rather than associating 'Theory' with a common object, which it has not, with an epistemic subject, which also varies significantly, or with a language, which tends to depend on the other two, one might approach it as the emergence of a renewed[3] intellectual attitude, or as what I would call an ethics of thought.

Such an ethics concerns the cultivation of an intellectual deportment characterised by a particular operation which, after Kant, Husserl, and Derrida, he calls the 'transcendental reduction' or *epochē*. 'The transcendental reduction', Hunter argues, 'is the act of suspending one's commitments to all empirical views and positivistic formalisms, thereby preparing oneself for the irruptive appearance of the noematic transcendental phenomenon' (Hunter 2006: 83). In other words, the gesture of the *epochē* which Hunter associates with the moment of theory characterises a particular mode of philosophising or theorising which situates the theorist *away from* the world which she attempts to think, forbidding her from asking questions or making claims that would presuppose the empirical world as a ground for the posing of the question itself. Conversely, it invites the theorist to problematise the very acts and processes of grounding, the transcendental or archaeological conditions, that would make a certain understanding of the world possible as a foundation for knowledge.

The implications of the *epochē* as an intellectual gesture become thus clear—they involve the incessant questioning, through a philosophical or theoretical technique performed upon oneself and upon others, of all forms of empirical knowledge from the point of view of their transcendental or 'archeological' conditions. In this sense, it may be said to constitute a radicalised version of the ethics of estrangement I have been problematising in previous chapters. As Hunter (2007: 9) puts it elsewhere, what configures the persona of the theorist and justifies her exercise is not simply the *realisation* that things are never what they seem. By contrast, the theoretical exercise is that of disassembling the semblance

---

[3] Hunter (2006: 98) relates this emergence to a post-phenomenological renewal of seventeenth century European university metaphysics, which 'can be characterised as an academic discipline (or culture) whose thematics concern the relation between an infinite, atemporal, self-active, world-creating intellect and a finite, "duplex" (intellectual-corporeal) worldly being. Since the seventeenth century one of this discipline's central tasks has been to forestall the autonomy of positive knowledges by tethering them to philosophical reflection on this relation of finite to infinite being.'

of things: 'things do not lose their self-evidence; it has to be taken away from them'.

The relation between theory and experience is thus indeed a *critical* relation, establishing the former as a sounder of that which constitutes the latter as self-evident. If for empiricists direct experience is, as Whitehead (1955: 6) put it, 'infallible', such that '[w]hat you have experienced, you have experienced', if what remains to be constructed is not what makes direct experiences possible but the abstractions that may allow us to interpret and reconstruct it inventively, for Theory-as-we-have-come-to-know-it what is infallible is rather that any experience that can be called 'direct' is always already *in*direct.

The challenge was then that of interrogating the intellectual, pre-empirical operations by which experience can be constituted as such.[4] Theory's attitude and role in relation to the empirical knowledge-practices of the contemporary social sciences and the humanities was thus one of scepticism and suspicion, of unveiling the hidden mechanisms—epistemes, intertexualities, underlying structures, regimes of truth, plays of signification, unconscious processes, systems of signs, power-relations—whereby 'the empirical' could itself be constituted as an object of scientific knowledge in diverse ways. Once taken up by social researchers themselves, this attitude of scepticism and critique has been, as we have seen, transposed to the experience of their own objects of inquiry.

Because of its sceptical relation to experience, theory was seen as a means of producing what we could call a 'critical diagnostics' of our present. One could perhaps argue that what informed its task was a rather limited interpretation of Foucault's (1997b) famous essay on Kant's *What is Enlightenment?* one in which he sought to positively describe the philosophical *ethos* as a 'critique of what we are saying and doing through a

---

[4] This can be said to be the case at least to the extent that one retains 'theory' as a somewhat abstract characterisation of a mode of self-interrogation that might allow as to articulate a different ethics of thought. Like any abstraction from concrete fact, however, Hunter's characterisation omits part of the truth. So does mine, insofar as it takes his as a point of departure. Indeed, when one approaches the individual works of some of the authors loosely associated with the moment of Theory on the question of experience, as intellectual historian Martin Jay (2005) has done with Barthes, Foucault, and also Bataille, for instance, it becomes clear that these theorists' relation to experience was less straightforward and more ambivalent than here suggested. I will come back to this, concerning Foucault, below and in the Afterword.

*historical ontology of ourselves*' (1997b: 316). If I say that Theory's interpretation of Foucault's description was or is limited is because, if our depiction of Theory's ethics of thought is correct, then it would seem that this 'critical ontology of ourselves' was understood exclusively in its historical or genealogical dimension. That is, 'as a historical investigation into the events that have led us to constitute ourselves and to recognise ourselves as subjects of what we are doing, thinking, saying' (1997b: 316). This is perhaps why in the symposium mentioned above, for instance, feminist theorist Teresa de Lauretis (2004: 365) resisted the very invitation to think about the future of theory on the grounds that, in her view, 'the time of theory is always the now.' As she explained:

> What this means is, the time of theory, as articulated thought, is always the present, though its roots be found in the past, reaching across the contingent, material, social, sexual, racial, intellectual history of the theorizing subject and regardless of its uses and abuses in the undetermined future (2004: 365).

But Foucault's articulation of such a philosophical ethos also contained an 'experimental' dimension, one he connected very intimately to the question of freedom and one he would arguably explore in his later writings on sexuality, ethics, and truth. Besides the critical work produced by historical inquiries, Foucault (1997b: 317) argued, theory must 'put itself to the test of reality, of contemporary reality, both to grasp the points where change is possible and desirable, and to determine the precise form this change should take'. In the next section, I will argue that speculative experimentation is singularly attuned to this second dimension mentioned by Foucault and rarely taken seriously by theorists. As we will see, to add experimentation to theory not only complexifies theory's relation to experience, but forces us to consider that the time of speculation is never the present as a limit. Rather, the time of speculative experimentation is the sliding of the present into a possible future.

Given theory's ultimate distrust of empirical knowledges and of the question of the possible futures experience might herald, then, it is not entirely surprising that, in light of its demise, a powerful set of responses has given way to what has been termed a (re)turn to the empirical (Adkins and Lury 2009). To be sure, not all of the proposals that are or could be included within this reappraisal of experience have been anti-theoretical. One example of the latter concerns the emergence of an interest in questions of affect. Although itself a heterogeneous field grouping a number of very different approaches and thinkers, affect *theorists*—as they are commonly called, and not for no reason—particularly those in the tradition that emerges from Deleuze's readings of Spinoza and Bergson, have arguably sought provide theory with an empiricist inflection and a novel attention to pre-individual, pre- or sub-conscious, and pre-subjective experiences. It is this interest in the pre-individual realm that has arguably led some of these theorists to explore and attempt to think with the empirical evidence produced by some of the life sciences such as Neuroscience and Biology. Sciences which do study 'the human', but do so from the point of view of the many other pre-social, pre-cultural modes of existence that feed into the process of its own composition.

There has been some controversy as to how such empirical evidence is taken up in affect theory, suggesting that in these theoretical works biology and neuroscience are endowed with some kind of revelatory capacity that allows theorists to *ground* their more ambitious claims instead of approaching the evidence critically (see Leys 2011, Papoulias and Callard 2010). This might be true in some cases. But what these critiques often miss is that the best examples of affect theory involve not only an affirmative theoretical practice that seeks to connect empirical evidence of pre-individual experiences to the composition of individual, social, and cultural ones—a connection that itself requires inventive thinking—but also, and crucially, a transformation in the ethics of thought that drives theoretical activity (e.g., Connolly 2002; Massumi 2002; Stenner and Greco 2013). Namely, a mode of thought that does not oppose culture to biology, or nature, but that seeks to inventively attend to what Connolly (2002: 20) would call the interactive 'layering of culture'—a mode of inquiry that invites 'you to attend to the complex relays joining bodies, brains, and culture' in such a way 'the hubris invested in tight models of explanation and consummate narrative of interpretation becomes vivid'.

Other returns to 'the empirical' have been less sympathetic to the activity of theory and critique. In yet another of the many 'turns' that the contemporary social sciences and the humanities have for some time repeatedly hastened to proclaim, anti-theoretical or anti-critical responses have emerged under the umbrella label of a 'descriptive turn' (for a history of its early emergence see Dosse 1999). Again, these responses, which have emerged more prominently within social theory but that have also affected literary theory (e.g., Love 2010), are as heterogeneous as what they are responding to.[5] Some of them have turned critique and theory on their heads, that is, into objects of empirical study, while not necessarily endorsing their demise (Boland 2013; Boltanski 2011; Boltanski and Chiapello 2005; Heilbron 2011).

Others have gone one step further, attempting to kill off the theoretical or critical ethos[6] by replacing it with a purely descriptive one. If anything groups them together, however, is perhaps a gesture that associates theory and critique—when placed in the hands of 'professional' theorists and critics—with the hubris of monopolising interpretation, and regards them as ineffective modes of thinking and practice. Theory becomes a strategy that, according to Boltanski and Chiapello's (2005) argument, ends up becoming hunted by its prey, and mobilised by those discourses and practices it once sought to problematise.

Among those who *oppose* a descriptive ethos to a theoretical one, a most famous example is Latour's (1993a, 2004, 2005) declaration that critique has run out of steam, that it is redundant, similar to conspiracy theories, irredeemably modern, always operating by providing explanations that seek to monopolise the definition of a situation by replacing the causal forces at stake. Certainly, Latour is very aware of the fact that, first, what we have come to associate with theory and critique is to be conceived as a particular ethics of thought rather than a stable field with a common object or language; second, that one of the gestures that characterises this ethos is a retreat from the empirical:

> The mistake we made, the mistake I made, was to believe that there was no efficient way to criticize matters of fact except by moving away from them and directing one's attention toward the conditions that made them possible. But this meant accepting much too uncritically what matters of fact

---

[5] For a critical overview in social theory see Savage (2009).
[6] From the point of view of a characterisation of 'Theory' as a technique of self-problematisation, critiques of 'critique' or of 'Theory' appear as treating both terms interchangeably.

were. This was remaining too faithful to the unfortunate solution inherited from the philosophy of Immanuel Kant. (Latour 2004: 231–232)

As we saw in Chap. 2, his return to the empirical, or what he calls the 'realist attitude' (2004: 232), entailed the proposition that reality is not simply composed of matters of fact, but of what he calls *matters of concern*, whose coming into existence always involves the participation of a multiplicity of heterogeneous human and nonhuman agencies. The new attitude he proposes, then, is one that would concern itself with adding *more* reality to matters of fact by describing the many agencies that feed into the making of things. Description constitutes, according to Latour, 'the highest and rarest achievement' (2005: 137). It consists precisely in this activity of deploying as many actors composing a thing or situation as possible so that 'the uniquely adequate account of a given situation' may be provided (2005: 144). In this way, description involves the consequence that 'through the report concluding the enquiry the number of actors might be increased; the range of agencies making the actors act might be expanded; the number of objects active in stabilizing groups and agencies might be multiplied; and the controversies about matters of concern might be mapped' (2005: 138).

To the extent that it attempts to modify the ethos of scepticism concerning the empirical that is the characterising feature of what we have come to know as theory and critique, and to the extent that for him descriptions have a constructivist function, which is to say, that they *add* reality to matters of fact instead of replacing it for one of a different order, I appreciate Latour's empiricist call to devise a different relationship between intellectual practices and experience. Nevertheless, my sense is that the exploration of the question of relevance forces us to add some layers of complexity to his proposal, and to realise that the constructivist nature of descriptions is a fundamentally *theoretical* exercise, although of a different kind of theorising than the one we have associated with Theory thus far.

While I agree with him that when it comes to adding reality to matters of fact, '[r]elevance, like everything else, is an achievement' (Latour 2005: 138), I hope that my exploration of the question of relevance has made evident that the achievement of inventions that matter is not entirely dependent on *increasing* the number of actors, or on expanding the range of agencies. That might surely be required in some cases, as in Hetherington's (2013) encounter with the Paraguayan peasants and the killer soy beans (see Chap. 4), where an object of inquiry—a human, in this case—*objects* to an exceedingly narrow definition of a situation put forth by an anthropologist. But the risk belonging to the question of relevance goes, I think, beyond the question 'Have I assembled enough?' (Latour 2005: 136, n. 192). Achieving 'relevance' through inquiry is not so much about expanding the *quantity* of actors that compose a situation but about the event of a successful negotiation of the varying manners and degrees in which they matter to it and to each other. As I argued, this requires inventive encounters involving questions, objections, an experimentation with the manner in which an inquiry is *pre*positioned, and risks born of hesitant action.

Thus, although Latour (2005: 137) is right to say that explanations are hardly necessary, the image of descriptions as a prophylactic measure that, '[m]uch like "safe sex"', will 'protect us against the transmission of explanations' seems rather misleading. In fact, what to me is important about Latour's attempt to produce descriptions whose risk is that of adding to reality, is that this constructivist operation could in my view be directly associated with the 'experimental' dimension that Foucault emphasises. Although by the time of *Reassembling the Social* (2005) Latour seeks no longer to reform theory but to oppose it, I would argue that the constructivist nature of his descriptivism is still a theoretical exercise. It is a kind of theoretical exercise, however, that is not based on distrusting what one describes, but rather on establishing the unstable, experimental, and speculative link between the actuality of facts as encountered in the present and the immanent possibilities inherent in those facts, possibilities that exhibit in the present a transition to a future (Whitehead 1967a).

In other words, if the kind of empiricism I am trying to outline here may be called 'speculative' it is also because the experience of the present is not just one of things 'as they are' but also includes the experience of things 'as they could be'. It is this unfinished nature of the present or, in other words, this experience of the present as itself exposed to the becoming of a future, as a transition between past and future, that is both crucial to this kind of empiricism and that opens up a space for the positive characterisation of an experimental, future-oriented mode of theorising that I here want to associate with the notion of speculation.

## To Make Thought Creative of the Future: On Speculative Experimentation

What does it mean to say that the present is itself exposed to the becoming of a future? Let us briefly go back to the characterisation of events that I explored at some length in the last chapter. As I showed, insofar events *make* time rather than happen *in* time, they are never reduced to what *is happening*, but include simultaneously what has happened and what is about to happen. To the extent that the becoming of events requires the inheritance of past events and the exposure to the possibility of future events, then, the experience of the present is itself a mode of transitioning between events. As Whitehead (1967a: 192) put it, '[e]ach moment of experience confesses itself to be a transition between two worlds, the immediate past and the immediate future'.

Now, as I argued, the past inheres in the present as completed events that demand to be inherited but which do not dictate the terms in which its heirs will do so. To the extent that they *demand* to be inherited, and insofar as their inheritance is a requirement for the becoming of a future event, however, it follows that a future, or better, the necessity of a future, inheres in the demand of past events that contribute to constituting our present. Events beget future events. Again, this is neither to say that the past efficiently *causes* the future, nor that the future is already constituted as a determined component in the present. As SF writer Margaret Atwood (2011: 5) has argued, 'the future is an unknown: from the moment *now*, an infinite number of roads lead away to "the future", each heading in a different direction.'

To say that futures inhere in the present, that the latter is fundamentally unfinished by reason of its exposure to a future, is simply to assert that the constitution of the present 'necessitates that there be a future' (Whitehead 1967a: 193). This is why I said in the previous chapter that a practice that inhabits a world of events is *simultaneously* situated by an ethics of inheritance of the past and an ethics of exposure to possible futures. Because the present 'arises as an effect facing its past and ends as a cause facing its future' (Whitehead 1967a: 194). In this way, the future inheres in the present as the experience of immanent *possibilities* to be actualised.

With this characterisation of futures in the present we can begin to approach a first definition of speculative experimentation. For while all practices oriented towards events must learn to become *exposed* to the possibility of a future event, speculation designates, in a nutshell, those practices that actively and constructively experiment with possibilities. By so doing, their aim is that of inventing tools, however abstract, that in leaping into the possibilities of what is not-yet, may contribute to directing a transition from the givenness of the present towards a future that is more than the mere conformation to that givenness.

In fact, this is precisely what sets speculation, as I am attempting to characterise it,[7] apart from probabilistic forecasting techniques familiar to the future-oriented practices of many social scientists, policymakers, financial brokers, and insurance companies. For as historians and philosophers of science have crucially shown (Bergson 2011; Hacking 1990; Whitehead 1967a), any probabilistic estimation about future events presupposes a linear relationship between present and future whereby the latter is understood as the mere extension of the former. Indeed, what allows for a probabilistic forecast to be understood as providing knowledge of

---

[7] The mode of speculation that I am seeking to articulate here differs in various ways from what in recent years has acquired the name of 'Speculative Realism' (SR) and 'Object-oriented ontology' (OOO) (e.g., Bryant 2011; Harman 2010; Meillassoux 2008). One of SR's central claims is the rejection of the Kantian and Husserlian gesture that Meillassoux (2008: 5) termed 'correlationism'. Namely, 'the idea according to which we only ever have access to the correlation between thinking and being, and never to either term considered apart from the other'. As Graham Harman (2013: 23) argues, correlationism is thus the adoption of an intermediate position between idealism and realism, suggesting that 'we cannot say that the world either exists or fails to exist outside human thought'. This is another way of approaching the same sceptical position we have explored above. To that extent, the anti-correlationism of SR and the form of speculation I am attempting to outline share a common point of departure. The speculative realist project that ensues from this, however, constitutes an attempt to both affirm the possibility and explore the implications of a thought of reality that is independent from human knowledge, it is an attempt to think the 'in-itself' of things. For speculative empiricsm, on the other hand, human and other-than-human thinking is not a mere correlation to the facts but 'a factor in the fact of experience' (Whitehead 1958: 80). Thus, it is a practical tool for the experimental actualisation of possible futures (for different speculative projects see Bryant et al. 2011).

the future is the presupposition that the present facts upon which the calculation is performed will be conserved in the future state toward which the calculation is said to offer insight (Whitehead 1967a: 125–126).

In a world of events, however, this conservative relationship between present and future cannot be taken for granted. Thus, while the stability of temporal patterns presupposed by probabilistic forecasting may *occasionally* be of help for the orientation of action during limited periods of stability, it should never be confused, as it often is, with a structural law of regularity (Hacking 1990). Stability is always an immanent and precarious achievement of a succession of ordinary events that conform to each other. And the presupposition of continuous stability becomes decreasingly robust and reliable in a world characterised by an accelerated pace of events (Connolly 2013). In this sense, it is not that probabilistic forecasting provides us with certainties as to the actual becoming of the future. What makes them 'probable' rather than certain is also not just that the present knowledge upon which the calculation is performed is by necessity incomplete. Rather, the methods of probabilistic forecasting incorporate in themselves a *gamble* on the conformation of the future to the present. They pass judgement on the present, or the immediate past, and *bet* that the future will conform to the judgement.

To the extent that the future does *sometimes* conform to the present, we should not rush into a disqualification of probability *tout court*. The question is whether probabilities suffice, and whether it is in them that our social, cultural, and political theories should invest its inventive attention. Connolly (2002: 137–138), for instance, proposes that '[c]oncentration on probabilities alone can be left to bureaucrats and consultants', while '[p]olitical and cultural theory should focus first and foremost on possibilities that speak to pressing needs of the time.' I am of a similar mind. For to speculate is to wager on the possibility, however implausible or unlikely from the point of view of our present knowledge, that the future might be more than a mere continuation of the present. Speculation is not, then, the facile attitude of ascribing unwarranted meanings to uncertainties when scientific evidence is lacking (cf. Ericson and Doyle 2004). Neither is it the introduction of the 'intuitive' within the calculation of probability that characterises political and economic judgements based on algorithmic analyses (Amoore 2013). Speculation here designates a constructivist, experimental mode of thought whose role is no other than 'creating possibles, that is of making visible the directives, evidences, and rejections that those possibles must question before they themselves can become perceptible' (Stengers 2010: 12).

To be sure, possibilities are not always, in and of themselves, a cause for celebration. Some of the possible and perhaps even likely futures to which we are exposed may not include the social sciences or the humanities among their existents, at least not as we have come to know them. It may well be that some futures do not even include 'us', humans, as part of their living inhabitants. Indeed, the possibilities to which we become exposed may be tragic. Yet, it is precisely in the face of the uncertain and problematic nature of the many possibilities to which we are exposed that the need for speculative modes of theorising makes itself felt. As Dewey (2004: 80) has argued, it is precisely this problematic encounter with the perplexing questions that the world poses that forces us to think:

> men (sic) do not, in their natural estate, think when they have no troubles to cope with, no difficulties to overcome. A life of ease, of success without effort, would be a thoughtless life, and so also would a life of ready omnipotence. Beings who think are beings whose life is so hemmed in and constricted that they cannot directly carry through a course of action to victorious consummation.

Not any problem, however, demands to be thought. In fact, for Dewey (2004: 82), whenever a problem is 'completely actual and present, we are overwhelmed. We do not think, but give way to depression.' In contrast, for it to demand a speculative mode of thought a problem needs to present itself as an 'impending problem', one that makes felt a present that is unfinished and developing, orienting us to what is yet to come. To that extent, '"[t]hought' represents the suggestions of a way of response that is different from that which would have been followed if intelligent observation had not effected an inference as to the future' (2004: 83).

For his part, in *The Function of Reason* (1958) Whitehead distinguishes between two forms of speculative thought. One of them, which arguably he would comprehensively undertake in his *magnum opus*, *Process and Reality*—not accidentally subtitled 'An Essay in Cosmology'—constitutes the construction of 'a cosmology expressing the general nature of the world as disclosed in human interests' (1958: 85). Its aim is to 'frame a coherent, logical, necessary system of general ideas in terms of which every element of our experience can be interpreted' (Whitehead 1978: 3). The other mode of speculation is perhaps more modest and pragmatic. And while, for reasons that will become apparent below, it is not itself methodic, it constitutes 'speculative Reason in its closest alliance with the methodological Reason' (1958: 85). This second mode of speculation, Whitehead suggests, 'accepts the limitations of a special topic, such as a science or a practical methodology [and] then seeks speculatively to enlarge and recast the categoreal ideas within the limits of that topic' (1958: 85).

While drawing on James, Whitehead, Deleuze, and others for the cultivation of a sensibility and an awareness to a speculative cosmology, I have sought throughout the preceding chapters to experiment with the second, more modest and practical mode of speculation. Thus, by confronting the impending problem of the future of the contemporary social sciences as put into question by multiple demands for relevance, I have experimented with a speculative proposition that is doubly related to the question of how things matter, in what degrees and manners. For in inviting the practices of the social sciences to encounter a situation with the question 'how is it, here, that things matter?' and to inquire into the many ways and degrees in which the elements and relations that compose it come to matter, I have simultaneously speculated on how such a question itself *might matter* to possible modes of social inquiry and to the production of social scientific knowledge. This speculative question has situated my theoretical exploration itself into the realm of adventure, forcing me to think *scienceward*, for practices yet to come.

However, because speculative experimentation works by leaping into the possibilities emerging from the present beyond the limitations offered by the habits of thought and practice that have become built into the theories and methods of the social sciences, it would be a mistake, I would argue, to give in to the temptation of turning speculation into a method.[8]

---

[8] Unless we take method in its 'inventive', problem-sensitive version rather than in its traditional form (see Lury and Wakeford 2012, and especially Parisi 2012)

As Whitehead (1958: 66) argues, speculative reason questions established methods, refusing to let them rest:

> The speculative Reason is in its essence untrammelled by method. Its function is to pierce into the general reasons beyond limited reasons, to understand all methods as coordinated in a nature of things only to be grasped by transcending all method. This infinite ideal is never to be attained by the bounded intelligence of mankind. But what distinguishes men (sic) from the animals, some humans from other humans, is the inclusion in their natures, waveringly and dimly, of a disturbing element, which is the flight after the unattainable. This element is that touch of infinity which has goaded races onward, sometimes to their destruction. It is a tropism to the beckoning light—to the sun passing towards the finality of things, and to the sun arising from their origin. The speculative Reason turns east and west, to the source and to the end, alike hidden below in the rim of the world.

Now, to say that speculation is untrammelled by method is neither to suggest that it is *against* method, nor that it functions through guesswork or by means of a practice of wild, unconstrained, conjecturing. Quite the opposite is the case. In fact, I am speaking of a speculative experimentation precisely because I think it can best be understood as an experimental intellectual practice, where 'experiment' connotes the risky stakes of highly constrained creativity that Dewey (2008b) has associated with the experimental logic of inquiry.

As he argues, experimental modes of inquiry exhibit three main characteristics. First, they all involve overt doing, 'the making of definite changes in the environment or in our relation to it'. Second, they are never random activities, but are directed by ideas and propositions 'which have to meet the conditions set by the need of the problem inducing the active inquiry.' Last but not least, the outcome of experimentation is 'the construction of a new empirical situation in which objects are differently related to one another' (Dewey 2008b: 63). Let me approach the implications of the first two characteristics first, and I shall come back to the question of outcomes below.

To the extent that speculation can be said to be experimental, it cannot embrace the ethics of thought advocated by what we have come to know as 'Theory'. In other words, the speculative thinker does not act upon herself by distrusting and becoming estranged from experience, by being sceptical of the facts that compose the natural and cultural world, or by demanding compliance of it. What a speculative ethos requires of her is a different intellectual attitude, namely, to think *with* and *for experience*, that is, to take up the many experiences that constitute the present as a constraint upon her thinking. The exercise of speculation involves something akin to what, in *What is Philosophy?*, Deleuze and Guattari (1994) refer to as 'the empiricist conversion'. As they express it:

> [i]t may be that believing in this world, in this life, becomes our most difficult task, or the task of a mode of existence still to be discovered on our plane of immanence today. This is the empiricist conversion (we have so many reasons not to believe in the human world; we have lost the world, worse than a fiancée or a god). The problem has indeed changed. (Deleuze and Guattari 1994: 75)

The implications of the empiricist conversion[9] for a speculative mode of theorising involve a practice of thinking that is crucially grounded in both perceptual and *conceptual* experience—speculations must begin from the real possibilities emerging from actual facts and inventively construct abstract and practical tools capable of effecting a different mode of transitioning between present and future by providing an alternative path towards a *novel empirical situation*. Experience is thus not only the

---

[9] We should not be confused by Deleuze and Guattari's use of the term 'belief' in this passage. Indeed, to the extent that they are developing a philosophy of becoming thoroughly committed to an immanent world that is not just immanent to God, or any other transcendental value, but only immanent to itself, the term 'belief' here should not be interpreted in the Christian mode that we discussed in Chap. 5. It is not a belief in God, that might concern the transcendental existence of the latter, but one that concerns 'the infinite immanent possibilities brought by the one who believes that God exists' (1994: 75). It is this commitment to the radical immanence of the world—a plane of existence that William James (2003) would call 'pure experience'—that gives meaning to the notion of an 'empiricist conversion'. The shift is spiritual, for sure, as the term 'conversion' provocatively suggests. But it involves not the claim that there is a God beyond our immanent world, but the wager of a world that matters, and which includes the possibilities of those who believe in the existence of God as their inhabitants. Perhaps this is what Whitehead (1926: 49)—who, admittedly, was more of a theist than either Deleuze or myself—meant when he proposed that '[r]eligion is world-loyalty'.

beginning, but the end—speculation begins in experience, and it works with a view towards the composition of a new, transformed experience.

Beginning in experience, speculative experimentation is not sceptical of facts but encounters them with a docility that does not thereby involve complete submission to them. By virtue of the unfinished or transitional nature of the present, the facts of experience are approached as materials for speculation, as themselves exhibiting the possibility of an alternative that demands creative modes of intellectual experimentation. In so doing, it surveys the variety of contemporary experiences, no matter how minor, implausible, or rare these may be, so as to extract from them possibilities for a different composition to be actualised. In other words, the possibilities speculation works with are not, as in some cases of science fiction,[10] pure potentialities divorced from actuality. As we have already seen with Stengers (2011b: 313), a 'speculative possibility does not simply fall from the sky of ideas. Speculation originates in unique situations, which exhibit the possibility of an approach by the very fact that they have already undertaken it'. As my exploration of three very unusual encounters in contemporary social research has, I hope, suggested, what becomes material for speculation are *real possibilities* inherent in the present.

Showing docility to facts without succumbing to them means that the main function of speculative experimentation is neither simply to describe the facts that compose a present situation, nor merely to provide a rational explanation for their coming about. Thus, it resists the dogmatic fallacies involved both in theories that would revert every event to their own preferred explanatory framework, and in those other 'theories-of-no-theory' which would confine our experience of the world to what is merely 'observed'. Instead, it takes up the stubbornness of facts as a constraint upon its own creative activity.

This is where such form of speculation involves 'overt doing', constructively seeking to make possible changes in our relationship to a situation,

---

[10] I am here drawing on the distinction made by Atwood (2011: 6) between science fiction and speculative fiction. What she means by 'science fiction' is 'those books that descend from H.G. Wells's *The War of the Worlds*, which treats of an invasion by tentacled, blood-sucking Martians shot to Earth in metal canisters–things that could not possibly happen. 'Speculative fiction' by contrast, 'means plots that descend from Jules Verne's books about submarines and balloon travel and such—things that really could happen but just hadn't completely happened when the authors wrote the books.'

to a milieu, to the world. To engage in speculative experimentation is to think with facts. It is not to be sceptical of but to attempt to think *with* the sciences. But unlike the scientific reliance on methodological reason, hard or soft, speculative experimentation is characterised by the willingness to risk a thought about that which our habits would advise us against thinking, to cast off into what we may have not yet thought, to reclaim what we may have learned to forget, to construct elements for thinking what we do not yet know how to think.

In this way, its ultimate aim is that of producing concepts, words, or tools that may contribute to the rearrangement of the relationships, the modes of togetherness of the facts that compose a situation so that the latter might be experienced differently, opening a path to the composition of a different future. For this reason, the time of speculation is not the 'now' as a limit, but a fugitive now that is always passing too quickly to be held still, immediately begging the question of what might come after it.[11] In this way, the speculative attitude involves the gesture of combining the stubborn rigour of actuality with the freedom of the possible. Dewey (2008b: 63) emphasises this point when he argues that

> [t]here is a distinction between hypotheses generated in that seclusion from observable fact which renders them fantasies, and hypotheses that are projections of the possibilities of facts already in existence and capable of report. There is a difference between the imaginative speculations that recognize no law except their own dialectic consistency, and those which rest on an observable movement of events, and which foresee these events carried to a limit by the force of their own movement. There is a difference between support by argument from arbitrarily assumed premises, and an argument which sets forth the implications of propositions resting upon facts already vitally significant.

Marked by the empiricist conversion, then, the intellectual instruments that a speculative experimentation seeks to produce can never amount to

---

[11] To be sure, it may be that what comes after it involves a different form of inheriting the past. In this sense, to say that speculation is future-oriented is not to say that it is unconcerned with the past. As I have argued, that it takes the existence of the past as a stubborn fact that demands to be inherited does not mean that this fact determines 'how' it is to be inherited, or what the 'right' account of the past is. Thus, the future with which speculation is concerned might indeed involve the future of the past.

a new general framework that would, once and for all, resolve the problematic character of the many experiences that compose the world. To suggest the contrary would amount to sustaining that thought bears a structuring relationship to experience—that social theory can, by its own means, set limits to the question of what a society is capable of. If one is to remain an empiricist without becoming disdainful of thinking, one has to conceive of theories in the concrete, as being 'made of the same stuff as things are' (James 2003: 20). They are prompted by experiences, they allow us to reconstruct experience, and they *must themselves be experienced*. As they contribute to forging particular forms of sensibilities and to intensifying our sensitivity to possibilities that may allow for a different future to come, theories are felt and they involve feeling—they are, in Whitehead's words (1978: 184), lures for feeling. If speculations succeed in changing the mode of togetherness of the many facts and relations that compose a situation, it is not by inviting us simply to 'think differently' about that situation, but by *adding* to it the experience of a thought that connects some elements of the present to possibilities to be actualised in the future. That is, the force of speculative thinking is compositional—it adds itself to the making of a situation and in so doing shifts the intensities with which a future may be felt in the fugitive present. It participates in 'modifying old dispositions and forging new habits even as it expresses established habits and dispositions' (Connolly 2002: 99). This is arguably why Whitehead (1968: 36), who was always at pains to avoid fundamental bifurcations, once described the experience of thought as 'a tremendous form of excitement. Like a stone thrown into a pond', he suggested,

> it disturbs the whole surface of our being. But this image is inadequate. For we should conceive the ripples as effective in the creation of the plunge of the stone into the water. The ripples release the thought, and the thought augments and distorts the ripples. In order to understand the essence of thought, we must study its relation to the ripples amid which it emerges. (1968: 36)

As I suggested above, speculation begins in the midst of experience, and it constructively seeks to arrive at a novel empirical situation. It risks a thought that proposes itself to the world and in so doing affects the patterns by which things might come to matter. To be sure, the rippling effect may not always succeed in leading us towards better ends. It might not always affect the patterns of relevance in such a way that a path towards a future that be more than the mere extension of its immediate past can be opened up. In this sense, speculative *propositions* or theories should be taken less in a logical sense—as statements containing a subject and a predicate whose primary function is to be judged as to their truth or falsehood, in terms of how they correspond to a given state of affairs[12]—and might be better approached in a political sense, that is, as an invitation that is put into play in relation to a problematic situation from which it extracts its sense and which it seeks to modify.

As 'tales that perhaps might be told about particular actualities' (Whitehead 1978: 256), the putting into play of speculative propositions is always doubly risky. Like with other inventions, the milieus to which speculative propositions relate constitute themselves a risk, placing the question of their efficacy as an unknown that, as I argued above, cannot be tamed by the guarantees of a method. But as Judith Schlanger (1983: 255) has noted, moreover, with speculative propositions the failure to modify the experience of a situation also oftentimes leads to a failure to gain admission into a pre-existent standard of rationality. That is, they face the risk of being disqualified as nonsense, or as mere theoretical exercises that do not matter to anyone, anywhere.

To characterise the risks of speculation in this way is to suggest, then, that making thought creative of the future is neither a process of unilateral effectuation or 'performativity' that simply takes the effect of intellectual efforts for granted, nor a process of probabilistic anticipation that relies too firmly on the supposed security of a given method. Rather, it involves the wager, but never the promise, that a situation might become responsive to our thinking. That our propositions, launched into the developing edge of the present, might find a response so that they themselves might become practically responsive to the problems that the pres-

---

[12] This is not to say that speculative propositions are not to be judged as to their truth or falsehood. What this means is that their possible truth is not *primary* nor inherent in them, but is an event that can happen to them. As James (2011: 141, emphasis in original) was at pains to argue, 'truth *happens* to an idea, it becomes true, it is made true by events. Its verity is in fact an event, the process namely of verifying itself, its veri*fication*.'

ent poses. Speculative experimentation affirms the world and attempts to make a contribution, however small or modest, to the world's own adventures of ideas. We all know by now that we can never be sure where an adventure might take us.

## Conclusion: It Matters What Tales We Tell Other Tales With

Speculative experimentation constitutes a mode of thought that surveys the variety of contemporary facts of experience and constructively experiments with the possibilities that inhere therein by producing propositions that wager upon the becoming of a different future. Now, to the extent that it bets on a different mode of transitioning between present and future to the one that might obtain without the intervention of thought, the experimental mode of speculation that I have proposed is not the name for what we would normally call a method, for to call it a method in that sense would presuppose that all bets are off. That it has itself some secure foothold on the becoming of the future. And neither does this pragmatic mode of speculation designate a new grand theory, for although it may rely on more abstract speculative cosmologies, the latter have no transcendental footholds either—immanently, they seek to articulate worlds, thoughts, and thinkers.

If speculative propositions are tales that might be told about the world and its inhabitants, tales that might allow for the construction of new experiences, what thinking speculatively *for* speculation entails, rather, is an attempt to begin to cultivate a different mode of thought, another set of intellectual sensibilities, another ethics of theoretical imagination.

By affirming thinking as both an element and factor in the fact of experience, a speculative ethic of theoretical imagination seeks to incorporate and expand Donna Haraway's (2011: 4) lesson,[13] that '[i]t matters what matters we use to think other matters with; it matters what stories we tell to tell other stories with; it matters what knots knot knots, what thoughts think thoughts, what ties tie ties. It matters what stories make

---
[13] A lesson she herself learned from Marilyn Strathern (1992: 10).

worlds, what worlds make stories.' Thus, precisely *because* the future can only be waged upon, precisely because it requires the risking of a thought whose success is never guaranteed but whose sheer possibility is a lure for an opening towards a different experience, that theory, in this speculative key, matters. It matters what tales we might tell other tales with. To make its possibility perceptible, to allow speculation to come to matter, is already to engage in it, to propose propositions, to experiment with experiments, to risk thinking thoughts that may allow us to take the risk of thinking.

# 8

# Afterword: Becoming an Apprentice

By undertaking a speculative exercise in reconstruction, in this book I have sought to produce a series of intellectual instruments that might make possible a different care of knowledge in the contemporary social sciences. The speculative task of making possibles has here forced me to reconsider the place that the concept of relevance has, and may have, in relation to the articulation of a different mode of social inquiry. One that rather than understanding itself as an exercise in estrangement from the facts of experience, would embark on the adventures that are opened up in the transitions between events, a transitional present characterised by the double challenge of inheriting a past while becoming exposed to the possibilities of a different world to come. It is such an ethics of inquiry, one that might find expression in the situated question of 'how is it, here, that things matter?' that I have associated with the adventure of relevance and which I have attempted throughout the preceding chapters to endow with some of the constraints that may enable its possibility to be made perceptible.

Some of these constraints have led me to explore and seek to articulate a series of propositions concerning the inventive nature of knowledge-practices, as requiring a coming to terms with the immanent obligations that objects of inquiry may pose; the need to articulate, in practice, the taking of risks in the articulation of a manner of encountering objects of inquiry such that the encounter might prove fertile; an account of the efficacy of knowledge that does not forget the active roles of the many milieus with which the former connects and which is attentive to the emergent, circulating, and often perplexing forms of causality that connections set in motion; a concern for a more-than-human world of events that does not disavow our attachments to human experience nor the possibility of emergent and always precarious forms of order; as well as the possibility of a mode of theorising characterised not by the distrust of experience but by the active experimentation with the possibles that experiences in the present may herald, such that paths to novel empirical situations may be opened up.

As I suggested in the introduction to the book, the ethical question to be entertained here was not the normative, general question of 'what is the good?' or 'what is evil?' but rather the practical, situated question of 'how is one to live?'. Above all, then, the ethics of inquiry that I have here sought to cultivate is one that will find no foothold in stable, universal, anonymous foundations, but which can only extract its possible sense from the very situations from which it seeks to learn, in relation to which it immanently operates, by virtue of which it might become alive.

If the adventure of relevance could be said to be a way of responding, or perhaps more appropriately, a mode of inheriting and entertaining the question 'how is one to know?' that I associated with the care of knowledge, it does so not by offering a final response which could be said to be 'ethical', but rather by attempting to make the question resonate with each encounter. It thus forces one to come to terms with the fact that the question does not tell one how to respond, even though it demands that responses be invented. What is at stake, rather, is the possibility of enabling the question itself to exist in its own right, as an open problem to be developed. Taking the question of relevance seriously, then, does not involve the acquisition of a piece of knowledge, a procedure, or a faculty that might provide social scientists with ready responses to how they are to know. Rather, it attempts to situate those who do take it seriously in a process of *learning*, immanently and without recourse to transcendental principles, how to invent responses that matter. To embark on an adventure of relevance is, in effect, to conjoin the challenge of knowing with the challenge of learning how to know.

I will return to this issue below, but for now it should be noted that this double challenge does not *only* concern a care of knowledge but, simultaneously, a care of the self and a care of the world. As I have suggested in the introduction to the book, if the task of reconstruction is to become more than a mere theoretical exercise that, as Dewey (2008b: 39) would say, 'makes no difference anywhere', these two dimensions cannot be conceived as disentangled. Knowledge-practices are neither just technologies of the self, nor simply practices of world-making, but what we might call *techniques of habitation*—habits that inventively articulate a multiplicity of other habits, of ways of existing in the world, and of heterogeneous patterns of relevance that compose a situation—that is, a habitat—while they themselves become added to, and thus alter, the composition of the situation.

What might follow from this is that the site of a care of knowledge belongs to what Stengers (2011c: 164) has named 'etho-ecology'—the conjunction of '*ethos*, the way of behaving peculiar to a being, and *oikos*, the habitat of that being and the way in which that habitat satisfies or opposes the demands associated with the ethos or affords opportunities for an original ethos to risk itself.' To cultivate a care of knowledge, as I have tried to articulate it, is to explore the intimate connections between a care of the self and care of the world; it is to think in terms of habitation. That is, to conjoin, in one and the same problem, the mutation of the habits that animate certain ways of response with the constraints and possibilities of transformation that their respective habitats may provide. Thinking in terms of habitation is, I believe, crucial, for it may help us avoid two distinct but complementary dangers that emerge as a consequence of overemphasising, deliberately or not, only one of these dimensions at the expense of the other.

The first danger was already alluded to in the Introduction. It is that which emerges from over-emphasising the dimension of the care of the self at the expense of the care of the world. The later work of Michel Foucault (1984a, 1990) on ethics, subjectivity, and truth has, for example, been the focus of such a reading. Having centred his later work around practices of self-problematisation and self-formation in the

Greco-Roman period as ethical 'exercise[s] of self on the self by which one attempts to develop and transform oneself' (Foucault 1997a: 282), a number of readers of Foucault have taken his explorations as having a certain culture of the self, that is, an aesthetics of self-fashioning, as their sole aim.

While some authors have endorsed such a turn, arguing that it constitutes a welcome move away from a pervasive habit in the humanities of overstating claims as to the *political* effects of their practices of knowledge-making (Guillory 2000), others have suggested that the turn to the care of the self poses the danger of reducing thought to a therapeutics (Myers 2013: 21–52). In this sense, philosopher and classicist Pierre Hadot (1995: 207)—from whose work Foucault took inspiration to develop his inquiry into the techniques of the self of the Greco-Roman period—has argued that, when compared to the ancient texts on which such a project is based, Foucault's concerns are 'precisely focused far too much on the "self," or at least on a specific conception of the self.' According to Hadot, what Foucault's particular emphasis ignores is that '[t]he psychic content of these exercises seems […] to be something else entirely. In my view, the feeling of belonging to a whole is an essential element: belonging, that is, both to the whole constituted by the human community, and to that constituted by the cosmic whole' (Hadot 1995: 208).

This is hardly the place for me to judge how accurate Foucault's readings of the Stoics and the Platonists might be, or whether this overemphasis on the culture of the self can in fact be ascribed to his work or not. It seems to me, however, that the danger is nevertheless present for anyone who engages the question of ethics in these terms. Beyond the matter of the exegesis of the Greeks, what Hadot's quotation above makes present is that in order to avoid turning the care of the self into a therapeutics, into a question of an exercise by the self in order to heal oneself, one must conceive of such exercises as simultaneously involving a certain care of the world, a practice that is not simply 'of the self on the self' but with the self, with others, and with the world. In other words, once the very distinction between self and world that becomes troubled, an exercise of transforming one's own manner of existing in the world does not set aside, but requires a reciprocal transformation, however modest, of the world's own manner of existing. The troubling of the self-world distinction in ethics must avoid, however, a second potential danger, which is that of *grounding* a care of the self and a care of knowledge on a pre-established definition of what it means to take care of the world. By this I do not mean to say that in order to entertain the question of the care of knowledge one has to avoid any and every ontological commitment. I agree with Connolly (1995: 9) that the issue is not whether one cultivates certain ontological commitments or not, but whether one belongs to those 'who suppress the "onto" in political interpretation' as well as in epistemic, ethical and ecological thinking, or to 'those who diverge about how to engage it.' The crucial point, however, is to avoid simply deducing one's thinking from those commitments, and instead to seek to articulate and cultivate thinking, commitments and sensibilities, together. Thus, to suggest that the care of knowledge involves a care of the world does not mean that the latter precedes and informs the former, but that the two are, precisely, *involved*—entangled, folded with each other.

As I have shown in preceding chapters, the particular care of knowledge that I have called an 'ethics of estrangement' involves the modern metaphysical presupposition that Whitehead (2004) termed the 'bifurcation of nature'—a world split into two realms that distribute and organise causes and effects, subjects and objects, facts and values, nature and culture, appearance and the really real, and so forth. I have suggested that the bifurcation of nature and the ethics of estrangement could be seen as having contributed to some of the challenges—intellectual, institutional, and ecological—that the contemporary social sciences are now confronted with. In order to begin to cultivate a different ethics of inquiry, I argued, it was required that we question *both* their ethos and their metaphysical assumptions, and entertain the question of 'how is one to know' in way that involved a non-bifurcated, eventful world.

To say that a different ethics of inquiry *requires* putting aspects of modern metaphysics into question is to foreground the fact that the questioning is a *pragmatic* one, that is, one founded on nothing but an art of consequences. For this reason, I have at all times attempted to refrain from suggesting that 'we have never' lived in such a bifurcated world. In contrast, by discussing the assumptions underpinning contemporary demands for relevance as well as by entertaining the implications that may follow from the idea of the Capitalocene, I have been more interested in the *consequences* of such metaphysical assumptions and of such an ethics of inquiry than in whether or not they have ever been 'true' or adequate *in principle*.[1] They certainly have had effects, and it is those effects that matter. It is in relation to them, and not in spite of them, that a reconstruction is to be carried out.

In order to attempt to resist those effects and to open up the possibility of alternative futures—and thus, of alternative consequences—from the outset I have sought to produce some of the instruments required to *propose* a different care of knowledge that would directly *involve* a different care of the world—a care for a world characterised by the relevance of existence and the existence of relevance, a care for what Whitehead (1968: 111) would otherwise call 'value experience', the experience that things matter, that '[e]verything has some value for itself, for others and for the whole' such that '[e]xistence, in its own nature, is the upholding of value intensity' (1968: 111).

Thus, if the adventure of relevance cultivates commitments that can be associated with a certain process metaphysics, it does so only on condition that one does not forget the *speculative* nature of Whitehead's—and in my reading, of James's—philosophy. By this I mean, of course, that neither my commitments nor theirs need to be accepted as incontestable matters of fact. By contrast, as Stengers (2009b: 104) has argued in relation to Whitehead's propositions: '[t]hat which decides between their failure and success is indeed the transformation of emphasis that they must be able to produce with regard to the powerful and pragmatically justified abstractions which lure and sometimes dominate our experiences'. As I argued in Chap. 7, speculative propositions do not work by making us think differently, as if by the flick of a Gestalt-switch, but they work by *proposing* themselves to a situation such that a path to a novel experience, composed by different contrasts, by different patterns of relevance, may become available. Whether such propositions will be taken

---

[1] Put differently, what has indeed been contested is the upholding of such assumptions as true by virtue of a transhistorical, infallible, universal principle. Thus, I can entertain the modern ethos and its metaphysical assumptions only to the extent that they are seen as involving *weak* rather than *strong* ontological assumptions. Namely, assumptions that are fallible, open to contestation, and open to historical transformation (on weak ontologies see White 2000).

## 8 Afterword: Becoming an Apprentice

up or not by those who might entertain them is another matter, one that no argument could here guarantee.

Be that as it may, it seems to me that, having dealt with the question of the care of the world at some length throughout the preceding chapters, what needs to be explored in these remaining pages is the question of *who* might emerge from an adventure, what kind of social scientist—to be cultivated—an inquiry into a world of events that matter might involve. Indeed, as I have suggested, there is no telling where an adventure might take us. But it *can happen*, Cortázar's (2011: 57, emphasis added) poem intimates, 'it can happen that we might enter parks in Jaipur or Delhi, or in the heart of Saint-Germain-des-Prés *we might brush against another possible profile of man*'. Thus, what I shall attempt as a manner of concluding is a brief delineation—just as speculative; or perhaps more than speculative, 'to be read in the interrogative', as Cortázar (1997) would put it elsewhere—of a possible scientific *persona* that such a care of knowledge might involve.

I should first make clear that in addressing the question of a *persona*—rather than of a 'self'—I am not attempting to explore the individual experience of embarking on an adventure of relevance, of which the encounters discussed in Chap. 4 might perhaps provide a much better account than I ever could, for the concrete form of adventure and of its experience depends on the specificity of the encounter in question. By contrast, as some historians of science have suggested by drawing on the seminal work of Marcel Mauss (see Daston and Sibum 2003: 2. see also Daston and Galison 2010), the persona is an '[i]ntermediate between individual biography and the social institution […] a cultural identity that simultaneously shapes the individual in body and mind and creates a collective with a shared and recognizable physiognomy.' Rather than individual persons, what is at stake then is the possibility of a *type* of scientist.

But here another distinction is called for. For in the work of historians, the scientific persona, if still conceptual, is *actual*, emerging from the encounters of the biographical, institutional, and public routes of inheritance that bring certain scientific figures into existence. Thus, '[p]ersonae are creatures of historical circumstance; they emerge and disappear within specific contexts. A nascent persona indicates the creation of a new kind of individual, whose distinct traits mark a recognized social species' (Daston and Sibum 2003: 3). They are 'an ethical and epistemological code imagined as a self' (Daston and Galison 2010: 204).

What Lorraine Daston and H. Otto Sibum (2003) call 'scientific personae', or 'scientific selves' (Daston and Galison 2010), are thus akin to what Deleuze and Guattari (1994: 67) would call 'psychosocial types'. Namely, empirical types emerging from socio-historical fields, whose discernment may teach us something about the movements and forces that characterise such fields, or equally, about the collective habits, cultivated epistemic virtues and ideals, and the shared fears, dreams, and hopes, that identify certain scientific and social scientific practices.

In this way, by advancing the hypothesis that 'all epistemology begins in fear', Daston and Galison (2010: 372) show that, '[d]epending on which threat to knowledge was perceived as most acute at that moment, the scientific self was exhorted to take epistemological precautions to redress the excesses of both the active and the passive cognition of nature, and to practice four-eyed or blind sight.' While '[f]or Enlightenment savants, the passivity of the sensationalist self was problematic', for 'nineteenth-century scientists the subjective self was viewed as overactive and prone to impose its preconceptions and pet hypotheses on data. Therefore, these scientists strove for a self-denying passivity, which might be described as the will to willnessness, or as a multitude of techniques of 'self—imposed selflessness' (Daston and Galison 2010: 203).

But because psychosocial types depend upon a milieu of socio-historical forces, of disciplinary habits and of biographical features, they cannot be entirely determined by an exercise in speculative thought. Indeed, to the extent that they constitute regulative ideals that operate at given historical and disciplinary moments, to propose a 'new' psychosocial type that would correspond to the care of knowledge that I have called an adventure would turn the latter into a highly normative and disciplinary proposition, or indeed into a moral injunction for contemporary social scientists to inhabit a predefined mode of being.

To the extent that I am here experimenting with the possibility of giving a provisional, personalised name to this project, my sense that is one should think of it in terms closer to what Deleuze and Guattari (1994) would call *conceptual personae*, which, for their part, 'are irreducible to psychosocial types, even if here again there are constant penetrations'

(1994: 76). For, unlike psychosocial types, conceptual personae do not emerge out of empirical, psychological, and social determinations, but are the sole product of thinking, or perhaps more appropriately, they are those characters of which thinking is a product. Conceptual personae are do not emerge from a certain manner of thought without simultaneously *animating* it, such that '[a] particular conceptual persona, who perhaps did not exist before us, thinks in us' (1994: 69). Thus, between conceptual personae and psychosocial types there is 'a conjunction, a system of referrals or perpetual relays.' While they relate to each other and combine, they never merge. For conceptual personae 'become susceptible to a determination purely of thinking and of thought that wrests them from both the historical state of affairs of a society and the lived experience of individuals, in order to turn them into [...] *thought-events* on the plane laid out by thought or under the concepts it creates' (1994: 70).

How might we characterise the figure animating and being animated by an adventure? What name may we give to that conceptual persona that wanders in the night, wondering about how things matter in a given situation, about how to inherit an event, asking questions, putting them at risk, becoming exposed, making mistakes, inventing errantly towards the possibility that something might be learned? Which character, in other words, might be capable of merging the challenge of knowing with the challenge of learning how to know?

As I have suggested in previous chapters, it is certainly not a hero, but someone—or something—whose existence is entirely dependent upon encounters. Surely, neither can it be that of the public sociologist as characterised by Burawoy and others, because this character is concerned with the challenge of making sociology audible rather than wondering about how to listen. It is also not, or not yet, a 'diplomat', a conceptual persona Stengers (2011b) and Latour (2004b, 2014) have proposed in relation to their attempt to cultivate a 'non-modernist' social science. For the diplomat is the one who inhabits the tensions inherent in the problem of translation and the risk of betraying those she represents (Stengers 2011b: 374–385), but who seems to know how to read that which requires translating. While there might be some family resemblances, its name can neither be that of the 'idiot', a conceptual persona that Deleuze (with and without Guattari), Stengers (2005) and others have proposed and developed. For the idiot is the one responsible for provoking thought, for slowing others down, rather than letting his or her thinking be provoked by an encounter.

My sense is that all of these conceptual personae have crucial affinities and may, at specific points, require each other, and work together. So rather than replace them, I propose to add to them another character whose name I will borrow, again, from Deleuze (1994), but who also sometimes can be seen animating the thought of Dewey (1922), Serres (1997) and Cortázar (2011)—this is *the apprentice*. The apprentice is not the one who knows, not even the one who learns, but the one whose *problem* is that of learning, of inquiring, of learning how to know. Because she exists only in relation to practical and speculative problems that demand inquiry (Deleuze 1994: 164), and '[n]o learning can avoid the voyage' (Serres 1997: 8), the apprentice always finds herself after events she has to construct ways inheriting, in encounters with problems she has to invent a way of developing, and she wonders about how to sense and respond to the patterns of relevance that compose them.

She wonders because what she does know about learning—or rather, about failing to learn—is that the risk is either to become *one* with the problematic situation, or to force the situation to become one with herself, to reduce it by approaching it in terms of what she already knows. In contrast, she has to inquire, to learn to invent a manner of coming to know a situation, bearing in mind that '[w]e never know in advance how someone will learn: by means of what loves someone becomes good at Latin, what encounters make them a philosopher, or in what dictionaries they learn to think' (Deleuze 1994: 165), and that there is no telling as to what may bring about the event of knowing. Nevertheless, she keeps on trying. Because learning is that which occurs only in relation to problematic situations, and because it requires becoming *with* them—which is not to say becoming *them*—she inquires so as to allow the situation to become her teacher—she inquires into it so as to learn, in her own manner, how to know about it. As Deleuze (1994: 23) puts it, 'we learn nothing from those who say: "Do as I do". Our only teachers are those who tell us to "do with me", and are able to emit signs to be developed in heterogeneity rather than propose gestures for us to reproduce.'

To be sure, the apprentice has many techniques and methods at her disposal, but she is not in possession of a procedure that would lead her safely to knowledge. For if that were the case, learning would not be part of her problem but simply the means to an end. What she does instead is attempt to cultivate, by putting herself at risk in the encounter, by effecting piecemeal, practical transitions upon the situation and upon herself, the manner by which to learn how to relate to the demands that the situation poses. Thus, she cultivates a certain docility to that which demands to be learned, a docility that, as Dewey (1922: 97) reminds us, should not be confused with conformity, or with submission to the power of education, but with a humble yet inventive capacity to 're-make old habits, to re-create': '[t]o be truly docile is to be eager to learn all the lessons of active, inquiring, expanding experience' (Dewey 1922: 64). The aim of the apprentice is not to provide a solution to the problem that identifies a situation, but to risk inventing a manner of understanding how the problem may be defined, and how it might be developed. There is no other solution.

Occupying the problem of learning, of learning how to know and of knowing how to learn, the apprentice risks propositions, attends to the objections that the situation poses, makes mistakes; has to start over, alter the questions, try again without guarantees. Exposed to the possibility that her efforts might bring about something new, sometimes they do contribute to making the encounter fertile, and her inventions become successful, allowing for the problem to be experienced differently, in a way that matters for those with whom it is concerned. It is this event that she calls 'knowledge'. Events, however, are as much achievements as they are openings, and 'knowing' does not mark an end but a transition, the beginning of a new adventure.

# References

Adkins, L., & Lury, C. (2009). Introduction: What is the empirical? *European Journal of Social Theory, 12*(1), 5–20.

Allport, F. H. (1919). Behavior and experiment in social psychology. *Journal of Abnormal Psychology, 14*, 297–306.

Althusser, L. (1971). *Lenin and philosophy and other essays*. New York: Monthly Review Press.

Althusser, L. (2006). *Philosophy of the encounter: Later writings, 1978–1987*. London: Verso.

Amoore, L. (2013). *The politics of possibility: Risk and security beyond probability*. Durham, NC: Duke University Press.

Asad, T. (1993). *Genealogies of religion: Discipline and reasons of power in Christianity and Islam*. Baltimore: Johns Hopkins University Press.

Attridge, D., Bennington, G., & Young, R. (1989). *Post-structuralism and the question of history*. Cambridge: Cambridge University Press.

Atwood, M. (2011). *In other worlds: SF and the human imagination*. London: Virago.

Austin, J. (1975). *How to do things with words*. Cambridge, MA: Harvard University Press.

Barad, K. (2007). *Meeting the universe halfway: Quantum physics and the entanglement of matter and meaning*. Durham, NC: Duke University Press.

Barnes, B., Bloor, D., & Henry, J. (1996). *Scientific knowledge: A sociological analysis*. Chicago, IL: University of Chicago Press.

Becker, H. (2007). *Telling about society*. Chicago, IL: University of Chicago Press.

Bell, V. (2007). *Culture and performance: The challenge of politics, ethics and feminist theory*. Oxford, England: Berg.

Bell, V. (2008). From performativity to ecology: On Judith Butler and matters of survival. *Subjectivity, 25*, 395–412.

Bensa, A., & Fassin, E. (2002). Les sciences sociales face à l'événement. *Terrain: Revue d'ethnologie de l'Europe, 38*, 5–20.

Bergson, H. (2007). *The creative mind*. Mineola, NY: Dover Publications.

Bergson, H. (2011). *Time and free will*. Mineola, NY: Dover Publications.

Bijker, W. E., & Law, J. (1992). *Shaping technology/building society: Studies in sociotechnical change*. Cambridge, MA: Harvard University Press.

Blackman, L. (2012). *Immaterial bodies: Affect, embodiment, mediation*. London: Sage.

Bloom, H. (1997). *The anxiety of influence: A theory of poetry*. New York: Oxford University Press.

Bloom, H. (1999). *Shakespeare: The invention of the human*. London: Fourth Estate.

Bloom, H. (2003). *Genius: A mosaic of one hundred exemplary creative minds*. New York: Warner Books.

Bloor, D. (1977). *Knowledge & social imagery*. London: Routledge & Kegan Paul.

Boland, T. (2013). Critique is a thing of this world: Towards a genealogy of critique. *History of the Human Sciences, 27*(1), 108–123.

Boltanski, L. (2011). *On critique: A sociology of emancipation*. Cambridge, MA: Polity Press.

Boltanski, L., & Chiapello, E. (2005). *The new spirit of capitalism*. London: Verso.

Bourdieu, P. (1992). *Language & symbolic power*. Cambridge, MA: Polity Press.

Braudel, F. (1982). *On history*. Chicago, IL: University of Chicago Press.

Brenkman, J., Lloyd, E., & Albert, D. (2000). *The Sokal hoax: The sham that shook the academy*. Lincoln, NE: University of Nebraska Press.

Brewer, J. D. (2013). *The public value of the social sciences: An interpretive essay*. London: Bloomsbury Academic.

Brown, S. (2011). Rats, elephants, and bees as matters of concern. *Common Knowledge, 17*(1), 71–76.

Brown, S., & Stenner, P. (2009). *Psychology Without Foundations: History, Philosophy and Psycho-Social Theory*. London: Sage.
Bruce, S. (1992). *Religion and modernization: Sociologists and historians debate the secularization thesis*. Oxford, England: Clarendon.
Bryant, L. (2011). *The democracy of objects*. Ann Arbor, MI: Open Humanities Press.
Bryant, L., Srniceck, N., & Harman, G. (2011). *The speculative turn*. Melbourne, VC: re.press.
Burawoy, M. (2005). For public sociology. *American Sociological Review, 70*(1), 4–28.
Burrows, R. (2012). Living with the h-index? Metric assemblages in the contemporary academy. *The Sociological Review, 60*(2), 355–372.
Butler, J. (1990). *Gender trouble: Feminism and the subversion of identity*. London: Routledge.
Butler, J. (1997). *The psychic life of power: Theories in subjection*. Stanford, CA: Stanford University Press.
Butler, J. (2005). *Giving an account of oneself*. New York: Fordham University Press.
Butler, J. (2007). Performative agency. *Journal of Cultural Economy, 3*(2), 147–161.
Butler, J., Guillory, J., & Thomas, K. (2000). *What's left of theory? New work on the politics of literary theory*. New York: Routledge.
Bynum, C. W. (2001). *Metamorphosis and identity*. New York: Zone Books.
Callon, M. (1986). Some elements of a sociology of translation: Domestication of the scallops and the fishermen of Saint Brieuc Bay. In J. Law (Ed.), *Power, action and belief: A new sociology of knowledge?* (pp. 196–233). London: Routledge and Kegan Paul.
Callon, M. (1998). *The laws of the markets*. Oxford, England: Blackwell Publishers.
Callon, M. (2007). Performativity, misfires and politics. *Journal of Cultural Economy, 3*(2), 162–169.
Canguilhem, G. (2008). *Knowledge of life*. New York: Fordham University Press.
Caso, J., & Sanders, P. B. (1977). *Rodin's sculpture: A critical study of the spreckels collection*. Rutland: Charles E. Tuttle.
Cassin, B. (2014). *Sophistical practice: Toward a consistent relativism*. New York: Fordham University Press.
Certeau, M. (1985). What we do when we believe. In M. Blonsky (Ed.), *On signs* (pp. 192–202). Baltimore: Johns Hopkins University Press.

Certeau, M. (1992). *The writing of history*. New York: Columbia University Press.
Certeau, M. (1997). *The capture of speech & other political writings*. Minneapolis, MN: University of Minnesota Press.
Chakrabarty, D. (2008). The public life of history: An argument out of India. *Postcolonial Studies, 11*(2), 160–190.
Chakrabarty, D. (2012). Postcolonial studies and the challenge of climate change. *New Literary History, 43*(1), 1–18.
Clairborne Park, C. (2005). Author! Author! reconstructing Roland Barthes. In D. Patai & W. H. Corral (Eds.), *Theory's empire: An anthology of dissent* (pp. 318–330). New York: Columbia University Press.
Clark, E. (2004). *History, theory, text*. Cambridge, MA: Harvard University Press.
Clifford, J. (1986). Introduction: Partial truths. In J. Clifford & G. E. Marcus (Eds.), *Writing culture: The poetics and politics of ethnography* (pp. 1–26). Berkeley, CA: University of California Press.
Clifford, J., & Marcus, G. E. (1986). *Writing culture: The poetics and politics of ethnography*. Berkeley, CA: University of California Press.
Colander, D., Goldberg, M., Haas, A., Juselius, K., Kirman, A., Lux, T., et al. (2009). The financial crisis and the systemic failure of the economics profession. *Critical Review: A Journal of Politics and Society, 21*(2-3), 249–267.
Colebrook, C. (2014). *Death of the PostHuman: Essays on extinction* (Vol. 1). Ann Arbor, MI: Open Humanities Press.
Collins, P. H. (2000). *Black feminist thought: Knowledge, consciousness and the politics of empowerment*. London: Routledge.
Collins, P. H. (2007). Going public: Doing the sociology that had no name. In D. Clawson, R. Zussman, J. Misra, N. Gerstel, R. Stokes, A. L. Douglas, & M. Burawoy (Eds.), *Public sociology: Fifteen eminent sociologists debate politics and the profession in the twenty-first century* (pp. 101–113). Berkeley, CA: University of California Press.
Collins, H. M., & Yearley, S. (1992). Epistemological chicken. In A. Pickering (Ed.), *Science as practice and culture* (pp. 301–326). Chicago, IL: Chicago University Press.
Connolly, W. (1995). *The ethos of pluralization*. Minneapolis, MN: University of Minnesota Press.
Connolly, W. (2002). *Neuropolitics: Thinking, culture, speed*. Minneapolis, MN: University of Minnesota Press.
Connolly, W. (2011). *A world of becoming*. Durham, NC: Duke University Press.

Connolly, W. (2013). *The fragility of things: Self-organizing processes, neoliberal fantasies, and democratic activism.* Durham, NC: Duke University Press.
Cortázar, J. (1966). *Hopscotch.* New York: Pantheon Books.
Cortázar, J. (1997). *Save twilight: Selected poems* (pp. 3–5). San Francisco, CA: City Light Books.
Cortázar, J. (2011). *From the observatory.* Brooklyn, NY: Archipelago Books.
Crutzen, P. J., & Stoermer, E. F. (2000). The 'Anthropocene'. *Global Change Newsletter, 41,* 17–18.
Danziger, K. (1990). *Constructing the subject: Historical origins of psychological research.* Cambridge: Cambridge University Press.
Daston, L. (2009). Science studies and the history of science. *Critical Inquiry, 35*(4), 798–813.
Daston, L., & Galison, P. (2010). *Objectivity.* Brooklyn, NY: Zone Books.
Daston, L., & Park, K. (2003). *Wonders and the order of nature, 1150–1750.* Brooklyn, NY: Zone Books.
Daston, L., & Sibum, O. (2003). Introduction: Scientific personae and their histories. *Science in Context, 16*(1-2), 1–8.
Deleuze, G. (1994). *Difference and repetition.* New York: Columbia University Press.
Deleuze, G. (2004). *The logic of sense.* London: Continuum.
Deleuze, G. (2007). *Two regimes of madness: Texts and interviews 1975–1995.* New York: Semiotext(e).
Deleuze, G., & Guattari, F. (1987). *A thousand plateaus.* Minneapolis, MN: University of Minnesota Press.
Deleuze, G., & Guattari, F. (1994). *What is philosophy?* London: Verso.
Deleuze, G., & Parnett, C. (2006). *Dialogues II.* London: Continuum.
Derrida, J. (1976). *Of grammatology.* Baltimore, MD: Johns Hopkins University Press.
Derrida, J. (1992). *Limited Inc.* Evanston, IL: Northwestern University Press.
Derrida, J. (2001). *Writing and difference.* Chicago, IL: University of Chicago Press.
Despret, V. (2004). *Our emotional makeup: Ethnopsychology and selfhood.* New York: Other Press.
Despret, V. (2008). The becomings of subjectivity in animal worlds. *Subjectivity, 23,* 123–139.
Dewey, J. (1922). *Human nature and conduct: An introduction to social psychology.* New York: Henry Holt and Company.
Dewey, J. (1989). *The public and its problems.* Athens, OH: Ohio University Press.
Dewey, J. (1998). *Experience and nature.* Mineola, NY: Dover Publications.

Dewey, J. (2004). *Reconstruction in philosophy*. Mineola, NY: Dover Publications.
Dewey, J. (2008a). *Logic: The theory of inquiry*. Carbondale, IL: Southern Illinois University.
Dewey, J. (2008b). *The quest for certainty*. Carbondale: Southern Illinois University Press.
Didier, E. (2007). Do statistics "perform" the economy? In D. MacKenzie, F. Muniesa, & L. Siu (Eds.), *Do economists make markets? On the performativity of economics* (pp. 276–310). Princeton, NJ: Princeton University Press.
Didi-Huberman, G. (2012). *Images in spite of it all: Four photographs from Auschwitz*. Chicago, IL: University of Chicago Press.
Dosse, F. (1999). *Empire of meaning: The humanization of the social sciences*. Minneapolis: University of Minnesota Press.
Dosse, F. (2010). *Renaissance de l'événement. Un défi pour l'historien: entre sphinx et phénix*. Paris: PUF.
du Gay, P. (2007). Performatives: Butler, Callon and the moment of theory. *Journal of Cultural Economy, 3*(2), 171–179.
Eagleton, T. (2003). *After theory*. London: Penguin Books.
Eakin, E. (2003). The latest theory is that theory doesn't matter. *The New York Times* (online). Retrieved May 2, 2014, from http://www.nytimes.com
Eco, U. (1992). *Interpretation and overinterpretation*. Cambridge: Cambridge University Press.
Economic and Social Research Council. (2014). Social science disciplines (online). Retrieved July 1, 2014, from http://www.esrc.ac.uk/about-esrc/what-is-social-science/social-science-disciplines.aspx
Elliot, J., & Attridge, D. (2011). *Theory after 'Theory'*. Abingdon, England: Routledge.
Ericson, R. V., & Doyle, A. (2004). Catastrophe risk, insurance and terrorism. *Economy & Society, 33*(2), 135–173.
European Commission. (2014). Societal challenges-horizon 2020. Retrieved July 1, 2014, from http://ec.europa.eu/programmes/horizon2020/en/h2020-section/societal-challenges
Faubion, J. D., & Marcus, G. E. (2009). *Fieldwork is not what it used to be: Learning anthropology's method in a time of transition*. Ithaca, NY: Cornell University Press.
Felt, U. (2014). Within, across and beyond: Reconsidering the role of social sciences and humanities in Europe. *Science as Culture, 23*(3), 384–396.
Feyerabend, P. (2010). *Against method*. London: Verso.
Flinders, M. (2013). The tyranny of relevance and the art of translation. *Political Studies Review, 11*(2), 149–167.

Foucault, M. (1980). *Language, counter-memory, practice: Selected essays and interviews*. Ithaca, NY: Cornell University Press.
Foucault, M. (1981). The order of discourse. In R. Young (Ed.), *Untying the text: A post-structuralist reader* (pp. 48–78). London: Routledge & Keegan Paul.
Foucault, M. (1984a). *The use of pleasure: The history of sexuality* (Vol. 2). London: Penguin.
Foucault, M. (1984b). Politics, polemics and problematizations: An interview with Michel Foucault. In P. Rabinow (Ed.), *The Foucault reader* (pp. 381–390). London: Penguin.
Foucault, M. (1990). *The care of the self: The history of sexuality* (Vol. 3). London: Penguin.
Foucault, M. (1994). *The order of things: An archeology of the human sciences*. London: Vintage.
Foucault, M. (1997a). The ethics of the concern for the self as a practice of freedom. In P. Rabinow (Ed.), *Ethics, subjectivity and truth: Essential works of Foucault 1954–1984* (pp. 281–302). New York: The New Press.
Foucault, M. (1997b). What is enlightenment? In P. Rabinow (Ed.), *Ethics, subjectivity and truth: Essential Works of Foucault 1954–1984* (pp. 303–320). New York: The New Press.
Foucault, M. (2002). *The archeology of knowledge*. London: Routledge.
Foucault, M. (2007). *Security, territory, population: Lectures at the College the France, 1977–78*. Hampshire, England: Palgrave Macmillan.
Fraser, M. (2009). Experiencing sociology. *European Journal of Social Theory, 12*, 63–81.
Fraser, M. (2010). Facts, ethics and event. In C. B. Jensen & K. Rödje (Eds.), *Deleuzian intersections: Science, technology, anthropology* (pp. 57–82). New York: Berghahn Books.
Garcia, T. (2014). *Form and object: A treatise on things*. Edinburgh: Edinburgh University Press.
Geertz, C. (1973). *The interpretation of cultures*. New York: Basic Books.
Gibbons, M., Limoges, C., Nowotny, H., Schwartzman, S., Scott, P., & Trow, M. (1994). *The new production of knowledge: The dynamics of science and research in contemporary societies*. London: Sage.
Ginzburg, C. (2012). *Threads and traces: True, false, fictive*. Berkeley, CA: University of California Press.
Gilbert, N., & Mulkay, M. (1984). *Opening Pandora's Box: A sociological analysis of scientists' discourse*. Cambridge: Cambriddge University Press.
Guggenheim, M. (2012). Laboritizing and de-laboritizing the world: Changing sociological concepts for places of knowledge production. *History of the Human Sciences, 25*(1), 99–118.

Guillory, J. (2000). The ethical practice of modernity: The example of reading. In M. Garber, B. Hanssen, & R. Walkowitz (Eds.), *The turn to ethics*. New York: Routledge.

Gupta, A., & Ferguson, J. (1997). Discipline and practice: "The field" as site, method, and location in anthropology. In A. Gupta & J. Ferguson (Eds.), *Anthropological locations: Boundaries and grounds of a field science* (pp. 1–46). Berkeley, CA: University of California Press.

Hacking, I. (1983). *Representing and intervening: Introductory topics in the philosophy of natural science*. Cambridge: Cambridge University Press.

Hacking, I. (1986). Making up people. In T. Heller, M. Sosna, & D. Wellbery (Eds.), *Reconstructing individualism: Autonomy, individuality and the self in western thought* (pp. 222–236). Stanford, CA: Stanford University Press.

Hacking, I. (1990). *The taming of chance*. Cambridge: Cambridge University Press.

Hacking, I. (1999). *The social construction of what?* Cambridge, MA: Harvard University Press.

Hadot, P. (1995). *Philosophy as a way of life*. Oxford, England: Blackwell Publishers.

Halewood, M. (2011). *A.N. Whitehead and social theory: Tracing a culture of thought*. London: Anthem Press.

Hamilton, C., Bonneuil, C., & Gemenne, F. (2015). *The anthropocene and the global environmental crisis: Rethinking modernity in a new epoch*. Oxon, MD: Routledge.

Haraway, D. (1991). *Simians, cyborgs, and women: The reinvention of nature*. London: Free Association Books.

Haraway, D. (2008). *When species meet*. Minneapolis: University of Minnesota Press.

Haraway, D. (2011). *SF: Science fiction, speculative fabulation, string figures, so far*. Acceptance comments. The Pilgrim Award, Lublin, Poland. Retrieved May 2, 2014, from: http://people.ucsc.edu/~haraway/Files/PilgrimAcceptanceHaraway.pdf

Haraway, D. (2012, October 26) *Cosmopolitical critters: Companion species, SF, and staying with the trouble*. Lecture. Institute for Advanced Studies, University of London, Senate House.

Haraway D. (2014, July 8–10). *Anthropocene, Capitalocene, Chthulucene: Staying with the trouble*. Lecture. 'Arts of living in a damaged planet' Conference. Santa Cruz, California. Retrieved July 10, 2015, from http://vimeo.com/97663518

Harding, S. (1991). *Whose science? Whose knowledge? Thinking from women's lives*. Ithaca, NY: Cornell University Press.

Harding, S. (2008). *Sciences from below: Feminisms, postcolonialisms and modernities*. Durham, NC: Duke University Press.
Harman, G. (2010). *Towards speculative realism: Essays and lectures*. Hants, England: Zero Books.
Harman, G. (2013). The current state of speculative realism. *Speculations: A Journal of Speculative Realism, IV*, 22–28.
Hays, S. (2007). Stalled at the alter? Conflict hierarchy, and compartimentalization in Burawoy's public sociology. In D. Clawson, R. Zussman, J. Misra, N. Gerstel, R. Stokes, A. L. Douglas, & M. Burawoy (Eds.), *Public sociology: Fifteen eminent sociologists debate politics and the profession in the twenty-first century* (pp. 79–90). Berkeley, CA: University of California Press.
Hayward, E. (2010). Fingeryeyes: Impressions of cup corals. *Cultural Antrhopology, 25*(4), 577–599.
Heilbron, J. (1995). *The rise of social theory*. Minneapolis, MN: University of Minnesota Press.
Heilbron, J. (2011). Practical foundations of theorizing in sociology: The Case of Pierre Bourdieu. In C. Camic et al. (Eds.), *Social knowledge in the making* (pp. 181–208). Chicago: University of Chicago Press.
Henning, B. (2005). *The ethics of creativity: Beauty, morality and nature in a processive cosmos*. Pittsburgh: University of Pittsburgh Press.
Herrera, C. D. (1997). A historical interpretation of deceptive experiments in American psychology. *History of the Human Sciences, 10*(1), 23–36.
Hetherington, K. (2013). Beans before the law: Knowledge practices, responsibility, and the paraguayan soy boom. *Cultural Anthropology, 28*(1), 65–85.
Hindess, B. (2008). Been there, done that.... *Postcolonial Studies, 11*(2), 201–213.
Horst, H. A., & Miller, D. (2012). *Digital anthropology*. London: Berg.
Hunter, I. (2006). The history of theory. *Critical Inquiry, 33*(1), 78–112.
Hunter, I. (2007). The time of theory. *Postcolonial Studies, 10*(1), 5–22.
International Social Science Council. (2013). *World social science report 2013: Changing global environments*. Paris: UNESCO. Retrieved July 2, 2014, from: http://unesdoc.unesco.org/images/0022/002246/224677e.pdf.
Ingold, T. (2008). 'Anthropology is Not Ethnography'. *Proceedings of the British Academy, 154*, 69-92.
Jacoby, R. (2005). Thick aestheticism and thin nativism. In D. Patai & W. H. Corral (Eds.), *Theory's empire: An anthology of dissent* (pp. 490–508). New York: Columbia University Press.
James, W. (1956). *The will to believe and other essays in popular philosophy*. Mineola, NY: Dover Publications.

James, W. (1957). *The principles of psychology* (Vol. 1). Mineola, NY: Dover Publications.
James, W. (1996). *Some problems of philosophy.* Lincoln, NE: University of Nebraska Press.
James, W. (2003). *Essays in radical empiricism.* Mineola, NY: Dover Publications.
James, W. (2011). *Pragmatism and the meaning of truth.* Milton Keynes: Watchmakers Publishers.
Jameson, F. (1990). *Postmodernism, or the cultural logic of late capitalism.* Durham, NC: Duke University Press.
Jay, M. (2005). *Songs of experience: Modern American and European variations on a universal theme.* Berkeley, CA: University of California Press.
Jullien, F. (1995). *The propensity of things: Toward a history of efficacy in China.* New York: Zone Books.
Jullien, F. (2004). *A treatise on efficacy: Between Western and Chinese thinking.* Honolulu, HI: University of Hawai'i Press.
Kauffman, S. A. (2008). *Reinventing the sacred: A new view of science, reason, and religion.* New York: Basic Books.
Knorr-Cetina, K. (1981). *The manufacture of knowledge: An essay on the constructivist and contextual nature of science.* Oxford, England: Pergamon Press.
Koselleck, R. (1988). *Critique and crisis: Enlightenment and the pathogenesis of modern society.* Cambridge, MA: MIT Press.
Kuhn, T. (2012). *The structure of scientific revolutions.* Chicago, IL: University of Chicago Press.
Kuklick, H. (1997). After Ishmael: The Fieldwork Tradition and Its Future. In A. Gupta & J. Ferguson (Eds.), *Anthropological locations: Boundaries and grounds of a field science* (pp. 47–65). Berkley, CA: University of California Press.
Latour, B. (1988). *Science in action.* Cambridge, MA: Harvard University Press.
Latour, B. (1993a). *We have never been modern.* Cambridge, MA: Harvard University Press.
Latour, B. (1993b). *The pasteurization of France.* Cambridge, MA: Harvard University Press.
Latour, B. (1999). *Pandora's hope: On the reality of science studies.* Cambridge, MA: Harvard University Press.
Latour, B. (2004). Why has critique run out of steam? From matters of fact to matters of concern. *Critical Inquiry, 30*(2), 225–248.
Latour, B. (2005). *Reassembling the social: An introduction to actor-network theory.* Oxford: Oxford University Press.

Latour, B. (2009). *The making of law: An ethnography of the Conseil d'Etat*. Cambridge: Polity Press.
Latour, B. (2010). *On the modern cult of the factish gods*. Durham, NC: Duke University Press.
Latour, B. (2014). *An inquiry into modes of existence: An anthropology of the moderns*. Cambridge, MA: Harvard University Press.
Latour, B., & Woolgar, S. (1986). *Laboratory life: The construction of scientific facts*. Princeton, NJ: Princeton University Press.
Lauretis, T. (2004). Statement due. *Critical Inquiry, 30*(2), 365–368.
Law, J. (1999). After ANT: Complexitiy, naming and topology. In J. Law & J. Hassard (Eds.), *Actor-network theory and after* (pp. 1–14). Oxford, England: Wiley-Blackwell.
Law, J. (2002). *Aircraft stories: Decentering the object of technoscience*. Durham, NC: Duke University Press.
Law, J. (2004). *After method: Mess in social science research*. London: Roultedge.
Law, J., & Urry, J. (2004). Enacting the social. *Economy & Society, 33*(3), 390–410.
Lee, N., & Brown, S. (1994). Otherness and the actor network: The undiscovered continent. *American Behavioral Scientist, 37*(6), 772–790.
Lévi-Strauss, C. (1963). *Structural anthropology*. New York: Basic Books.
Leys, R. (2011). 'The Turn to Affect: A Critique'. *Critical Inquiry, 37*, 434–472.
Lloyd, E. (2008). *Science, evolution and politics*. Cambridge: University of Cambridge Press.
Love, H. (2010). Close but not deep: Literary ethics and the descriptive turn. *New Literary History, 41*, 371–391.
Lury, C., & Wakeford, N. (2012). *Inventive methods: The happening of the social*. London: Routledge.
MacKenzie, D. (2004). The big, bad wolf and the rational market: Portfolio insurance, the 1987 crash and the performativity of economics. *Economy & Society, 33*(3), 303–334.
MacKenzie, D., Muniesa, F., & Siu, L. (2007). *Do economists make markets? On the performativity of economics*. Princeton, NJ: Princeton University Press.
Marcus, G. E. (2012a). The contemporary desire for ethnography and its implication for anthropology. In R. Hardin & K. M. Clarke (Eds.), *Transforming ethnographic knowledge* (pp. 73–92). Madison, WI: The University of Wisconsin Press.
Marcus, G. E. (2012b). The legacies of writing culture and the near future of ethnographic form: A sketch. *Cultural Anthropology, 27*(3), 427–455.

Marres, N. (2005). Issues spark publics into being. A key but often forgotten point of the Lippmann-Dewey debate. In B. Latour & P. Weibel (Eds.), *Making things public: Atmospheres of democracy* (pp. 208–217). Cambridge, MA: The MIT Press.

Marres, N. (2012). *Material participation: Technology, the environment and everyday publics*. London: Palgrave Macmillan.

Massey, D. (2007). The strength of weak politics. In D. Clawson, R. Zussman, J. Misra, N. Gerstel, R. Stokes, A. L. Douglas, & M. Burawoy (Eds.), *Public sociology: Fifteen eminent sociologists debate politics & the profession in the twenty-first century* (pp. 145–157). Berkeley, CA: University of California Press.

Massumi, B. (2002). *Parables of the virtual: Affect, movement, sensation*. Durham, NC: Duke University Press.

Massumi, B. (2011). Perception attack: The force to own time. In J. Elliot & D. Attridge (Eds.), *Theory after 'Theory'* (pp. 75–89). Abingdon, England: Routledge.

Megill, A. (1994). *Rethinking objectivity*. Durham, NC: Duke University Press.

Meillassoux, Q. (2008). *After finitude: An essay on the necessity of contingency*. London: Bloomsbury.

Mignolo, W. (2009). Epistemic disobedience, independent thought and decolonial freedom. *Theory, Culture & Society, 26*(7-8), 159–181.

Milgram, S. (2004). *Obedience to authority: An experimental view*. New York: Harper-Collins Publishers.

Mills, C. W. (2000). *The sociological imagination*. Oxford: Oxford University Press.

Mitchell, W. J. T. (2004). Medium theory: Preface to the 2003 *critical inquiry* symposium. *Critical Inquiry, 30*(2), 324–335.

Mol, A. (2002). *The Body Multiple*. Durham & London: Duke University Press.

Moore, J. W. (2014). The capitalocene. Part I: On the nature and origins of our ecological crisis. Retrieved July 2, 2014, from http://www.jasonwmoore.com/uploads/The_Capitalocene__Part_I__June_2014.pdf

Morton, T. (2010). *The ecological thought*. Cambridge, MA: Harvard University Press.

Morton, R. B., & Williams, K. C. (2010). *Experimental political science and the study of causality*. Cambridge: Cambridge University Press.

Motamedi-Fraser, M. (2012). Once upon a problem. *The Sociological Review, 60*, 84–107.

Myers, E. (2013). *Worldly ethics: Democratic politics and the care of the world*. Durham, NC: Duke University Press.

Nandy, A. (2001). A report on the present state of health of gods and goddesses in South Asia. *Postcolonial Studies, 4*(2), 125–141.

Nora, P. (1972). L'événement monstre. *Communications, 18,* 162–172.

Nowotny, H., Scott, P., & Gibbons, M. (2001). *Re-thinking science: Knowledge and the public in an age of uncertainty.* Cambridge: Polity Press.

Osborne, P. (2011). Philosophy after theory: transdisciplinarity and the new. In J. Elliot & D. Attridge (Eds.), *Theory after 'Theory'* (pp. 19–33). Abingdon, England: Routledge.

Osborne, T., & Rose, N. (1999). Do the social sciences create phenomena? The example of public opinion research. *British Journal of Sociology, 50*(3), 367–396.

Papoulias, C., & Callard, F. (2010). Biology's gift: Interrogating the turn to affect. *Body & Society, 16*(1), 29–56.

Parisi, L. (2012). Speculation: A method for the unattainable. In C. Lury & N. Wakeford (Eds.), *Inventive methods: The happening of the social* (pp. 232–244). Abingdon, England: Routledge.

Patai, D., & Corral, W. H. (2005). *Theory's empire: An anthology of dissent.* New York: Columbia University Press.

Pickering, A. (1995). *The mangle of practice: Time, agency & science.* Chicago, IL: University of Chicago Press.

Pink, S. (2009). *Doing sensory ethnography.* London: Sage.

Porter, T. (1996). *Trust in numbers: The pursuit of objectivity in science and public life.* Princeton, NJ: Princeton University Press.

Potter, J. (1996). *Representing reality: Discourse, rhetoric and social construction.* London: Sage.

Proctor, R. (1991). *Value-free science? Purity and power in modern knowledge.* Cambridge, MA: Harvard University Press.

Rabinow, P. (2003). *Anthropos today: Reflections on modern equipment.* Princeton, NJ: Princeton University Press.

Rabinow, P. (2008). *Marking time: On the anthropology of the contemporary.* Princeton, NJ: Princeton University Press.

Rabinow, P., & Stavrianakis, A. (2013). *Demands of the day: On the logic of anthropological inquiry.* Chicago, IL: University of Chicago Press.

Rabinow, P., & Sullivan, W. (1987). *Interpretive social science: A second look.* Berkeley, CA: University of California Press.

Rao, A. (2008). Affect, memory, and materiality: A review essay on archival mediation. *Comparative Studies in Society and History, 50*(2), 559–567.

Rappert, B. (1999). The uses of relevance: Thoughts on a reflexive sociology. *Sociology, 33*(4), 705–723.

Readings, B. (1996). *The University in Ruins*. Cambridge, MA: Harvard University Press.
Rheinberger, H. (1997). *Toward a history of epistemic things: Synthesizing proteins in the test tube*. Stanford, CA: Stanford University Press.
Rabinow, P., & Marcus, G. (2008). *Designs for an Anthropology of the Contemporary*. Durham and London: Duke University Press.
Sahlins, M. (2005). *Culture in practice: Selected essays* (pp. 293–351). Brooklyn, NY: Zone Books.
Santos, B. (2004). A critique of lazy reason: Against the waste of experience. In I. Wallerstein (Ed.), *The modern world-system in the Longue Durée* (pp. 157–198). Boulder: Paradigm Publishers.
Santos, B. (2009). A non-occidentalist west?: Learned ignorance and the ecology of knowledge. *Theory, Culture & Society, 26*(7-8), 103–125.
Savage, M. (2009). Contemporary sociology and the challenge of the descriptive assemblage. *European Journal of Social Theory, 12*(1), 155–174.
Savage, M., & Burrows, R. (2007). The coming crisis of empirical sociology. *Sociology, 41*(5), 885–899.
Savransky, M. (2012). Worlds in the making: Social sciences and the ontopolitics of knowledge. *Postcolonial Studies, 15*(3), 351–368.
Savransky, M. (2014a). Of recalcitrant subjects. *Culture, Theory & Critique, 55*(1), 96–113.
Savransky, M. (2014b). In praise of hesitation: "Global knowledge" as a cosmopolitical adventure. In W. Keim, E. Çelik, C. Ersche, & V. Wöhrer (Eds.), *Global knowledge production in the social sciences: Made in circulation*. London: Ashgate.
Savransky, M. (2016). Modes of Mattering: Barad, Whitehead and Societies. *Rhizomes: Cultural Studies in Emerging Knowledge*. 29.
Schachter, S., & Singer, J. (1962). Cognitive, social, and physiological determinants of emotional state. *Psychological Review, 69*(5), 379–399.
Schatzki, T., Knorr-Cetina, K., & von Savigny, E. (2001). *The practice turn in contemporary theory*. London: Routledge.
Schlanger, J. (1983). *L'Invention Intellectuelle*. Paris: Fayard.
Schlanger, J. (1994). How old is our cultural past? In C. McDonald & G. Wihl (Eds.), *Transformation in personhood and culture after theory* (pp. 13–24). University Park, PA: The Pennsylvania State University Press.
Schutz, A. (1970). *Reflections on the problem of relevance*. New Haven: Yale University Press.
Scott, J. (2005). Who will speak, and who will listen? Comments on Burawoy and public sociology. *The British Journal of Sociology, 56*(3), 405–409.

Searle, J. (1996). *The construction of social reality*. London: Penguin.
Serres, M. (1982). *The parasite*. Minneapolis, MN: University of Minnesota Press.
Serres, M. (1995). *The natural contract*. Ann Arbor, MI: The University of Michigan Press.
Serres, M. (1997). *The troubadour of knowledge*. Ann Arbor, MI: The University of Michigan Press.
Serres, M. (2001). *Hominiscence*. Paris: Éditions Le Pommier.
Serres, M. (2003). *L'incandescent*. Paris: Éditions Le Pommier.
Serres, M. (2012). *Biogea*. Minneapolis, MN: Univocal.
Serres, M. (2013). *Times of crises: What the financial crisis revealed and how to reinvent our lives and future*. London: Bloomsbury.
Serres, M., & Latour, B. (1995). *Conversations on science, culture, and time*. Ann Arbor, MI: The University of Michigan Press.
Seth, S. (2004). Reason or reasoning? Clio or siva? *Social Text, 22*(1), 85–101.
Seth, S. (2007). *Subject lessons: The western education of colonial India*. Durham, NC: Duke University Press.
Sewell, W. (2005). *Logics of history: Social theory and social transformation*. Chicago, IL: University of Chicago Press.
Simondon, G. (2005). *L'individuation à la lumière des notions de forme et d'information*. Grenoble: Éditions Jérôme Millon.
Smith-Lovin, L. (2007). Do we need a public sociology? It depends on what you mean by sociology. In D. Clawson, R. Zussman, J. Misra, N. Gerstel, R. Stokes, A. L. Douglas, & M. Burawoy (Eds.), *Public sociology: Fifteen eminent sociologists debate politics and the profession in the twenty-first century* (pp. 124–134). Berkeley, CA: University of California Press.
Sokal, A., & Bricmont, J. (1998). *Intellectual impostures*. London: Profile Books.
Sontag, S. (1966). *Against interpretation*. New York: Octagon Books.
Sperber, D., & Wilson, D. (1995). *Relevance: Communication and cognition*. Oxford, England: Blackwell.
Stacey, J. (2007). If I were a goddess of sociological things. In D. Clawson, R. Zussman, J. Misra, N. Gerstel, R. Stokes, A. L. Douglas, & M. Burawoy (Eds.), *Public sociology: Fifteen eminent sociologists debate politics and the profession in the twenty-first century* (pp. 91–100). Berkeley, CA: University of California Press.
Stam, H., Radtke, R., & Lubek, I. (2000). Strains in experimental social psychology: A textual analysis of the development of experimentation in social psychology. *Journal of the History of the Behavioral Sciences, 36*(4), 365–382.
Steinmetz, G. (2005). *The politics of method in the human sciences: Positivism and its epistemological others*. Durham, NC: Duke University Press.

Stengers, I. (1997). *Power and invention: Situating science.* Minneapolis, MN: University of Minnesota Press.
Stengers, I. (2000). *The invention of modern science.* Minneapolis, MN: University of Minnesota Press.
Stengers, I. (2002). Beyond conversation: The risk of peace. In C. Keller & A. Daniell (Eds.), *Process and difference: Between cosmological and postructuralist postmodernisms* (pp. 235–256). Albany: State University of New York Press.
Stengers, I. (2005). The cosmopolitical proposal. In B. Latour & P. Weibel (Eds.), *Making things public: Atmospheres of democracy* (pp. 994–1003). Cambridge, MA: The MIT Press.
Stengers, I. (2008). Experimenting with refrains: Subjectivity and the challenge of escaping modern dualism. *Subjectivity, 22,* 38–59.
Stengers, I. (2009a). *Au temps des catastrophes: Résister à la barbarie qui vient.* Paris: Editions La Découverte.
Stengers, I. (2009b). A constructivist reading of process and reality. *Theory, Culture & Society, 25*(4), 91–110.
Stengers, I. (2010). *Cosmopolitics I.* Minneapolis, MN: University of Minnesota Press.
Stengers, I. (2011a). Wondering about materialism. In L. Bryant, N. Srnicek, & G. Harman (Eds.), *The speculative turn: Continental materialism and realism* (pp. 368–380). Melbourne: Repress.
Stengers, I. (2011b). *Cosmopolitics II.* Minneapolis, MN: University of Minnesota Press.
Stengers, I. (2011c). Sciences were never "good". *Common Knowledge, 17*(1), 82–86.
Stengers, I. (2011d). *Thinking with whitehead: A free and wild creation of concepts.* Cambridge, MA: Harvard University Press.
Stengers, I., & Pignarre, P. (2011). *Capitalist sorcery: Breaking the spell.* Baisngstoke: Palgrave Macmillan.
Stenner, P. (2008). A.N. Whitehead and subjectivity. *Subjectivity, 22,* 90–109.
Stenner, P., & Greco, M. (2013). Affectivity. *Informática na Educação: teoria e prática, 16*(1), 49–70.
Stinchcombe, A. L. (2007). Speaking truth to the public, and indirectly to power. In D. Clawson, R. Zussman, J. Misra, N. Gerstel, R. Stokes, A. L. Douglas, & M. Burawoy (Eds.), *Public sociology: Fifteen eminent sociologists debate politics and the profession in the twenty-first century* (pp. 135–158). Berkeley, CA: University of California Press.
Stocking, G. W. (1983). The ethnographer's magic: Fieldwork in British anthropology from Tylor to Malinowski. In G. W. Stocking (Ed.), *Observers observed:*

*Essays on ethnographic fieldwork* (pp. 70–120). Madison: University of Wisconsin Press.

Stoller, P. (1989). *The taste of ethnographic things: The senses in anthropology*. Philadelphia: University of Pennsylvania Press.

Strathern, M. (1992). *Reproducing the future: Anthropology, Kinship and the new reproductive technologies*. Manchester: Manchester University Press.

Strathern, M. (2000). *Audit culture: Anthropological perspectives in accountability, ethics and the academy*. London: Routledge.

Teo, T. (2012). Psychology is still a problematic science and the public knows it. *American Psychologist, 67*(9), 807–808.

Thrift, N. (2005). *Knowing capitalism*. London: Sage.

Trent, J. E. (2011). Should political science be more relevant? An empirical and critical analysis of the discipline. *European Political Science, 10*, 191–209.

Tsing, A. (1993). *In the realm of the diamond queen: Marginality in an out-of-the-way place*. Princeton: Princeton University Press.

Turpin, E. (2013). *Architecture in the Anthropocene: Encounters among design, deep time, science and philosophy*. Ann Arbor, MI: Open Humanities Press.

Valins, S. (1966). Cognitive effects of false heart-rate feedback. *Journal of Personality and Social Psychology, 4*(4), 400–408.

Vásquez, M. A., & Marquardt, M. F. (2000). Globalizing the rainbow Madonna: Old time religion in the present age. *Theory, Culture & Society, 17*(4), 119–143.

Veyne, P. (1984). *Writing history: Essay on epistemology*. Middletown: Wesleyan University Press.

Vilnius Declaration. (2013). Vilnius declaration—horizons for social sciences and humanities. Retrieved July, 2014, from http://horizons.mruni.eu/vilnius-declaration-horizons-for-social-sciences-and-humanities

Viveiros de Castro, E. (1998). Cosmological deixis and amerindian perspectivism. *The Journal of the Royal Anthropological Institute, 4*(3), 469–488.

Wagner, P. (2001). *A history and theory of the social sciences: Not all that is solid melts into air*. London: Sage.

Wagner, P., Wittrock, B., & Whitley, R. (1991). *Discourses on society: The shaping of the social science disciplines*. Dordrecht: Kuwer Academic Publishers.

Wallerstein, I. (1999). *The end of the world as we know it: Social science for the twenty-first century*. Minneapolis, MN: University of Minnesota Press.

Wallerstein, I. (2001). *Unthinking social sciences: The limits of nineteenth-century paradigms*. Philadelphia, PA: Temple University Press.

Wallerstein, I. (2007). The sociologist and the public sphere. In D. Clawson, R. Zussman, J. Misra, N. Gerstel, R. Stokes, A. L. Douglas, & M. Burawoy (Eds.), *Public sociology: Fifteen eminent sociologists debate politics and the pro-*

*fession in the twenty-first century* (pp. 169–175). Berkeley, Los Angeles & London: University of California Press.

Wallerstein, I., Juma, C., Fox Keller, E., Kocka, J., Lecourt, D., Mukimbe, V. Y., et al. (1996). *Open the social sciences: Report of the Gulbenkian commission on the restructuring of the social sciences*. Stanford: Stanford University Press.

Watson, M. (2011). Cosmopolitics and the subaltern: Problematizing latour's idea of the commons. *Theory, Culture and Society, 28*(3), 55–79.

Weber, M. (2009). *From Max Weber: Essays in sociology*. London: Routledge.

Webster, M., & Sell, J. (2007). *Laboratory experiments in the social sciences*. Burlington: Academic Press.

Wellek, R. (2005). Destroying literary studies. In D. Patai & W. H. Corral (Eds.), *Theory's empire: An anthology of dissent* (pp. 41–52). New York: Columbia University Press.

Whetherell, M., & Potter, J. (1987). *Discourse and social psychology: Beyond attitudes and behaviour*. London: Sage.

White, H. (1973). *Metahistory: The historical imagination in nineteenth-century Europe*. Baltimore, MD & London: Johns Hopkins University.

White, S. K. (2000). *Sustaining affirmation: The strengths of weak ontology in political theory*. Princeton, NJ: Princeton University Press.

Whitehead, A. N. (1926). *Religion in the making*. Cambridge: Cambridge University Press.

Whitehead, A. N. (1955). *Symbolism: Its meaning and effect*. New York: Fordham University Press.

Whitehead, A. N. (1958). *The function of reason*. Boston: Beacon Press.

Whitehead, A. N. (1967a). *Adventures of ideas*. New York: Free Press.

Whitehead, A. N. (1967b). *Science and the modern world*. New York: Free Press.

Whitehead, A. N. (1968). *Modes of thought*. New York: Free Press.

Whitehead, A. N. (1978). *Process and reality: An essay in cosmology*. New York: Free Press.

Whitehead, A. N. (2004). *The concept of nature*. Mineola, NY: Dover Publications.

Wolfe, C. (2011). Theory as a research programme—The very idea. In J. Elliot & D. Attridge (Eds.), *Theory after 'Theory'* (pp. 34–48). Abingdon, England: Routledge.

Zalasiewicz, J., Williams, M., Smith, A., Barry, T., Coe, A., Bown, P., et al. (2008). Are we now living in the Anthropocene. *GSA Today, 18*(2), 4–8.

Zalasiewicz, J., Williams, M., Steffern, W., & Crutzen, P. (2010). The new world of the Anthropocene. *Environmental Science & Technology, 44*(7), 2228–2231.

# Index

## A

Actor-Network Theory (ANT), 20, 72, 74–77
    actant, 74–77
Adventure, ix, v–vi, viii, 23, 48, 51, 53, 62, 134, 217
    as care of knowledge, 20, 22, 55 210, 215
    definition of, 40–41
    and eels, 2–3
    and encounters, 89–90, 95–97, 160, 215
    ethics of, 20, 89, 120, 122, 139, 154, 155, 160, 173 (Ethics)
    and events, 165, 167, 172
    and radical empiricism, 22, 185
    and social sciences, 29, 41, 71–72, 77, 96, 105–107, 111, 114–118, 172, 215
    and speculation, 58, 186, 199, 206, 214
    and transitions/possible futures, 120, 179, 209
Aesthetics, 168–169, 171
Affects (theory of), 191–192
Althusser, Louis, 91, 187
Anthropocene, 41, 43–44
    *see also* Capitalocene
Anthropology/anthropological, 21, 27, 68, 105–106, 110–111
    and difference, 43, 52–53
Apprentice, viii, 23, 218–219
    *see also* Personae (conceptual)
Archive, 114–118
Area studies, 14
Art theory, 187
Austin, John, 112n, 125–127, 130, 132–134

## B

Barad, Karen, 60n, 100
Barthes, Roland, 112n, 187, 189n
Beliefs', 43, 110, 201n
  scientific, 66
  Western invention of, 22, 142–149
Bell, Vikki, 132
Bergson, Henri, 176n, 191, 196
Bifurcation of nature, viii, 15–16, 35–36, 42, 67, 71, 213
Biology, 191
Bloom, Harold, 168–169, 171
Bourdieu, Pierre, 134, 187
Braudel, Fernand, 157–158
Brewer, John, 12, 26
Burawoy, Michel, 27n, 28–32, 37–38, 43, 217
Butler, Judith, 91–92, 127, 130–131, 134, 186

## C

Callon, Michel, 73, 127–128, 130–131, 134
Canguilhem, Georges, 136, 141
Capitalism, vii, 14, 41, 44, 157n, 171, 187
Capitalocene, 42, 44–47, 52, 123–124, 213
Care of knowledge, vii, 11, 12, 15–20, 22–23, 35–36, 40, 50–51, 55, 87, 95, 162, 178, 182, 209–216
Care of the self, 11, 23, 211–212
Care of the world, 11, 23, 178, 211–215
Causality/cause and effect, vii, 15, 64, 127, 137, 149, 157, 163–164, 170–171, 173–174, 195–196, 213
Certeau, Michel de, 143–144, 155
Chakrabarty, Dipesh, 27n, 43, 53
Chemistry, 93–94
Clifford, James, 106–107, 112
Colonial/colonialism, 22, 106, 145–146, 148–149, 151, 168
Connections, 39, 50, 54, 87, 120–121, 210
  and inventions, 135, 137, 141–142, 150–151, 190
  modes of, 133–135, 142, 145–150
  and performativity, 91n, 133, 138
Connolly, William, 10, 53, 156, 191, 197, 204, 213
Cortázar, Julio, 1–6, 23, 41, 52, 154, 172–173, 215, 218
Cosmopolitics/cosmopolitical, 52–54
Crisis, ecological, 7
  economic, 7, 41
  of modernity, 25n
  moral, 147–149
  of representation/reception, 107
  of scientific paradigms, 33–34n
  of social sciences, 7, 20, 22, 25, 41, 122–123, 183
Cultivation, of a care of knowledge, 16–23, 35–36, 39, 50–52, 87, 95, 162
  of an ethics of adventure, 89, 121, 206, 211, 213–214
  of efficacy, 138–139
  of perplexity, 119–120
  of possibilities, 150, 154

## D

Dance of agency, 79, 84, 87
Daston, Lorraine, 63, 64n, 68n, 69, 144, 170, 178, 215–218
Deleuze, Gilles, 18, 39, 61, 87, 155, 169, 170n, 181, 199, 216–217
  and causality, 171, 173
  and empiricist conversion, 191, 201
  and encounter, 90, 92, 120
  and event, 155–156, 173, 178
  and Felix Guattari, 135n, 136, 201, 216–217
  and virtual, 177n
Derrida, Jacques, 112, 127, 131, 134, 187–188
'Descriptive turn', 192
Despret, Vinciane, 83–84, 95
  and Valin's experiment, 100, 102–104
Dewey, John, 18, 32n, 120, 181, 198, 218
  and habits, 10n, 219
  and reconstruction, 5–8, 10, 12, 61, 211
  and speculation, 22, 198, 200, 203
Didier, Emannuel, 139–140
Didi-Huberman, Georges, 57–59
Dilthey, Wilhelm, 63n
Discourse/discursive, 69, 107, 111–114, 159
Disposition/dispositional, 204
  definition of, 137–140
Dosse, Francoise, 157–159, 192
Durkheim, Emile, 143, 158

## E

Economics/economic theory, 13, 27n, 41, 111, 128, 130, 134, 139
Eco, Umberto, 113n
Efficacy of knowledge, 18, 124, 127, 142–143
  of inventions, 21, 124, 129, 131, 133–135, 141, 147–150 (Performativity)
  as Shi, 137–139 (Shi)
Empiricism/empirical, 81, 176, 183, 189, 191, 193
  abstract, 7, 17–18
  conversion to, 201, 203–204
  radical, 16, 22, 33n, 47–49, 181, 185
  speculative, 186, 194
Encounters, viii, 31, 47–48, 58, 74, 85, 92–93, 215
  and connections/relationality, 120, 121, 136
  definition of, 94–95, 218
  and ethnography, 104–111
  and experimentation, 98–104, 140
  and invention in social sciences, 38, 75, 77, 79–83, 86, 95–98, 182, 199, 202
  and relevance, 50–51, 138
  thinking with, 21, 86–87, 89–90, 95, 217
  and words, 111–118
Environment/environmental, 45–46, 100, 135–136, 141, 200
Epistemology/epistemic, 17, 30, 36, 47, 50, 61–67, 69, 78, 99, 105, 112, 154, 165, 170, 216
  epistemic objects, 76

Ethical sensibility of knowledge/
inquiry, 10–11, 15, 18–19,
48, 50, 87, 95, 164–165,
178, 208–210, 213
Ethics/ethos, of adventure, 20, 89,
121, 153–154, 159
of estrangement, vii–viii, 15, 17,
20, 35–37, 40, 49, 65, 67,
74, 84, 95, 157, 161,
168–169, 185, 188, 213
of exposure, 22, 172–177, 196
of inheritance, 22, 170–172, 196
of thought, 188–192, 200, 206,
209
Ethnography, 94–95, 97, 105–110,
114–115, 119
Eurocentrism, 65, 107
Events, vi, 8–9, 20, 22, 32–34, 39,
41, 154, 157–159, 159–
161, 163
banalisation of the, 160–161
and connections (world of
events), 18, 133, 151, 162,
165, 197, 213, 215
(Connections)
cynicism of the, 161
definition of, 155–157
double temporality of the, 159,
162–163, 165, 195
and historiography, 157–159
and inheritance/exposure,
170–177, 195–196 (Ethics)
and invention, 79, 82–83, 85n,
140, 144, 150
and metaphysics, 160
and non-events, 164n
and Theory, 183–184, 202
and transformation of the
possible, 159, 164, 166–

167, 172–173, 179, 209,
219
Experience, 6, 8, 12, 58
and 'belief', 142–151 (Beliefs')
of immanent possibilities, 177,
196, 202, 204
of knowledge, 2, 18, 40–41,
141–142, 167, 204
modes of, 87, 104, 136
relevance of/relevance, viii, 15–17,
32–33, 54, 181
and speculation, 22, 183, 185,
190–191, 193–194,
201–202, 206–207
'subjective', 67, 71
'value experience', 33–34, 214
Experimentation/experimental, vi,
212, 233
experimental objects,
79, 82
and social sciences, 68, 96,
98–104, 140, 166, 174–175
speculative, 17, 22–23, 32, 181,
185–186, 190, 194–196,
199–200, 202–203,
206–207

F

Febvre, Lucien, 157
Feminism/feminist, 168–169, 190
Feyerabend, Paul, 63
Fieldwork, 105, 107
Flinders, Matthew, 27, 122
Foucault, Michel, 10–11, 18, 61, 63,
112n, 136–137, 149,
158–159, 168, 187,
189–190, 194, 211–212
Frankfurt School, 187

## G

Gay, Paul du, 132
Geertz, Clifford, 68
Ginzburg, Carlo, 114, 118
God, 201n
    Christian concept of, 144

## H

Hacking, Ian, 69n, 81, 99n, 128, 196–197
Hadot, Pierre, 10–11, 182n, 212
Halewood, Michael, 139n
Haraway, Donna, 13, 44, 64, 65n, 109, 131, 206
Harding, Sandra, 60, 65–66
Harman, Graham, 196n
Heidegger, Martin, 36
Hesitation, 108, 110, 162, 178
Hetherington, Kregg, 95, 107–111, 194
Hinduism, 145–148
Historiography, 27n, 157, 164–165
    and horror of the events, 157–158, 165–166
    and longue durée, 157–158
Humanities, 186–187, 212
Humans and other-than-humans, 7, 16, 18, 37, 42, 46–49, 52–53, 60n, 107, 109–110, 144, 147, 154, 182, 196n, 210
Hunter, Ian, 188, 196
Husserl, Edmund, 188

## I

Inheritance, 178
    ethics of, 22, 165, 169–172, 178

    of events, 195
    routes of, 93–94, 104, 138, 215
Invention (in social sciences), 6–8, 87
    definition of, 77–78
    efficacy of, 21–22, 39, 124–125, 131–134, 150
    of the human, 168–169 (Shakespeare)
    and milieus/connections, 135–142, 145–150, 205 (Milieus and Connections)
    and objectivity, 59–61, 72, 77, 82
    and propositions, 51, 76, 121, 129 (Language)
    and relevance, 20, 39, 51–53, 151, 176
    risks of, 21, 38, 55, 57, 77–80, 83–86, 110, 205
    and speculation, 83, 196
Iran, 115–118

## J

James, William, vi, viii, 5, 16, 18, 33n, 46–51, 54, 119, 120, 125, 151, 153, 176, 177, 181, 187, 199, 201n, 204–205, 214
Jay, Martin, 189n
Jullien, François, 137–138

## K

Kant, Immanuel/Kantianism, viii, 51, 59–60, 68, 168, 188–189, 193, 196n
Kauffman, Stuart, 36
Knorr-Cetina, Karin, 69–70

Knowledge, transitional, 178–179
  and the empirical, 188–190
  as technique of habitation, 211
Koselleck, Reinhardt, 25n
Kuhn, Thomas S., 25n, 63

L

Language/linguistics, 187
  and performativity/illocutionary, perlocutionary, 125–133, 141, 147
  and structuralism/post-structuralism, 91, 112–114, 141
  and words, 116 (Words)
Latour, Bruno, vi, 13, 36–37, 50, 62, 69–76, 80, 85, 94, 171, 183–184, 186, 192–194, 217
Lauretis, Teresa de, 185, 190
Law, John and John Urry, 127, 129–130
Learning, 23, 87, 154, 159, 164, 167, 169, 210, 217–219
Levi-Strauss, Claude, 106, 158, 187
Linguistic turn, 112–114
Literary studies, 168–169, 187, 192
Lloyd, Elizabeth, 64, 67
Luc Boltanski, 183, 187, 192–193
Lyotard, Jean-François, 187

M

MacKenzie, Donald, 127–128, 130n
Malinowski, Bronislaw, 106
Marcus, George E., 107, 112–113
Marxist, 16n, 91n, 169
Marx, Karl, 143, 168

Materialism, 91n, 160
  eliminative, 68n
Mauss, Marcel, 215
Meillassoux, Quentin, 196n
Metaphysics/metaphysical, 37, 139n, 159, 164, 170n, 188n, 213
  of the event, 160–164
  and process, 214
Methods/methodology, scientific, 15n, 31, 34
  and ethical sensibility, 96–98, 104, 114, 149, 199
  and objectivity, 63–64, 67–68, 70
  and speculation, 199–200
Mignolo, Walter, 65
Milieu/milieus, 7, 18, 21, 31, 40, 47, 59, 94, 107, 124–125, 133–138, 140–156, 159–160, 162, 164–165, 170, 191, 203, 205, 210, 216, 226, 232
Mills, Carl Wright, 6–7, 28
Modes of becoming, 121, 185
Modes of existence, 10, 50–51, 60, 78–81, 191
Modes of mattering, vi, 38, 48–49, 52–53, 60, 62, 83–85, 94, 107, 110, 123
Morton, Timothy, 49n
Motamedi-Fraser, Mariam, x, 95, 114–117

N

Nandy, Ashis, 146
Neurosciences, 68n, 191
Nietzsche, Friedrich, 168
Nora, Pierre, 161

## O

Objective/objectivity, vi–viii, 30, 36, 38, 54–55, 170, 174
  as 'god trick', 64, 77, 85
  and invention, 18, 21, 60–62, 86
  as 'ontological tyranny', 68, 70–71, 77, 85
  positivism, 63–64 (Positivism)
  in scientific atlases, 63
  as 'still objectivity', 71–72, 74, 77, 85
  weak and strong, 65–69
Ontology/ontological, 16, 213
  and events, 22 (Events)
  and objectivity, 64, 67–68, 70 (Objectivity)
  of ourselves, 190
Osborne, Thomas & Nikolas Rose, 70, 127, 129

## P

Paraguay, 107–111, 194
Pasteur, Louis, 74–85
Peirce, Charles S., 113n
Performativity, 21, 125
  in economics, 129–130
  and efficacy, 131–132, 134, 173 (Efficacy)
  and illocution/perlocution, 125–126, 128–129, 131, 141, 147, 151
  and knowledge, 124, 140
  and propensity, 138
  and subject, 91
Perplexity, cultivation of, 2, 58, 87, 119–120, 139, 178
Personae, conceptual, 23, 216–218

apprentice, viii, 23, 209–219 (Apprentice)
  diplomat, 217
  idiot, 217
  scientific, 216
Physics, 36, 50, 93
Pickering, Andrew, 79, 87, 183n
Poetry, 169
Politics, 13, 64–65, 208
  and ANT, 74, 78
  ethico-politics of prepositions, 94, 105, 109, 115
  of knowledge-production, 48, 52–54, 62–63, 71 (Cosmopolitics)
Positivism, 63–64, 124, 138
  in anthropology, 68
  formalism in, 188
  neo-positivism, 111
Possible/possibilities, 23, 41, 49, 59, 96, 142, 144, 148, 171–172
  cultivation of, 150
  and events, 173–178
  and probabilities, 155, 196–197, 205
  and social sciences, 62, 80, 102, 110 (Social Sciences)
  and speculation, 119, 185, 197, 202
  transformation of, 153–155, 164–168, 179, 188, 190–196, 198, 204, 211, 214
Postcolonial studies, 27, 64
  decolonial, 65
Postmodernism/postmodern, 62, 178
Post-structuralism/post-structuralist, 16n, 91, 112, 166, 168, 185

Pragmatism/pragmatists, vii, 18, 125
  see also Dewey and James
Process/processual, 6, 46–47, 133,
  150, 156, 159–160, 198,
  214
Psychoanalysis, 168

R

Reconstruction, 5–10, 12, 17,
  20–21, 27–29, 61, 214
  see also Dewey
  speculative, 12, 21, 32, 87, 96,
    153, 209 (Speculation)
Reflexive turn, 107
Relationality, 21, 38, 40, 47–49, 52,
  90–91, 93
Relevance, v–viii, 11–12, 214
  as care of knowledge, 16, 20, 55,
    97, 153–154, 182, 210
  as demand for social sciences,
    8–9, 25–29, 37, 39, 54,
    176, 199
  as event of the world, 22, 32–34,
    39, 54, 167
  and inventions, 20–21, 58,
    77–78, 80, 96, 104,
    193–194, 210
  as public communication/impact,
    29–32, 35–36, 122–123,
    132
  relational patterns of/connections,
    21, 26, 38, 42–43, 46–47,
    50–51, 53–54, 90, 135–
    136, 138, 140, 146,
    149–150, 211, 214, 218
  and subject/object, 61–62, 66,
    71–72, 86–87

Religion, 143–144, 146–148, 225n
  as belief, 143, 146–147
Rheinberger, Hans-Jorg, 76, 79
Rodin, Auguste, 182
Rorty, Richard, 187

S

Sahlins, Marshal, 157
Santos, Boaventura de Sousa, 147
Saussure, Ferdinand de, 158
Schlanger, Judith, 14, 182n, 205
Schutz, Alfred, 31
Searle, John, 130
Serres, Michel, 43, 46, 93–95, 135,
  163–164, 175, 177, 179,
  218
Seth, Sanjay, 65, 143–149
Sewell, William, 157–158,
  170–171
Shakespeare, William, 168–169
Simondon, Gilbert, 19
Social constructivism, 71–72, 75,
  112, 151
Social sciences, and capitalocene,
  44–47, 52 see also
  Capitalocene
  and ethics of inquiry, 10, 12, 15,
    17, 19, 55, 68, 84, 87, 97,
    157–158, 164, 171, 209, 213
  and (pragmatics of) events, 22,
    164–166 (Events)
  and experience, 177, 182
  experimentation in, 23, 55, 96,
    98–104
  invention in, 21, 85–87, 122,
    124, 135, 139, 141, 150
  non-modernist, 217

objectivity in, vii, 54, 61, 63–65, 67–68, 81–82, 124, 176–177 *see also* Objectivity
and performativity, 125–134
public, 29–42, 123
reconstruction of the, 5, 7–9, 27, 153
relevance in, 7–9, 20–21, 26–29, 45, 48, 50, 60, 77, 84, 96, 119, 153–154, 199
risks in, 82–83
and theory, 183–184, 186–187, 189 *see also* Theory
Society/societies, as objects for social sciences, 13, 68–69, 72, 144
in Whitehead, 81, 92–94
Sociology, 27n, 28–30, 35–36, 69, 158, 217
Sontag, Susan, 106
Soybeans, 21, 104, 108–111, 194
Speculation/speculative, vi, viii
and propositions, 205–206, 214
and reconstruction, 12, 17, 21, 32, 87, 96, 153, 209
and social inquiry, 58, 83, 119, 199
speculative experimentation, 185–186, 190, 196, 199–203, 206
'Speculative Realism' / SR, 196n
and time, 172, 194–195, 197–198, 203–204
Spinoza, Baruch, 191
Stengers, Isabelle, v–viii, 18, 22, 38, 41, 44, 47, 50, 53, 54, 60, 62, 64, 77–80, 82, 85n, 96, 134–135, 150, 155, 160, 162, 167, 174, 181, 198, 202, 211, 214, 217

Strathern, Marilyn, 122, 173, 206n
Structuralism/structuralist, 16n, 158, 166, 185, 187
Subject-object, 61–62, 66, 71–72, 86–87
pragmatic maintenance of the distinction, 77, 80

T
Theory, 14, 185–186, 188–194, 197, 201
death of, 186–187
mattering of, 22, 181–182, 207
Tilly, Charles, 158
Transitions, 136, 156n, 163, 178–179, 185, 194–196, 201–202, 206, 209, 219

V
Veyne, Paul, 163–164
Vilnius Declaration, 25–26

W
Wallerstein, Immanuel, 13–14, 26, 30n, 158
Weber, Max, 63n, 68, 143, 178
Whitehead, Alfred North, viii, 14–18, 22, 31, 33–35, 42, 46, 49–50, 80–81, 85n, 92–94, 136, 138–139, 141, 156n, 160, 163, 177, 181, 185, 189, 194–201, 204–205, 213–214
Wittgenstein, Ludwig, 112n
Woolgar, Steve, 70, 72

Words, 111–118
World, 6, 11
   of connections, 21, 39–41, 46–47, 49, 121, 133, 150–151, 206
   and culture, 41, 46, 201
   modern, 44, 178
   and nature, 41, 42, 45–46, 67, 201
   plurality of the, 106, 135, 150, 162–163, 204
   processual, 156, 159
World Social Forum, 167
Wundt, Whilhelm, 98–99, 104

The manufacturer's authorised representative in the EU is Springer Nature Customer Service Centre GmbH, Europaplatz 3, 69115 Heidelberg, Germany. If you have any concerns regarding our products, please contact ProductSafety@springernature.com

Printed and bound by CPI Group (UK) Ltd, Croydon, CR0 4YY

23/03/2026

02076459-0002